Praise for Craig Robinson and
A GAME OF CHARACTER

"He helped elect a president."

—*The New York Times*

"Craig doesn't profess to know the specifics of politics the way he knows the X's and O's of basketball. But I think what he does understand is the need to wake up every morning doing your best and having a positive attitude. And him communicating that to me was always very helpful."

—President Barack Obama

"For many years, the role of family historian—the 'keeper of the family lore' as Craig puts it—had belonged to his father, my late husband, Fraser Robinson. Without Fraser here to keep those stories alive, they were in danger of becoming lost and Craig was determined not to let them go, but instead to take up his father's mantle of storyteller, motivator, and Philosopher-in-Chief. Craig has risen to the challenge with *A Game of Character*, a book that not only pays tribute to his parents (and to all parents, teachers, mentors, and coaches, for that matter) but also honors a beautiful brother-sister relationship and all sibling, family, and community relationships."

—Marian Robinson

"If anyone wonders how the First Lady can
and intelligent, yet down-to-ear
warming new book *A Game o*
incredible support system and a

D1113922

Currently the men's basketball coach at Oregon State University, **Craig Robinson** played his college ball at Princeton University under the legendary Pete Carril. He is also the brother-in-law of President Barack Obama. He lives in Oregon with his wife and children.

A GAME OF CHARACTER

A FAMILY JOURNEY FROM CHICAGO'S SOUTHSIDE TO THE IVY LEAGUE AND BEYOND

CRAIG ROBINSON
WITH MIM EICHLER RIVAS
FOREWORD BY MARIAN ROBINSON

GOTHAM BOOKS
Published by Penguin Group (USA) Inc.
375 Hudson Street, New York, New York 10014, U.S.A.

Penguin Group (Canada), 90 Eglinton Avenue East, Suite 700, Toronto,
Ontario M4P 2Y3, Canada (a division of Pearson Penguin Canada Inc.);
Penguin Books Ltd, 80 Strand, London WC2R 0RL, England; Penguin Ireland,
25 St Stephen's Green, Dublin 2, Ireland (a division of Penguin Books Ltd);
Penguin Group (Australia), 250 Camberwell Road, Camberwell, Victoria 3124, Australia
(a division of Pearson Australia Group Pty Ltd); Penguin Books India Pvt Ltd,
11 Community Centre, Panchsheel Park, New Delhi–110 017, India;
Penguin Group (NZ), 67 Apollo Drive, Rosedale, North Shore 0632, New Zealand
(a division of Pearson New Zealand Ltd); Penguin Books (South Africa) (Pty) Ltd,
24 Sturdee Avenue, Rosebank, Johannesburg 2196, South Africa

Penguin Books Ltd, Registered Offices: 80 Strand, London WC2R 0RL, England

Published by Gotham Books, a member of Penguin Group (USA) Inc.

Previously published as a Gotham Books hardcover edition

First trade paperback printing, May 2011

2 4 6 8 10 9 7 5 3 1

Gotham Books and the skyscraper logo are trademarks of Penguin Group (USA) Inc.

Photo credits:
Robinson family archives: insert 1, pp. 1-8; insert 2, pp. 2-3;
insert 2, p. 7 (bottom left); insert 2, p. 8
Scott DuJardin, Clark Photography, Chicago, IL: insert 2, pp. 2-5
Justin Sullivan/Getty Images News/Getty Images: insert 2, p. 6 (top and bottom right)
Chip Somodevilla/Getty Images News/Getty Images: insert 2, p. 6 (bottom left)
Brendan Smialowski/Getty Images News/Getty Images: insert 2, p. 7 (top)
Jaimee Colbert, Oregon State University Men's Basketball: insert 2, p. 7 (bottom right)

LIBRARY OF CONGRESS CATALOGING-IN-PUBLICATION DATA
Robinson, Craig, 1962-
A game of character: a family journey from Chicago's Southside to the Ivy League and
beyond / Craig Robinson; foreword by Marian Robinson.
p.   cm.
ISBN 978-1-592-40548-0 (hardcover)   978-1-592-40591-6 (paperback)
1. Robinson, Craig, 1962-   2. Basketball coaches—United States—Biography.
3. Robinson Family.   4. Obama, Michelle, 1964-   5. Obama, Barack.   6. Conduct of life.
I. Title.
GV884.R614A3 2010
796.323092—dc22
[B]   2010001666

Printed in the United States of America · Set in Bembo · Designed by Patrice Sheridan

*Penguin is committed to publishing works of quality and integrity.
In that spirit, we are proud to offer this book to our readers;
however, the story, the experiences, and the words
are the author's alone.*

IN LOVING MEMORY OF
FRASER ROBINSON III

AND

TO MY FAMILY—MY LIFE,
MY EVERYTHING

CONTENTS

FOREWORD

BY MARIAN ROBINSON

I'd like to begin by borrowing an idea that my son raised when he was asked to provide an introduction for his sister, my daughter, Michelle Robinson Obama, now our nation's First Lady, before she spoke on the opening night of the Democratic National Convention. He lovingly noted then, as a family member it is an honor to make such an introduction. So it gives me similar pleasure not just to introduce my son, Craig Robinson—the author of *A Game of Character*—but more important, to introduce my son to *you*.

As I think you'll discover the moment you dive into the stories ahead, Craig loves the game of basketball with a passion that is absolutely contagious. He truly believes that everyone and anyone can benefit from learning the lessons of character that the game can teach. And even if you know little or nothing about basketball, and have never contemplated the possibility of knowing more about it, be prepared for that to change! Oh yes, ever since he was a little boy, Craig has had an unusual ability to put his convictions to use—along with his enthusiasm and excellent skills of strategy—and to successfully persuade others to consider looking at something in a new and different way.

This may explain why my daughter enlisted Craig's help in persuading me to consider moving to the White House not long after Barack was elected president. There were many good and valid reasons that Michelle raised with me, not the least of which was the opportunity to continue spending time with my granddaughters, Malia and Sasha, and to assist in giving them a sense of normalcy that is a priority for both of their parents, and has been from the time Barack began his political career. My feeling, however, was that I could visit periodically without actually moving in and still be there for the girls.

"True," Craig agreed when he heard my reasons for not wanting to move to 1600 Pennsylvania Avenue. But then he argued, "Why not think about it as an opportunity to expand your horizons, to try something new? You might want to just give it a try." He had a point. And what made his argument so convincing was that, as usual, he was using a line of reasoning he had learned from me! Of course, not to overplay his hand, Craig then added, "But you should do whatever you think is right."

As a compromise, I opted to move to the White House after all, at least temporarily—while still reserving lots of time to travel and to maintain a certain amount of autonomy. So far, so good!

When I first heard that Craig was going to be writing this book, I couldn't have been more delighted. For one thing, he has a very distinctive point of view about the connection between basketball and character that comes from a lifelong, ongoing study of each of those areas of interest. Also, as he explained to me at the time, for many years the role of family historian—the "keeper of the family lore," as Craig puts it—had belonged to his father, my late husband, Fraser Robinson. Without Fraser here to keep those stories alive, they were in danger of becoming lost and Craig was determined not to let them go, but to instead take up his father's mantle of story-teller, motivator, and Philosopher-in-Chief.

Well, I can assure you, that is one tall order! But Craig has risen to the challenge with *A Game of Character*, a book that not only pays tribute to his parents (and to all parents, teach-ers, mentors, and coaches, for that matter), but also honors a beautiful brother-sister relationship and all sibling, family, and community relationships. In the process, Craig also brings to life long-forgotten memories for me that I suspect may spur your own family recollections. I'm confident that you will find the stories he uses to illustrate lessons learned, as I did, to be as moving, funny, honest, and instructive as they are en-lightening.

As a parent, I'm certainly not alone in feeling that there are few experiences more rewarding than watching your chil-dren go out into the world and go further than you could have ever dreamed of going yourself. Fraser and I used to talk about that all the time. It's something I have told Craig and Michelle on numerous occasions, whenever they've voiced concerns about how challenging it was for their dad to get up and go to work every day with the painful disability of mul-tiple sclerosis. What I've tried to tell them is that their father was overflowing with so much joy and pride just from being their dad that he felt like the luckiest person to walk the earth.

There are simply no words to say how proud Fraser would have been today of his daughter, Michelle, and his son-in-law, Barack, whom he had the pleasure of getting to know and of welcoming into our family early on in the young couple's courtship. What a proud grandfather he would have been of

Malia and Sasha Obama, as well as of his grandchildren Avery and Leslie Robinson, and of their baby brother, our newest family arrival, Austin Lucas Robinson, born January 4, 2010, to my daughter-in-law, Kelly, and to Craig.

More than anything, Fraser would have been so proud of the parents that our kids and their spouses have become. And I know he would have absolutely loved this book and how it reflects so much of the teaching he incorporated into his everyday interactions with others. He would have especially loved the fact that Craig reminds us throughout his book of the theme of unselfish basketball—and the opportunities we have to do more for one another and to win together as families, as communities, and as a nation.

Well, there is one other thing that I'm sure Fraser would have wanted me to add in this foreword, and that is to tell you just what an exceptional coach Craig Malcolm Robinson has become. I say that not as a mom or even as someone who has known him since he was born about forty-eight years ago. That comment comes from attending practices and games over the last fifteen years or so, and from watching Craig work with his players, using every teaching tool and resource at his disposal, coaching them to reach beyond their own limitations and to develop their own potential not only as athletes but as great human beings—inspiring them to go further than they may have even dreamed. And isn't that what character is all about?

PREGAME:
TESTS OF CHARACTER

The idea to write this book—as a way of paying tribute to a handful of very important individuals who have shaped my understanding of basketball and of life, and who have contributed to my ongoing search for what it truly means to have character—has been percolating in the back of my mind for years.

But it wasn't until the waning minutes before my appearance at the Democratic National Convention in Denver on Monday night, August 25, 2008, that I made the conscious decision to put pen to paper. Of course, writing a book was the last thing that I needed to be thinking about at that particular time for me and my family, not to mention in those very moments while standing backstage—where I was attempting to go through the equivalent of my pregame ritual that allows me, as a coach, to remove myself from the hubbub and become the calm within the storm for my players. But this night, for lack of a better description, was a whole other ball game!

Not that I was nervous about stepping out into the glare of history's spotlight. On the contrary, nothing could have been more gratifying than the opportunity to speak from my heart in introducing my sister, Michelle Robinson Obama, to the thousands of incredibly energized delegates at the Convention Center and to the millions of Americans watching. The weight of the moment, rather, had everything to do with the unbelievable responsibility that had fallen to Michelle. As the headliner of the convention's first night, my little sister, Miche, twenty months my junior, my only sibling, now wife of Senator Barack Obama—who was about to become the party's nominee for president of the United States of America—had to deliver the speech of her life. Intended not only to welcome the delegates and help reunite the party after what everyone agreed had been the most bruising primary season in modern times, the speech also had to deliver the most important character reference for the candidate that would be given throughout the general election season to come.

In basketball terms, at least in my thinking, Michelle was being asked to sink a three-pointer at the buzzer in a do-or-die game at the start of the championship. Everything to come, victory or disappointment, would hinge on this one shot. And all I could do to help was simply pass her the ball. And *believe*.

As if reading my mind, just as I turned to follow a production assistant to the spot from which I would enter onto the stage for my speech, a glowingly confident Michelle popped her head out of the green room and hurried over for a last-minute hug.

"Craig," she said, with a look in her eyes that spoke volumes, letting me know that she was ready to cross the threshold into the public eye and to become, potentially, the most influential woman in the world, "thank you."

"Thank you." I grinned in response, thrilled to be along

for the ride, as surreal as it all seemed. Both of us were probably thinking the same thing—how grateful we were to have
our mother, Marian Robinson, on hand for this occasion and
to take part in this most unlikely of journeys. And I was sure
that on this night, of all times, Michelle and I both missed our
dad, the late Fraser Robinson III, more than ever. Then again,
I was just as sure that he was very much present, smiling down
on us, reveling in the possibilities.

"Mr. Robinson," one of the staffers whispered with a mix
of politeness and urgency, pointing me toward the stage where
I would enter in darkness during the last minutes of a video
about our family. Before I turned to go, Michelle, playing
coach for a minute, gave me a last once-over, nodding with
approval at my choice of attire—a tailored black suit with an
orange tie that my wife, Kelly, had picked out, with input
from my son, Avery, and daughter, Leslie. Four months earlier,
in the midst of the fever pitch of the presidential primary
season, I had accepted the post as head coach of the men's
basketball program at Oregon State University. We had only
recently started to acclimate to Providence, Rhode Island,
where I'd spent the last two seasons as head coach at Brown
University, but the opportunity to move to a Pac-10 school
(its subbasement record at the time notwithstanding) was too
great to pass up. With the season set to start in days, I knew
what a boost it would be to wear the school colors as a shout-
out to Oregon State.

"Well?" I said, with a final it's-now-or-never shrug to
Miche, making sure that we were both good to go.

She answered by doing something either one of our parents might have done: She stepped forward to straighten my
tie, a gesture of love and pride, no words necessary, and then
turned to go toward the other side of the set from which she
would be entering.

Now it was time to take my place on the stage in the

darkness and wait for the lights to come up. Was this crazy or what? The question uppermost in my mind while I stood there in the dark was, *How had all of this happened?* It was one of those out-of-body experiences others had described before but that had been foreign to me until now—with floodgates opened and scenes of my life passing in front of my eyes, memories from the past coming at me from every direction. Everything was so vivid—all the stages of my own journey and those of loved ones, the critical turning points, the all-important counsel sought by me and by others, and then the everyday, ordinary family upbringing in the Robinson household on the Southside of Chicago that was the primary music of my childhood and youth.

As if no time at all had passed, what suddenly came into my awareness were word-for-word conversations shared with Dad over the course of many years about the game of basketball—which to him was indeed a game of character. This wasn't our only topic of philosophical interest, but because basketball was a personal passion and serious pursuit for me, I was especially attuned to his analysis as to how you could tell everything you needed to know about someone by how they played the game—whether it was the dog-eat-dog combat of street basketball in the neighborhood, or the more structured play at the high school level, or at the top tiers of collegiate and professional basketball, or in a more casual game of pickup ball.

As someone who embodied character in its truest sense, Fraser Robinson spoke with authority. And without a doubt, I listened. Here was a man who never missed a day of work, sometimes doing double and swing shifts for the City of Chicago at the water filtration plant, and who would come home to spend time with the wife he adored and the two children he loved—as fully engaged in his role as husband and parent as he was at everything else in his life. It is noteworthy that I often have to remind myself that he did all this while he battled the debilitating disease of multiple sclerosis. Never once in any of my memories can I recall seeing him walk without a limp. Yet never once can I remember him complaining, even when he went from using one cane to two, and in those times when he needed help getting up and dressed in the morning and, later, more help just getting around.

When Dad made observations about how players revealed different parts of their personalities on the court, the point wasn't for me to agree wholesale with every opinion. Instead, he was encouraging me to do what both he and Mom wanted their kids to remember throughout life—to think for ourselves and come to our own conclusions. This was obviously great training for the basketball player and future coach in me; learning to see the subtleties in the code of ethics that different individuals brought to their game—whatever game it happened to be—would have other valuable applications along the way. I learned to see how certain players could be horribly selfish—and, in spite of certain skills, were not guys you wanted on your team—or how others were phonies and would keep up a front, only to undermine the team when the going got tough. On the flip side, I learned to spot the characteristics of players who could play well and who could raise everybody else's game around them. I developed my own theory about the spectrum that ran from those who played merely to have fun all the way to the other side, where you would encounter players who had to win at any cost.

"Remember, Craig," Dad told me on one occasion when I was disappointed a teammate had let me down during a game, "not everybody can do everything." That would be a recurring theme. Sometimes the guy with the most character couldn't shoot to save his life but was the ideal captain. Sometimes the star shooter who could hit the three-pointers from anywhere on the court was a ball hog and couldn't be relied upon to pass the ball when the pressure was on. This conversation also yielded the conclusion that it is usually as games wear on, when players are fatigued and have been in the trenches for a while, that their true colors really show.

Growing up, Michelle wasn't in on the details of these discussions. But given our proximity in small quarters and as a tight-knit family, through osmosis she must have just absorbed the notion Dad and I had embraced that you can tell a man's character through the game of basketball. Or at least that's what I suspected when she came to me with a very odd request several months after she had started dating one young man by the name of Barack Obama.

As I stood there in the darkness at the Denver Convention Center that momentous August night, thinking back to Michelle's request eighteen years earlier, circa 1990, I can honestly say that there was nothing about this very bright, handsome, poised new beau of my sister's that bespoke of some auspicious destiny. But let me quickly add that judging others based on what or who they might grow up to be was not the Marian and Fraser Robinson way. We were taught to recognize others for who they were, not for who they could become in the future or who their pedigree or résumé presented them as. At both college and graduate school—not to mention in earlier stints as a professional ballplayer and as an investment banker before changing course to pursue my true dream of being a coach—I'd met plenty of guys with impressive pedigrees and CVs whom I would have never considered worthy of my sister. So I wasn't looking for her to date someone who could become president of the United States of America or who would provide for her in material or impressive ways. I wasn't worried about that. Whatever she decided to do, Miche could provide for herself and forge her own future. What I wanted for Michelle was what our parents had and what I would later find in my second marriage, when I met Kelly—to be in a partnership with an ability to provide for each other, to build a home and family together. What mattered most of all was that they loved each other and had similar values and aspirations, could balance decisions with teamwork, develop the ability to compromise—and every attribute of marriage that makes a relationship a great relationship.

Granted, it wasn't easy to pass the approval test in the Robinson household—although I have to admit that the first time we met Barack, he couldn't have made a better impression. On a memorably hot Chicago summer evening, my parents and I were sitting out on the front porch when the two of them strolled up, stopping by to say hello on their way to a movie.

Out of earshot as they approached, Mom said, "Well, he's tall." With my sister being five-eleven, that was a good thing.

Dad nodded, adding, "Not a bad-looking guy either."

Michelle introduced him, no differently than she would have anyone else she dated, and he was very self-possessed, I thought—with a nice smile and a firm handshake. He asked questions and answered them with ease, as if he was used to jumping into new situations and genuinely liked people. I could relate. But it was when he talked about his family—even though his experiences were different from ours—that I saw a similarity in values that could definitely work to his advantage in their relationship. At the least, I concluded he was the kind of guy my sister wouldn't run over!

But no sooner had Michelle and Barack left for their date than Mom and Dad exchanged knowing glances and I let out a sigh.

"Too bad," Mom said.

"Yep," Dad and I said in unison. Then my father added, "She'll eat him alive."

Mom gave the relationship six months to last.

It was almost a year later—at the point we were taking bets about when she was going to move on, as usual—when

Miche came to ask for this favor that nearly floored me. From what she could tell, there was nothing not to like about Barack. But now she wanted to have some insight about what kind of guy he was when she wasn't around. And since Dad and I had preached the gospel of basketball being the true revealer of character, Michelle had come up with the idea that I include Barack in a game of pickup basketball and check him out.

Normally, I would have laughed at such a preposterous suggestion or complained bitterly about being put in the position of having to basically create an audition situation. But I was so happy that she really liked this guy that I agreed (albeit begrudgingly) to arrange a pickup game with a group of guys who played at mixed levels—mainly from their college days in the Ivy League and in Division I basketball, but also a couple who hadn't gone further than high school, and then a player or two who had played professionally.

We all gathered a week later on a sunny Saturday spring morning at a neighborhood high school gym at the University of Chicago Lab School. It was here, in this beautiful old gymnasium—with the tall, thin windows I loved for their view of the trees and the graceful campus outside—that I had spent many hours in a volunteer coaching job back in those days when I was not yet ready to leave my career in the financial field. Our pickup games often took place here, so there was nothing forced or unusual about the vibe as everyone arrived, on time, ready to play. Barack strolled in without any apparent intimidation, thankfully unaware that he was being vetted. Nor did he seem to detect anything out of the ordinary when I made sure that he was on my team—so I could keep an eye on him—as we began a series of five-on-five games intended to take us all through the paces for the next hour and a half.

My initial concern was that Barack would be so far out of

his element that I'd have to protect him on the court—not wanting him in any way to lose face. The other worry was that he might turn out to be one of those jerks who is oblivious to everyone else on the floor but himself. Almost as soon as we started playing, it was clear that I didn't have to worry about his competence. He was a typical basketball player who could hold his own, though there was more to be determined in terms of skill and character. The first test, however, had been passed.

Then, as we played on, came the next set of clues that he had definitely attained experience in the game at some point—which turned out to be high school basketball. And, lo and behold, Barack Obama proved to have some skills. He had a nice little shot and liked to go to the basket. He played with guts. Interesting. He also knew how to find the open shot. Excellent. Definitely a very left-handed player—not like some lefties who have developed right-handed maneuvers and can even outdo other righties. But Barack used his strengths to compensate for his weaknesses. Self-awareness! The more we played, the more he showed his basketball intelligence—the fact that he had knowledge of the game. He didn't have to constantly score to show he could play. He knew when to pass and when not to pass (even if he preferred going for that open shot). He knew when to cut, when to set a pick, and what to do after the pick. In my terminology, he knew the x's and o's, the nuts and bolts, of basketball.

Better still, Barack conformed to the unspoken rules of integrity that apply in these friendly but highly competitive gatherings where there are no refs. That meant when he fouled somebody else and was called for it, he didn't argue, but gave it up, acknowledging the push or the trip he'd committed with a mea culpa nod or by saying in a very cool, matter-of-fact way, "My bad"—and then allowing play to continue. When he was fouled, depending on the degree, he called it without overdoing the dramatic indignation or flopping that are usually signs of bad habits.

It should be mentioned that compared to most of us out there that day—me at six feet six plus, then at a medium build, and guys like the muscular Arne Duncan at six-five, who had been cocaptain of his team at Harvard (later to become secretary of education for the Obama administration)—Barack was definitely on the slight side. Now, not everyone in our group was a big guy. My longtime friend and colleague John Rogers—who was captain of the team at Princeton when I arrived to play there and who opened doors when I entered the business world—was only six feet tall, more than an inch shorter than Barack. Then again, Rogers packed so much power into how he moved and shot the ball that he would later famously beat Michael Jordan in a game of one-on-one. So, looking at Obama as he was then, you might have come to the conclusion that he'd be hitting the hardwood most of the time. Not so. Of course, I knew that in basketball—as in life—you never want to infer too much from appearances. That said, I gave him brownie points for toughness.

What was revealing as we reached the midway point—with each team having lost some and won some—was that Barack had come to play and that he knew the object was to *keep playing*. For that, I was willing to conclude he had passed the test with flying colors. But two other character traits didn't go unnoticed. One of these showed up after over an hour of playing and some of the guys were starting to tire. Not Barack. He seemed to have a quality that I've seen in leaders throughout my life—a capacity for what I call being relentless, for drawing from some inner wellspring of energy when others are running out of gas. And the clincher, even though he had no clue he was on an audition, was the fact that he was dating my sister, and he could have done any number of things to try to impress or kiss up to me, and he didn't! If he was a phony, by the time he started to fatigue toward the end, he would have done or said something embarrassing to either try to boost my ego or assume a level of closeness that wasn't there yet or showboat in some way. None of that happened. We were three-quarters of the way through the session when I gave in to major relief. Phew! I could report back to my sister that he was a *normal* player, someone who could continue on in our regular game, no problem. He was real, down-to-earth, a good guy.

Again, Michelle and Barack were only dating at the time. It wasn't as if they were engaged or, worse, that this was happening at the bachelor's party. Or at least that was in my thoughts when I began to appreciate the method to the madness and went to give my sister a glowing report. Summing it all up, I gave her the verdict: "He's very confident without being cocky." He had passed the test with a definitive thumbs-up on his playing and his character.

To what extent this input helped give Barack the edge a short time later when he proposed to Michelle and she accepted, I can't say. But the bottom line was that she said yes!

As much as I might have grumbled at the time, in hindsight, I could only feel honored that my sister trusted my assessment enough to ask for it. And that was the same sense of honor I felt some sixteen years later, in late 2006, when Barack came to me for advice and direction on an issue of great importance to him—a possible run for the White House.

"You mean—right now, for the '08 election?" was my immediate reaction when, without any prelude, he brought the subject up after I'd stopped by the Chicago Obama household to pick up Avery and Leslie, who were visiting with their cousins and spending time with their grandmother.

By this stage of the game, Barack was two years into his role as the junior senator from Illinois in the United States Senate, and I was just starting as head coach at Brown. My brother-in-law and I were used to conversations on the fly about our eventful lives—in this case literally on the fly, since I'd just flown into town. Barack and I had gravitated, as usual, to the kitchen, the hearth of the home, for something to eat and to get caught up on the concerns of the day. Of course, it hadn't been inconceivable that someday in the future he might be a candidate. But this was sudden.

Barack answered me by saying that, yes, he was referring to '08 and that there was meaningful interest in him as a candidate. Advisors who had worked on his Senate race, along with new partners, were telling him that this might be the right time to mount a bold, different kind of campaign built on grass roots and the nation's growing desire for change.

"There is a window of opportunity," Barack said thoughtfully, letting me know that while he certainly hadn't signed on yet, he was seriously looking at the pros and cons. Then he surprised me by asking, "What do you think?"

All I could think at that moment was what came out of my mouth—"Wow!" He had brought it up so matter-of-factly, without fanfare or drumroll, that I was caught off guard. But as I found my bearings, I went further, telling him, "I think it's fantastic!"

My only frame of reference, yet again, was from basketball. To me this was along the lines of being considered the Most Valuable Player ever of the NBA championships. There had to be a better analogy I could offer. Since my present career had begun with an assistant coaching position at Northwestern and I had only recently advanced to head coach at Brown—with the intended turnaround just getting under way—then, for me the coaching version of being considered for president would have to be this: to be appointed head coach of the winningest men's college basketball team in the country, the University of Kentucky Wildcats.

That was why, as we discussed the reasons that Barack

might not be ready for a presidential run, I had to argue, "You know what? I may not be ready for the Kentucky job, but if somebody offers it to me, I'm taking it!"

After all, as we both knew, when windows of opportunity open, you can't count on them staying that way. At the same time, given the landscape at this point, even a political outsider like me knew that the field of candidates was already crowded. But long shot though it was, my feeling was—why not? Between asking what the next steps were and how I could help, I had to add, "You're right, this is a window of opportunity to do good on behalf of a whole lot of people who really need it."

Barack seemed to take these words to heart and smiled as though encouraged. But then, less certainly, he added, "There's no way I can do this without having your sister and mother on board." He indicated that Mom wasn't as adamant as Michelle— who was none too happy about the prospect of having to go through an ordeal that would be exponentially more grueling for her and the girls than the Senate race had already been. Barack then put it to me directly when he asked, "Would you mind talking to your sister?"

"Well, no, but if you can't convince her, I don't see how I can."

"You don't have to convince her. But let her know how you feel. She trusts you."

With that, I took on the herculean assignment of assisting Barack by approaching two of the strongest women in the world—Michelle Robinson Obama and Marian Robinson— and employing arguments and lessons that they both had helped teach me over the years.

Much back-and-forth followed and eventually, as evidenced by where we had gathered in August of 2008, impossible though it had once seemed, the effort paid off. Even so, as the final seconds ticked by before the lights came back up in the convention center, with the tidal wave of memories gone and my senses focusing back on the present, I still had to laugh that even with my sister and brother-in-law both being Harvard-trained lawyers, the basketball coach was called in to help negotiate the deal!

Let me hasten to add, however, that it was the courageous actions taken by our current First Family and by every single person involved in the historic campaign that led to its final outcome. Which leads me to a fundamental teaching my parents always emphasized—that life happens to you, putting choices in your path that offer an abundance of opportunities as well as challenges (and sometimes both), and that the best choices are usually the ones that require courage. They may demand that you raise your level of play beyond anything you ever knew you were capable of, but those are the choices most worth taking.

And really, that's what most inspired me to write *A Game of Character*—not only to share with you what I've learned (and hopefully passed on to my children and to my players), but also to help reclaim the value of character that I believe is as intrinsic to basketball as it is to life. What's more, as the pages ahead will elaborate, true character is a quality that can be found everywhere and anywhere, in some of the least likely places—including the Southside of Chicago, which is exactly where we're headed next.

A GAME OF CHARACTER

PART I

FUNDAMENTALS

1

MEET THE
HOME TEAM

To the best of my knowledge, my parents never consciously set out to develop a game plan for educating their children as to the importance of character. Nor, for that matter, would Marian or Fraser Robinson claim to have had any special knowledge or inherent parenting gifts for creating what I believe was the greatest start in life that my sister and I could have ever wanted. And yet, the more time passes, the more amazed I am by how much they really did seem to know what they were doing.

To me, now as then, they were practically magical—with *practical* being the operative word. In fact, when I once asked Mom how she and Dad came up with their remarkable parenting approach, she shrugged and said, "We didn't see it that way. We were just trying to find what worked." They never presumed to be any different from most normal working-class families in our neighborhood—or from most parents everywhere. Mom's simple way of putting it was, "We were just trying to make a better life for our children."

Still, when I retrace my steps of learning to as far back as I can consciously recall—to somewhere in the vicinity of my third birthday—I can spot one of the guiding principles my parents used in what was clearly a purposeful coaching strategy. The main focus was to develop something I did hear Mom mention a lot over the years, long before I knew what it meant—a prized commodity known as *self-esteem*.

In my parents' playbook, self-esteem wasn't only a measure of feeling good about yourself and developing your own potential. It was also about cultivating unselfishness. Self-esteem, in these fundamental terms, came with having a sense of belonging to our family, of being loved and valued; and it came from the knowledge that we each had a role to play as a contributing member of the family—the original home team.

Family was everything. It was a constant and dominant strand woven into all of my childhood memories. One of the earliest of these took place a short while after April 21, 1965, the date of my third birthday, when my parents announced they had exciting news they wanted to share with me and Michelle.

Of course, since Miche, born January 17, 1964, was only a year and a half at the time, including her in the discussion was more to let me understand that this was a subject of importance to the whole family. Then again, since my sister happens to be one of the most fiercely intelligent individuals I've ever met, she may have followed the conversation much more than we realized.

In any event, when Dad proceeded to explain that we were going to be moving to another house—over on Euclid Avenue, farther east and closer to Lake Michigan—I couldn't see why this was exciting. The center of my universe was where we were living then, at the Parkway Garden Homes, a housing cooperative in the Woodlawn area on the Southside of Chicago. It was not the typical housing project becoming afflicted by urban blight in these years, but it was a project nonetheless and in one of the poorer neighborhoods in this era. But at three years old, what did I know? It was familiar. Why rock the boat?

Well, one reason to shake up the status quo, it turned out, had to do with the self-esteem curriculum designed by Mom and Dad. They wanted us to be open to new and even challenging experiences. That's how this opportunity to move up in the world was presented to me. Wanting to address my fear of the unknown, my parents went on to give me some of the details as to how and why this was happening.

Mom began, "You know the house we visited on Euclid Avenue where your great-aunt Robbie and great-uncle Terry live?" She was referring to her aunt—the sister of my mother's father, Purnell Shields—and to Aunt Robbie's husband, Terry.

Of course, we had been to visit them on a few recent occasions. After years of hard work at their respective jobs—Aunt Robbie as a schoolteacher and Uncle Terry as a Pullman porter—the two had pooled their retirement pensions and had purchased a two-story, redbrick Chicago-style bungalow on Euclid Avenue in the South Shore area of the Southside. Without kids of their own, they wanted our family to move in upstairs.

Looking back, I can see even more clearly why accepting the offer was a significant decision. First of all, in addition to raising two young children, my parents would also be responsible for taking care of two elderly family members. Secondly, if opportunities arose to move into a place of our own later on, they might not have the same freedom to do so. Besides, Mom and Dad were still a young couple and had seen their lives change dramatically since meeting and marrying in 1960, two years before I was born—or so I would later learn from my grandma LaVaughn Robinson, my father's mother. Before meeting Marian Shields, Fraser Robinson may not have been the settling-down type. Tall, handsome, he was something of a man about town, into jazz clubs and the like—just a very cool cat with his dark sunglasses, well-groomed mustache and short hair, and his cigarettes that he held between thumb and forefinger in a very hip, manly way.

Mom, for her part, was a beauty, very self-possessed, then working as a secretary at Spiegel Catalog. With an independent streak, she had everything within her to become an executive—although I think her real passion was for teaching. Mom had actually attended two years of a teaching college and my assumption was that she intended to return to college once she saved the money to do so. But life came calling. To be specific, Fraser Robinson did!

From what little Grandma would be able to tell me of their courtship, I know that my parents met through mutual friends, and dated for a year before getting married. Upon later reflection, it did seem like a major turnaround for my father, then twenty-six years old, to give up the adventurous life of the cool cat he had been and choose to settle down into the routine of the same job doing shift work for the city's water department. Nor could it have been the easiest thing for my mother to give up her independence. But judging from photos of the period when they were dating, it's as clear as day in their faces what the two saw in each other, how thrilled they were to be in each other's company, and that they just cracked each other up! In particular, there is one strip of four funny shots from a carnival photo booth that really looks like they were having the best time two young people could ever have. That love for one another was simply a fact of our lives, the foundation of the strong family unit they chose to build, and the reason they always seemed to be happy to me—even when circumstances might have dictated otherwise.

This is all to say that when I heard the game plan for our move, provided by Mom and Dad in a way that made sense logically to my three-year-old brain, all that was left was for them to then introduce the element of adventure. This wasn't only to entice me but also to make a lasting point: All kinds of fun and games might await us, but only if we were willing to give something new a try.

With that, I was sold. Little did I know, however, the degree to which the upper-floor residence of the two-family home on Euclid Avenue would become the Shangri-la of upbringings. True, there were rules, chores, and hard-won lessons about discipline that didn't seem remotely fun back then. Still, what most stands out for me as I think back to these formative years was the enthusiasm for life, another essential for self-esteem, that filled the household—from sunup to sundown, day in and day out.

Enthusiasm! For a player on any team, in any game, that is a quality of character, much underrated, that can compensate for a whole lot of other shortcomings. It came naturally to my parents and was something they taught more by example than by lecture. Not only that, but I remember it as a trait shared by most everyone in our extended family, and it could even be seen as a characteristic of the working-class neighborhood we inhabited.

With the weather alone, you had to muster some kind of upbeat attitude just to survive, especially when it was below zero with bone-freezing winds blasting in from Lake Michigan, or when summer's heat came on with a vengeance, with humidity at 100 percent and the thermostat even higher. And without air-conditioning! Or at least that was our situation. Maybe there was also something in this mix that came from the Chicago personality of being the "second city"—

always in the shadow of New York—with the we-try-harder mentality of needing the enthusiasm to compete. It was a quality I loved about our hometown teams—particularly the Bears, the team I watched religiously with Dad when I considered football a first love. Later, baseball took over when I started to play the game, when cheering for the Cubs (in spite of a chronic losing record) definitely became a test of enthusiasm. And then, when I eventually made basketball my focus, how could having the Bulls in my backyard be anything other than motivating?

But whether or not a case can be made for Chicago having its own brand of enthusiasm, I'm not the authority. What I do know is, that was the temperament of most folks around us in our section of redbrick bungalow-lined and tree-adorned blocks—some of whom were white families when we moved in, although a lot of our area of the Southside was becoming predominantly black. As I recall, people were generally optimistic, energetic, and hardworking—making the most from modest means. In this respect, you could detect a quality of character in the neighborhood—in the way that you might walk down a street and describe buildings as having character.

Interestingly enough, when the different styles of redbrick bungalows were being built in Chicago in the decades before World War II—to house the influx of workers in the steel industry and other manufacturing sectors, many of them blacks migrating from the South, along with a mix of immigrants—the architects considered certain design elements as being conducive to developing harmonious neighborhoods. In appearance, the houses were designed to be pleasing to the eye but also unpretentious; functionally they were built to be comfortable but practical. Though the bungalows had distinctive touches that gave them their individuality, they shared similar features—red brick, for one, along with plenty of windows that made good use of natural light. Not quite town houses, many bungalows were built closely to one another on narrow lots, with peaked rooftops that, instead of facing the street, were perpendicular to it. And some, like ours, had a main entrance that was on the side of the house, not the front. Actually, ours had two side entrances next to each other—one that went into Great-Aunt Robbie and Great-Uncle Terry's first-floor home, and then a second one that opened to the stairway that led up to what had probably been designed as a bachelor apartment for one person.

To be more precise, it was probably intended for one *short* person—not a family of two tall adults and two active children who would become taller in no time. Just how cramped it was would only be apparent in my grown-up years—when I'd be shocked on visits home that my shoulders could barely make it through the doorways and I'd have to bend down so as not to hit my head. But back in the day, I had no clue that it was such a small, modest abode. And to make it seem even more expansive, Dad made up a game that he introduced to me soon after we moved in.

"Cat," he said to me one weekend morning after breakfast, using the affectionate nickname he'd made up for me that he never explained, "come over here."

Taking me by the hand, Dad walked me slowly from the kitchen table down the hall to the doorway that led into the bedroom that Miche and I shared. As this was the only bedroom, Dad and Mom put us in here and converted the living room into their bedroom—another instance of how they often put our well-being ahead of theirs. The slow stutter-step of my father's, as he limped along down the hall, was already a part of who he was, as far as I knew. He had recently undergone back surgery for disk problems—to which I attributed the limp and his inability ever to run or even walk fast. It wouldn't be until our teens that we would hear anything having to do with MS.

But again, there was nothing about his limp or his pace

that diminished his enthusiasm or true abilities, which were nearly akin to superpowers in my eyes. Even in hindsight, I marvel at the high level of emotional intelligence that was within him, how everyone in the community and in our extended family looked up to him, and how he connected to others so strongly. He had an uncanny way of speaking the truth that people might not want to hear but needed to know—such that his serious counsel was frequently sought. What can I say? He was my hero.

"Well?" Dad asked with a twinkle in his eye when we reached the door to our bedroom. "Do you see what I see?" Pointing up to the trim above the door, he guided my eyes toward something shiny and metallic sparkling up there.

It was a quarter—twenty-five cents! That was a fortune in treasure to a four-year-old who had little concept of money. Though it was some time before I realized that Dad had put the quarter up there to create this game, it was easy to see that our job was to retrieve it. How? By jumping with all my might. Again, again, and again. Impossible! Dad eventually gave me a boost so that I could get to the quarter finally and not be totally frustrated. But as time went on and I grew, he kept putting quarters on the trim above all the doors and left their retrieval up to me. It wasn't that long before I developed a formidable vertical leap—thanks to this game. Not bad training for working on jump shots down the road!

Mom had similarly inventive devices up her sleeve, ready whenever we were. Such was the case when, at the age of four, I ran into the kitchen one morning and asked, "Mom, how do you tell time?"

Calmly, Mom replied that as soon as she finished the breakfast dishes she'd show me. The next thing I knew, she brought out a learning toy that she had obtained for just this occasion—a wooden windup clock that played an invigorating "Pop Goes the Weasel" if you successfully set it to a desired time. By the end of the day, I was the king of telling time, ready to demonstrate to my father when he came home.

A few months later, when I asked, "Mom, how do you read?" she was just as prepared—this time with a box of flash cards for teaching the alphabet and the sounds associated with each letter. She sat and worked with me all day long, and with the same diligence—to the point that not only did I learn to read at the age of four, but I did so in a very short period of time. Not surprisingly, by the time I started Bryn Mawr Elementary School, I was head and shoulders above where my classmates were—both heightwise and academically! Nor was it a surprise that I ended up skipping the third grade. And Michelle—having had the same early education from Mom at home—accelerated faster than me. She skipped second grade.

If you could make a game out of learning, my parents apparently thought—why not? We played everything from hide-and-seek to practical jokes, from sophisticated board games involving strategy to athletic contests, from games we made up to research information in dictionaries and encyclopedias to camping expeditions staged overnight on our own back porch. Mom and Dad loved the games as much as we did. It was almost a game to see who could be the most creative at turning something ordinary into a special occasion.

We had several ongoing games that lasted from early childhood into our late teens—like the one my father instigated the time he got off work early and went to hide in our bedroom to wait for us to come up from downstairs, where Mom, Miche, and I had gone that evening for our piano lessons. At seven years old, I was in the second grade and Michelle, five years old, was in kindergarten. Not only was Aunt Robbie giving us piano lessons, but we were part of an operetta workshop she had created for children in our school district, and we were rehearsing our singing parts for the Christmas production of *Hansel and Gretel* coming up in weeks. Occupied as we were with music and preparations, none of us heard Dad opening the outside door and going slowly up the stairs.

When lessons and rehearsal were over, Mom led the way, reminding us to put our music where it belonged in our room and then wash up for supper. In those days, the walls of our long, skinny bedroom had been festively decorated with clowns and cheerful circus designs and the furniture had been set up with Miche's bed and mine head-to-head—separated by a small table. This was to suggest that we had separate areas of the room but we were still together. It was the team approach, after all. In many ways, it was almost as if we were twins rather than siblings close in age. But as the older, responsible brother, I would have naturally been the first into the bedroom, with Miche following fast behind me. And Mom, being the disciplinarian, happened to be right behind us in making sure that we didn't throw our music books on the floor. No sooner had I flipped on the light switch and the three of us stepped foot into the room than Dad appeared from behind the bed—and shocked us all into speechlessness!

"Fraser!" my mother finally said, after catching her breath, and suppressing her amused smile. "You scared us to death."

Miche and I agreed that he had scared us to death too. And we loved it! From then on, it became a contest to see who could scare the others the most. Miche and I were usually on the same team to scare our parents, since we knew each other too well to figure out hiding places the other wouldn't suspect.

We were such a team, in fact, that whatever happened on a day-to-day basis to one of us would directly impact the other. If either one of us was happy for some reason, then the other was happier. We had an unwritten law that neither one of us could get up until the other was awake on Christmas morning—as was the case the year when I was seven and a half and I opened my eyes to see her standing at the side of the bed waiting for me. Dad met us as we were coming out of our room, excitedly informing us, "Hey, I think I heard Santa Claus down in the basement!"

We flew down the stairs in robes and slippers, where we were met by the sight of a brand-new bike with training wheels. Miche started cheering before I could say a word. But it wasn't really Christmas for me until I laid eyes on the tricycle that Santa had left for her.

The flip side of being happy for each other when either one of us had reason to celebrate was that we were even more upset at any injustice suffered by the other one. For instance, when Michelle was five and came home from kindergarten earlier than I did, she insisted on waiting for me at the gate to our yard right beside Mom, where she was horrified to see me one afternoon racing around the corner followed by a pack of girls from my class.

I was too young to explain that being chased by cute girls might not have been the worst feeling in the world. But to my sister this was an outrage and she began to call at the top of her lungs, "Come on, Craig, run faster! Come on!"

Run faster I did, which put me through the gate with seconds to spare—enough time for five-year-old Michelle Robinson to firmly push the gate closed and shrug confidently to the five out-of-breath girls, who then turned and stomped away in defeat. The next day, the aggressive girls were at it again, but in vain. This went on for weeks. Between my longer legs and Miche's fast, determined reflexes, they never got me.

In spite of my parents' protestations that they were no different from their peers, they really were unusual for their generation in the extent to which they spent time with us.

This wasn't from obligation but because, frankly, they seemed to enjoy our company. As a matter of fact, Mom and Dad almost never went on dates and left us with babysitters. Maybe three times in my life can I recall them going out and leaving us with other caretakers. It wasn't just that we didn't have money for extravagances like that. I think they really preferred being with their kids and including us in whatever entertainment they had in mind—whether it was to go to the drive-in as a family or to head over to a relative's house.

Dad's usual MO was to casually announce, "I'm going to stop over at Grandpa's house, who wants to come?"

By the time I was seven and Michelle was five, we had a fast response to that question, invariably asking in unison: "Which grandpa?" We were excited to go, no matter what, but if we were going to see my mother's father, that was one entirely different experience than if we were going to go see Dad's father.

Going to visit the home of Fraser Robinson II meant we could prepare to be "edified." That was one of the words that our grandfather had used in front of me and my sister—and then, with his signature scowl, asked us if we knew what that meant.

A real disciplinarian and very stern, he had worked at the post office for many years and was as precise as a drill sergeant when it came to the use of the English language. He seemed to look for every opportunity to use words that we'd never heard before. Then when we'd admit that we had no idea what that meant, he'd say, "Go look it up."

On one visit, I went to greet him and as soon as I said hello, Grandpa barked, "Well, that was perfunctory!"

Oh, no. I knew where this was headed. Sure enough, before I could respond, he asked, "Do you know what *perfunctory* means?"

"No, I don't know."

"Then go look it up!" my grandfather said, predictably. But then he smiled—which was not only shocking, since it was so rare, but also made me wonder if it made him happy to use a word we didn't know. Though he was not always enjoyable to be around, I will give him credit for significantly increasing our vocabulary.

When we were very young, we distinguished our grand-fathers by where they lived. As Dad's father lived on the Southside, not far from where we used to live, and Mom's father, Purnell Shields, lived on the Westside, we gave them nicknames in tribute to the neighborhoods. Grandpa Fraser became Southside and Grandpa Purnell became Westside.

But then one day when one of my father's five siblings, his youngest and only sister, Francesca, was leaving their par-ents' house, she said, "Bye, Dandy," as a slip of the tongue when she meant to say, "Bye, Daddy." From then on, we all called Grandpa Fraser "Dandy."

Meanwhile, my mother's father moved from the Westside to the Southside, about two blocks from where we lived on Euclid Avenue. We were over visiting one afternoon when a cousin on the Shields side of the family referred to Grandpa as Westside, which struck me and Michelle as hilarious.

"Westside lives over here on the Southside now," I pointed out.

"We should call him Southside," Miche declared per-suasively.

From then on, my mother's father was Southside and my father's father was Dandy.

So when our dad announced on a Friday night some-time around my ninth birthday, in the spring of 1971, that we were going over to Southside's house to drop off some tools, we knew from past experience that this seemingly spontaneous errand could possibly turn into a much bigger event.

For one thing, Dad and Mom like to propose spur-of-the-moment outings that had actually been planned—partly so as not to get our expectations up in case things didn't come together and partly for the surprise value. Second, there was always something cooking over at Southside's house. Literally! I'm talking whatever delicious feast was on the menu that day. On special occasions that would be his unsurpassed barbecue you could smell two blocks away at our house—chicken, ribs, and sausage on the grill that he'd fashioned from a big old garbage can.

That was Southside—by profession a carpenter and handyman but by calling a chef, drummer, and jazz aficionado, an impresario and all-around magnet who made everyone in the family gravitate to his side. Everyone, that is, except for my mother's mom, Grandma Rebecca.

After having seven children together—Carolyn Ann, Robbie Joyce, Adrienne, Marian (Mom), Gracie, and then David and Steve—my grandparents had separated, for reasons never discussed. Possibly they just weren't compatible. Where Southside was gregarious and loved to blast Charlie Parker and Miles Davis on his record player so loud that I think he lost some hearing in one ear as a result, Grandma Rebecca was a former nurse and a very reserved, though kindly, woman who preferred reading the paper quietly from cover to cover rather than entertaining the masses. Of course, she loved us and enjoyed visits with her many grandchildren, though she wasn't a get-down-on-the-floor kind of grandma that way.

After they separated, even though Grandma Rebecca lived around the corner from Southside with her youngest daughter—my aunt Gracie—and Gracie's husband, my mother's parents almost never saw each other again. One time when Southside was at our place, helping to remodel the bedroom that Michelle and I shared—installing a half wall between us so we could have a bit more privacy—we thought he'd like to know that it was just his luck that Grandma Rebecca was coming over for dinner and we were having Mom's fried chicken that we all loved.

Michelle and I had assumed he'd be delighted to see Grandma, but Southside got his tools together so fast to leave he almost fell down the stairs. We spotted Grandma a half block from our gate at about the same moment he dashed out of it and raced off in the opposite direction. According to family lore, the only time Purnell and Rebecca were knowingly in the same place at the same time was years later at the funeral for my great-grandmother, Southside's mom—otherwise known to her numerous grandchildren and great-grandchildren as Mamaw.

The Friday evening when Dad and Mom decided to stop over at Southside's, not surprisingly, most of the family on the Shields side of the aisle were also just stopping by. We were greeted by the sound of Ella Fitzgerald scat-singing on the record player and the sight of Southside presiding over his grill. Mamaw, still alive, was comfortably perched on a chair to watch the different generations enjoying themselves—aunts and uncles sitting down to card games or to talk politics and current events, and us kids running off to create skits complete with dialogue, singing, and dance moves. On that evening, as I recall, Southside had set up microphones to go with his stereo equipment and we were able to perform a medley of Jackson 5 songs—not too badly either!

After that, we all hung out, mixing in with the adults, not listening so much as absorbing the general attitude of enthusiasm they had toward whatever they were doing or talking about. Everybody did something outside of his or her work life—whether it was like Dad being a precinct captain for the Democratic Party or Mom volunteering at school, or Aunt Carolyn being the choir director at church, or Great-Aunt Robbie teaching her operetta workshop. Nobody called it service, per se. Rather, it was the idea of unselfishness and contribution—not to impress others with how giving you could be but because you genuinely had that to give and to offer.

That night, as usual, it was Mom who piped up at around ten P.M., letting Dad know, "We need to get these kids home to bed."

Dad took the cue and stood, giving us the gesture that it was time to go. And one thing about Fraser Robinson III that he took away from his stint in the military was timeliness. When it was time to go, we didn't like to keep him waiting—a pattern that was handed down to me in my dislike of tardiness and continues to this day with my players and my children.

Nonetheless, on this occasion, Southside held the trump card—as he often did—by pointing out to Mom, his daughter, "Marian, these kids don't have school tomorrow. What's the rush?"

Not waiting for an answer, he beckoned to us to follow him into the kitchen, where he promptly prepared a hearty snack of grilled steak and eggs and whipped up homemade malteds for whoever wanted one. The next thing we knew the storytelling began all over again, which meant Dad was in his element, and time was all but forgotten. Two and half hours later, we were headed home, tired but gratified that an outing to return tools to Southside had turned into another memorable night.

Just because trips to go visit Dandy and Grandma La-Vaughn didn't promise the same level of entertainment didn't mean that we resisted going. As it so happened, everyone on that side of the family was just as enthusiastic and as involved in activities as on Mom's side. Grandma LaVaughn—who was employed for many years by Moody Bible Institute's bookstore in Chicago—was a devout Baptist and quite scholarly when it came to scripture. Sweet and loving as she could be,

Grandma also had the gift for storytelling that she passed on to my father. Earlier on, she didn't talk much about family history, but in later years I'd go visit her and was able to fill in a lot of gaps. A primary question in my mind as a child was where Dandy had gotten the names for his five children. Being the oldest son and firstborn, my father lucked out by being the third Fraser Robinson. But Dandy named their second-born son "Nomenee Bednor."

Grandma didn't have the answer for where that came from. Several years intervened before the next three children were born. The youngest and only daughter—who would also attend and graduate from Simmons College—was named with the fittingly lovely name of Francesca. But no one knew what Dandy was thinking when he named the two boys who were born right before her—Andrew Cohen and Carlton Durant. Eventually, I learned that some of the names had come from tracing the Robinson family tree back to the days of slavery in South Carolina, to our great-great-grandfather Jim Robinson, a freed slave, whose son Fraser married Rose Ella Cohen. Hence, Andrew's middle name. But not all the names had historic explanations. My hunch was that my grandfather had come across certain words and names during his frequent browsing in dictionaries and encyclopedias—and used them to honor his children with names that definitely weren't run-of-the-mill.

Whatever the actual reason, it was always edifying to visit with the different members of that side of my family. My father's three younger siblings weren't much older than me. Andrew and Carlton were coming of age as young men in the late sixties and early seventies—when the country was in the midst of racial turmoil—and talked a great deal about black activism and the culture of the era. Later, when I was getting into my teens, my uncles, in their twenties, were full of advice about how to dress and stand so as to appeal to the opposite sex. Very useful.

The best part of going to visit any of my relatives was the very idea my parents introduced when we were preparing to move to Euclid Avenue—you never knew what it was going to be like until you stepped out of your comfort zone and took the ride. It didn't have to be earth-shattering or mind-blowing. One of the biggest surprises I can recall was the time we went over to have Easter dinner at Southside's house. Because his birthday sometimes fell on Easter and because he did all the cooking for every other holiday, this particular year my aunt Carolyn had volunteered to make dinner for everyone in her father's honor. Aunt Carolyn never married (although she had a steady boyfriend), but kept herself so busy directing the choir and looking after family members that this offer was considered very generous on her part, and all the adults appreciated it.

Excited to see Southside relaxing at his birthday Easter dinner, we were nonetheless dismayed when we arrived and detected the distinct smell of liver coming from the kitchen.

"Is that liver?" I asked Michelle quietly, throwing a look to Mom. In those days, my mother served liver every two weeks or so, as it was thought to be important for iron, healthy bones and teeth, and all the other reasons we forced ourselves to eat it—she and Dad included.

My father raised his eyebrows in surprise too. No one would seriously serve liver at an occasion like this.

"Probably they had liver last night," I proposed.

No such luck. Carolyn, probably from being cloistered with her choir and never having had to cook for a family, had no idea that she had committed the family faux pas. And of course, no one said a word to complain or to make her feel bad.

As soon as we got home to our house, we exploded with

laughter at how awful the liver had been, and we laughed about it for days. Mom was so appalled that she decided then and there never to serve liver again. And she never did. Which is why this particular tale of family folklore has such a happy ending for me!

It was a very short while after the liver incident that I was approached by a classmate at school who made a comment I'd never forget when he said, "If I had any wish to come true, it'd be to have a family like yours. You're rich!"

At nine years old, I didn't know what rich was. But I did suspect what he meant was that my sister and I had both a dad and a mom, and that my parents really cared. And if that was being rich, then there was no question that's what we were.

These days, whenever I confront a coaching or parenting challenge, I often think back to that classmate's comment and remind myself of the importance of feeling rich in self-esteem and family. Without that foundation, it's tougher to believe in yourself and to develop the confidence and unselfishness needed to thrive in life. It's a coach's or a parent's job, then, to go back to fundamentals to rekindle the belief in self and in team that will always win the day.

Now, as for whether we were really rich or not, my father had a lesson to teach me about that.

2

ROBINSON FAMILY VALUES: LOVE, DISCIPLINE, RESPECT

Over the years in my journey as a men's basketball coach—which has taken me from part-time volunteer status with high school youth to paid assistant coach at a major university and on to being head coach both in the Ivy League and at a Division I program—I have often been asked which coaches of mine most influenced how I approach the game. While there have been a handful of great basketball coaches who not only taught me how to build a strong, successful team but who also imparted lessons in character that definitely shaped my coaching style, two individuals stand above the rest. At the risk of sharing too many trade secrets, I confess that the way I coach the game today—though very much my own approach—comes as much from the Fraser and Marian Robinson school as it does from any of the other influences.

On the surface, such a statement may seem like a stretch. But as I dig deeper to recall fundamental values like love, discipline, and respect that Dad and Mom instilled in me and my sister—not in spot lessons or crash courses but consistently and insistently over time—I can see how so many of their strategies found their way into the Craig Robinson coaching style these many years later. One similarity that makes me laugh whenever I catch myself sounding just like Fraser or Marian is the tendency I have to seize on to any opportunity and turn it into a teachable moment.

Right about now I know that any of my players reading this are nodding their heads in agreement. Well, that's how I was trained! Mom and Dad were masters at taking something that happened in our day-to-day lives, good or bad, and turning it into a lesson with multiple levels of meaning. That was, in point of fact, how Dad reacted to my classmate's declaration that he wished his family were like ours because, as he suggested, we were rich. But even before Dad had a chance to seize the opportunity, I knew he was going to ask me what I thought about this statement.

So, were we rich? Before bringing it up to Dad I needed to mull the question over. On first glance, I figured my classmate had to be right. And the more I thought about how much fun we had as a family, the more certain I was that we really were rich. Then again, it wasn't like Miche and I were spoiled or anything. On the contrary, there were strict rules to follow and chores to handle every day of the week—especially weekends. So we couldn't be really rich. But would I want to trade my life for anyone else's? No way.

In fact, at almost ten years old, as I thought back over my childhood so far, there was only one really unpleasant memory that I could bring to mind—an event that had occurred back when I was eight years old in Mrs. Thompson's second-grade class at Bryn Mawr Elementary. This was the year when I was so far ahead of the rest of the class—because of how Mom had prepared me and Michelle, teaching us at home—

that I invariably whipped through my work and had to spend the rest of class time completely bored. Mrs. Thompson had done a survey of the reading levels and capacities of her top readers and I had scored 300 percent better than anyone else—thanks to Marian Robinson. Little wonder that Mrs. Thompson had decided to recommend that I do a double, as we then referred to skipping a grade.

But before that could happen, the end of the year was coming and the natives—such as we were, tromping up and down the stairs of the aging three-story brick building without much ventilation or air-conditioning—were growing restless. You could smell summer on its way. It wasn't just from the fragrance of trees in full bloom and the smell of fresh-cut grass mixing with the humidity as the mercury began its annual climb—causing hay fever symptoms to begin—but just a general need to break free. Or at least that's how I felt. And without anything to occupy my interest in class, I was primed for trouble.

I wasn't the only one. Another kid in my class decided he couldn't wait to dive into the gigantic bag of candy he had brought to school that day. But no sooner had he unwrapped a piece of bubble gum and popped it into his mouth than Mrs. Thompson was onto him like a hawk. As the rules dictated, she promptly confiscated the bag of candy and took it up to her desk, where, to everyone's titillation, she turned it over and dumped the entire contents into a pile just sitting there, sparkling in the almost-summer sunlight, like a mound of gold.

"Pssst, Craig," whispered one of the tougher boys in class who was in trouble all the time and liked to tease me for being a teacher's pet. "Dare ya to steal a piece!"

I put on my best scowl—an imitation of Grandpa Dandy's—just to show that I wasn't intimidated by the dare. Certainly I knew better than to steal a piece of candy. But when Mrs. Thompson turned her back to us and started to write on the chalkboard, and the kid dared me again, whispering, "You some kind of Goody Two-shoes? C'mon!" I succumbed to temptation.

Even at the age of eight I was already starting to shoot up, and had long arms and legs. And I did have a way of walking quietly that I'd developed trying to sneak up and scare my family members. Moving with impressive speed, I sprang into action and pounced on the pile of goodies, nabbing what looked like the sweetest piece of chewing gum I could get my hands onto and pop into my mouth. Within a split second—barely before my taste buds could even enjoy the sugar rush—a sensation of shame shot through me. Hundreds of years of history were suddenly brought into question. It was as if the entire Robinson and Shields extended families marched into the second-grade classroom with chagrin heavy in their hearts.

Of course, I knew this was wrong. After no more than five perfunctory bites, I spat it out—still shaped like a piece of gum almost just out of its wrapper—and threw it into the trash.

All of this went undetected by Mrs. Thompson. That is, until the kid who had dared me to steal it egged on the boy whose candy it was. Who then raised his hand and ratted on me to our teacher.

"Craig Robinson?" Mrs. Thompson exclaimed incredulously, as if about to burst into tears that her star pupil had committed such a heinous crime. "I can't believe you did that," Mrs. Thompson continued. "What are your mother and father going to think about this?"

Nothing she could have said would have made me feel any more horrible than I already did. Even when Mrs. Thompson summoned me to the front of the room to receive the three firm swats of the yardstick—usually reserved for the kids used to getting into trouble—that didn't take me any lower than I had already fallen in my own esteem. I will say it was such a shock for the class to witness Mrs. Thompson punishing her top student—the one who was always on his best behavior, usually finishing first and going on to help other students with their work—that no one said a word. Normally, they would have been howling with laughter.

That day, when I walked home and rounded the corner, where I spotted Mom and Miche waiting for me at the gate, it hit me like a thunderbolt that it was going to be impossible to keep the incident a secret. Mom must have figured something was up when she saw me walking like a guy on his way to the gallows. There was nothing to do but to tell her what had happened. Naturally, I waited to speak to her in private so that my little sister wouldn't suffer from hearing my tale of shame.

As soon as Michelle ran back inside, I spilled the beans to Mom, telling her about the theft, getting three smacks of the ruler, the whole nine yards. Later, she said that it was a challenge for her to keep from laughing at how well I had already punished myself. Not only that, but she turned out to be impressed by the fact that I was more upset with myself than worried about what others would think. This was a key piece of character training that my parents emphasized all the time—that knowing the difference between right and wrong needed to come from within.

That said, I had fully prepared myself for my mother to give me a serious spanking. Mom was, after all, the disciplinarian of the house and we did get spankings every now and then. For the record, my mother reminds us often that we didn't get as many as my sister and I apparently remember. But this was an occasion when a memorable spanking might have been warranted. Instead, Mom said, "All right, Craig. For now, why don't you go upstairs and get your homework done? We'll talk about this when your father gets home."

This was my mother's version of "Let's all just take a deep breath." Later on, whenever my own children were acting up, Mom's advice was, "Before you do anything, count to ten. Count to ten, no matter how mad you are."

When I went upstairs, in spite of the relief I felt over not getting a spanking from her, I knew that she was now going to confer with Dad. The two would then determine my fate. It should be noted that Dad didn't give spankings. But if he was disappointed, the whole house was disappointed. That was much worse! As you might expect, I spent the next few hours nervously waiting for the jury between my parents to come up with a fitting sentence for my crime.

Presenting the kind of unified front that is important for parents (as well as coaching staffs) to have—even when they disagree initially—Mom and Dad called me into their room to tell me what they had decided. Dad explained that a spanking was not in order. Phew! But then he went on, "You're on punishment for a week." By that he meant no hour of television a night as we were allowed at the time, no playing outside, no football, baseball, or basketball, and extra chores. So far so good. Dad added, "And tomorrow, you're going to have to go up to the school, pay for the candy you stole, and apologize to the entire class."

Not so good. But the law had spoken and it was up to me to take my lumps and not complain.

The next day, as per the terms my parents had set out, they accompanied me to school and came to my classroom with me. In front of them, Mrs. Thompson, my still-shocked classmates, and God, I repaid a penny for the stolen gum and apologized directly to Mrs. Thompson, to the boy whose candy I'd taken, and to the entire class. Then my teacher and my parents left the room and went into the hallway where—as I would later learn—they all broke down into hysterical laughter!

Interestingly enough, what might have been a scarring

event in my young, overly conscientious life turned into a positive opportunity to build the self-confidence that comes from making mistakes, failing, and falling down on the court but then having to pick yourself up and play on. In this regard, I should mention that my parents didn't favor the everyone-wins-and-gets-a-trophy school of self-esteem. Praise and awards become meaningless, they would have pointed out, when they're not attached to hard work, diligence, and challenges that have been met on the road. And on the other hand, the last thing that any kid needs, as we see all too often, is a parent who drives his or her children to distraction with the need to be perfect. It's tough enough when kids—like me and Michelle at times—put that pressure on themselves. Which is why my parents incorporated humor into all their teaching. In that way, the gum-stealing incident became a source of great teasing and laughter in the years to come—all done through love and affection.

For that reason, when it came to debating the question almost two years later over whether we were rich or not, the memory convinced me that we had to be. In reality, I had no clue that we were poor and wouldn't until leaving home for college. But what I did know was that I never had to want for anything that I needed or wished for. All there was left to do was to ask Dad if I was correct in my assessment.

Before he left for the swing shift that afternoon, I was able to put the question to him, catching him at the kitchen table. "Dad," I asked brightly, "are we rich?" Then I explained why I was asking.

"Well," he said thoughtfully, taking a beat, "what do you think?"

Having deliberated about it the whole way home, I gave him the reasons that it seemed to me we were—the fact that Mom didn't work outside of the house and could be a full-time mother, that he had a job with the city of Chicago, that everyone at school, in the neighborhood, and at church knew my parents and seemed to think highly of them.

Dad looked at me closely, as if to assess whether I was ready for what he had to say. From the look on his face, I could see that he was about to give me a reality check of some kind. Sure enough, he went on to say, "If you want to know what rich is, wait until I get my paycheck and I'll show you how much I bring home."

At the end of the month, instead of depositing his paycheck into the bank, Dad went there and cashed the entire amount and brought home a thick wad of cash. It was more money than I'd ever seen in my life. It couldn't have been much more than a thousand dollars—his after-taxes monthly salary. Still, when he spread it out in front of me on the foot of his bed, showing me the array of fresh twenties, tens, fives, and ones, I thought it looked like a fortune.

"Wow, we are rich!"

Dad then brought out a stack of bills, saying, "Now, Craig, wait a minute, what about what we owe every month?"

"What do you mean?"

"Well, the money gets spent on monthly expenses for things we need." He pointed to the phone bill and put the approximate cash in that envelope. Then he came to the gas bill. "See this? We have to pay for the gas we cook with." There went another part of the cash. "And we have the electricity bill, the car payment, the rent, and the money for groceries . . ." he continued, putting the money in various envelopes until there was little left. Dad went even further, listing miscellaneous expenses that weren't luxuries in the least, until he had exhausted what we spent every month, leaving only a twenty-dollar bill on the bed.

Well, that was still a lot, I thought. But just to be sure, I asked, "You get to keep twenty dollars every time you get paid?"

"No," Dad sighed. "I don't get to keep the twenty." He reminded me of our monthly splurges to the drive-in as a family and then how we all loved the occasional take-out food to give Mom a break from the kitchen. By this point, it was clear to me that just about every cent my father earned was spoken for.

The reality check wasn't just to teach me that we weren't rich, at least in monetary terms. It was also to help me better appreciate my parents' sacrifices to make our lives as secure and comfortable as possible. I didn't yet grasp how far they could stretch limited resources. But I did start to pay greater attention to things I'd previously taken for granted. The next time we went to the drive-in movies at the beginning of the summer, for instance, to one of the *Planet of the Apes* films, I noticed how Mom spent the afternoon cooking up the best fried chicken on the Southside of Chicago, and how right before we left she popped bags of homemade popcorn that would still be fresh and warm when we ate it. Meanwhile, I noticed the care Dad took making sure our car was spruced up and ready to roll.

We had recently said good-bye to the old maroon Chevy Bel Air that we had owned forever, replacing it with a much nicer car—a Buick Electra 225 ("a deuce and a quarter" was what Dad called it, letting his cool side show). One of the proudest moments in my childhood had taken place in this era when I was in the alley with a group of my friends and Dad pulled up in the Buick, just home from work, rolled down the window, and asked, "Hey, Cat, you want to park the car for me?" He'd been complimenting me on my thorough execution of chores and other responsibilities. And since he'd been teaching me how to park the car while sitting on his lap, he figured I could do it on my own. What a thrill!

On the night of our outing to the movies and at the appointed hour, we piled into the Buick—Dad and Mom in front, Michelle and me in our PJs in the back. Though it wasn't far to the drive-in, we knew that we ran the peril of having to stop at the railroad crossing, so the moment that my sister and I spotted a train up ahead, we urged Dad to drive faster.

"Relax," Mom hushed us. "We'll get there when we get there."

"But we're gonna miss the movie!" Michelle and I hollered in unison just as the crossing gate came down in front of us. There was nothing to do then but count the cars of the train and compete to see who could guess what the total was—anything to distract ourselves.

As usual, we arrived in plenty of time and didn't miss anything. Once we had secured the speakers in the car windows and Mom handed out napkins and snacks, my parents scooted close together in the front so they could cuddle up in the center, while Miche and I took our seats in the back on either side close to the windows. There was an unspoken competition between us kids to see who could outlast the other before conking out. This night, neither one of us made it past the first half of the movie. When we opened our eyes, it was the next morning and there we were: safe and sound in our beds at home.

That summer when I was ten years old turned memories into sharper focus the more I began to appreciate all the extras that our parents worked so hard to provide us. At the top of that list was our annual summer excursion to Dukes Happy Holiday Resort in White Cloud, Michigan. It was there that my real love affair with basketball had begun.

Of course, growing up on the Southside, where basketball was a way of life, there were plenty of outdoor courts in parks and playgrounds close to our house where I could learn the unwritten rules of street ball just from jumping into the mix and playing for dear life. But I really had my first exposure to the fundamentals of basketball during our vacations at Dukes— a quaint tourist resort of white frame cabins nestled in the woods that boasted both a swimming pool and a combination tennis/basketball court.

Even by the time that I was a worldly ten years old, being at Dukes was still to me like Christmas every minute! There was a constant chorus of crickets, frogs, and other forest creatures to entertain the ears, along with a host of smells to identify—trees, plants, flowers, all combining with the continual delicious aroma from whatever the different vacationing folks were cooking up on outdoor grills. The coolest part? Having the basketball court right outside of our cabin door, pretty much all to myself! That was enough to get me out of bed before anyone else. Within moments, I was washed, dressed, had a ball in my hands, and was stepping outside, onto the court. Swish!

This was the summer that I really began to see the importance of the connection between me and the basketball. In these early morning practices, it was a solo experience, not having anyone to play with me, but not a lonely one at all. The only comparison I could see was the relationship that Michelle had with the piano. Thanks to Aunt Robbie's lessons, I could play piano well. But not like my sister. She didn't just play notes by pressing down on the keys. Michelle at eight years old could already play music. That's how I sometimes felt about me and the basketball. There was a music and a beat that I could create out on the court alone from the sounds of the ball hitting down, and my sneakers scuffing and squeaking on the court, with a wonderful percussion created by the rhythm of my breathing and heartbeat. It was like the feeling of listening to Grandpa Southside's jazz records—an improvisation that I could control and change up all on my own. Still, if I really wanted to get the basketball to work with me like music, I was well aware that the secret was in practicing, practicing, practicing. That's what Dukes gave me—a couple of hours on my own before breakfast and then another few hours with Dad before lunch. Since we were on nobody's schedule but that of doing whatever we felt like, we could continue playing until dark.

Fraser Robinson on the court, playing all day with me, was a force of nature. Especially that summer, when I was starting to pay keener attention to everything that he provided by way of love and guidance and tireless enthusiasm. But I also had begun to recognize that his limp was becoming more pronounced and that it took him longer to get up the stairs at home. No complaints, no asking for special treatment for this increasing disability. The only clues that he needed any help at all were that sometimes he'd call up, "Hey, Cat, come on down and bring up these bags for me."

Let me quickly add that if anyone thought such concerns were going to stop Dad from playing full-out with me on the basketball court, well, they didn't know the true heart of Fraser Robinson. A natural athlete who had been a swimmer and a boxer, Dad wasn't necessarily versed in the intricacies of basketball. But he knew enough of the fundamentals to give me a proverbial head start in my education about the game, not to mention that he had a damn good two-handed set shot—although he never tried to make me shoot his way. Dad kept it much simpler. His mantra was, "If you're shooting and the ball's going in, let's not mess with that."

The emphasis in these years wasn't so much on basketball philosophy but more about lighting the flame of competition. Dad managed to draw from his own well of competitive energy to give me a serious run for my money—without actually running. Instead, he had a distinctive method of hopping and limping around the court that was much more in sync with the ball's movement than you might suspect. And his shot-blocking was intense. Sometimes too intense. While playing a game one late afternoon toward the end of our vacation, much to my horror, after Dad blocked my otherwise winning shot, he fell backward and smacked down onto the concrete court with a reverberating thud.

My heart stopped. Worry edged my voice as I asked, "Are you okay, Dad?"

Taking a beat before he answered, Dad told me he was fine and then shook it off as he bounced right back up, challenging me to play on. We did. And I won!

Inevitably, there was the usual letdown that our vacation was over when it came time to leave Dukes Happy Holiday Resort. Wise as they were, Mom and Dad started proposing other fun outings for the near future so we could begin to look forward to them. This took the edge off our feeling less than enthusiastic about returning to the everyday routine—all the chores and daily responsibilities that had been left behind.

But, again, now that my father had opened my eyes to the fact that we weren't rich, I had a better attitude about the chores. Michelle rarely complained about her duties, even though she laughed in agreement when I jokingly compared our household rules and regulations to army boot camp!

We were able to commiserate about such matters during what was often a nightly debriefing of the day's activities or just a brother-sister chat before falling to sleep. With the partition that Southside had built for us, we had our privacy, but we could still talk to each other as we always had. And in typical Robinson fashion, we could also use the time for a competitive game of pillow toss—or some other toy or stuffed animal we had on hand. The object of the game was to throw the small pillow over the wall as dictated by the opponent, in the dark, who then had to report honestly as to whether or not the catch had been successful.

Miche, for example, would catch first and then announce, "Left-handed catch, one hand." She would then throw the pillow, and call, "All right . . . right-handed catch."

A game of honor, it was my duty to report back, "Umm . . . right-handed catch attempted . . . unsuccessful."

This could go on forever until Mom would come and say, "That's it, you two, it's time to go to sleep!"

Our mother never singled one of us out over the other as the main instigator or transgressor of any misdeeds. The result was that Miche and I were even closer as a team. It was to our parents' credit that sibling rivalry was not a problem. Truly, we were each other's number-one fan. This never changed, even during heated battles of Scrabble, Password, or Stratego. Whatever the competition was, if I was good at it, nine times out of ten, Michelle LaVaughn Robinson was better. She could do just about everything and anything at the level of mastery without appearing to have to try. And yet she coupled talent with a ferocious work ethic.

Most of the time, I did well in school without really having to apply myself. Rather than read all the material, I might absorb the table of contents and the index and only skim the chapters. Not Michelle. No skating or skimping for her. She was a scholar—combining her deep intelligence with an intensity of focus and attention to detail in her studies that was just stellar.

There was only one area where my sister didn't compete at the level that I did, and that was sports. Michelle was an athlete and played well at everything from track to tennis to volleyball and basketball. But as a champion of justice and equality, my sister didn't like the fact that in team sports someone has to win and someone has to lose. Maybe the do-or-die mentality of players on the field took away from the enjoyment of the game for her. Whatever the cause, I didn't mind in the least, especially when she could take anyone in our family at most board games.

While Dad needed to have a discussion with me about whether we were rich or not, Michelle seemed to have a more realistic view of what things cost and why it was important to be frugal. Our respective habits when it came to our allowance illustrated our differences. Early on, we were given a quarter a week that was later raised to fifty cents and then eventually went up to a dollar in our teens. Money for me was spent on an as-needed basis. But Miche was a total saver! Her piggy bank was invariably stuffed full of coins and dollar bills. When we'd count up cash on hand, she usually had twice as much as me. Rather than being jealous of her thrifty ways, I had to admire her discipline. Oh, sure, there may have been a time or two (or three) when I tried to goad her into having a little less willpower and might have even let a mean comment like "stingy" or "tightwad" issue from my mouth.

No sooner would I utter such a word than out of nowhere, Mom would appear and say, "Well, how would you feel if your sister called you 'stingy'?" Two points for Mom!

Undoubtedly, the Southside Family Robinson household was run very much as a tight ship. In the early days, when Uncle Terry was physically able to keep up the yard and cut the grass, I didn't have to do too much outdoor work. Then, when his health started to decline, mowing the lawn, raking, and weeding became my responsibilities. From a young age, I swept and scrubbed our wooden stairs with a brush, Lysol, and soapy water, digging and scraping a week's worth of collected dirt from out of the crevices and corners. My other main job on Saturdays was cleaning the bathroom—scrubbing the sink and the tub, cleaning the toilet, mopping the floor, wiping down the counters, and making the mirrors shine, plus battling the mildew around the windows, between the tiles, and on the walls. Michelle had her list of duties as well. On weekdays, we took turns with the dishes, kept our bedroom neat, took out the garbage, and helped carry in and put away groceries.

To keep everything running smoothly and maintain the joyous spirit that prevailed—regardless of tough tasks on the agenda—Mom and Dad understood and utilized the most effecting training strategy ever invented: the power of demonstration. It was a lot more show than tell. Dad didn't just say that he wanted us to be on time, he modeled that behavior constantly. In fact, he was always early. Instead of battling time, since it took him longer to get going in the morning, Dad set his alarm a half hour earlier so that if we needed to leave the house at seven A.M.—he was ready to leave at six thirty. The habit of punctuality was thus so ingrained in me and Miche that it became part of our DNA.

Similarly, Mom and Dad not only encouraged us to develop diligent study habits but they demonstrated their own quest for knowledge—through reading the newspapers and books that fed their own curiosity about a multitude of subjects. Mom's familiar refrain was, "Knowledge acquired is something no one can take away from you." Dad would then underscore the value of hard work in striving for excellence in all things—whatever we chose to invest ourselves in. There was never any pressure that we had to study a particular subject, play this sport versus another, or aspire to a certain field of endeavor. Mom and Dad let us know at every stage of our development that they respected us enough to let us make those choices for ourselves. The point was, as Dad would say, "It doesn't matter what you do in life, what counts is being the best at whatever you choose." And then he would use the prime example, "If you have to be a ditchdigger, then be the very best ditchdigger." The secret to being the best? Hard work.

Miche and I had to laugh about that because, as far as we knew, there weren't many actual ditchdiggers being hired anymore. Nonetheless, we grasped the idea that the habit of hard work wasn't only what our parents exemplified but was something that had its own rewards for us. Every year, the proof of that was under the Christmas tree. Santa was obviously sending us the message that our parents knew what they were talking about. Mom and Dad continually reminded us not to get our hopes up too much because Santa had high standards. And yet, every year, we worked so hard to meet those standards, he left us three more gifts than we had asked for.

Sure, using Santa Claus to encourage niceness over naughtiness might be the oldest parenting trick in the book, but that didn't stop my parents from employing Saint Nick to the max. Then came the cold, dark winter of 1972, when I was ten and a half and Miche was about to turn nine, and our being stuck inside all day led us down to the basement, where a game of hide-and-seek led us to opening up the unplugged refrigerator. Inside were Christmas gifts bought at local stores—including a pair of boxing gloves for me—and still in their boxes. Right about then, our proverbial lightbulbs lit up about the Santa story. We later learned Mom had wanted to throw the boxes away but Aunt Robbie—a waste-not-want-not kind of woman—had insisted on saving them for future storage possibilities. Mom was not happy.

Now that Santa was out of the picture we would just have to be good for goodness' sake. The revelation only added to my appreciation of what Dad's demonstration with his paycheck had shown me.

There was one other repercussion of the conversation with Dad about whether or not we were rich that bears mentioning. Because he had opened my eyes to the weight of responsibilities that he shouldered in supporting the family, at around this age I started to feel an added sense of responsibility of my own—in the event something ever happened to him so that he couldn't provide for us. My worrying, unfortunately, would progress as I got into my teens, when it would be aggravated by the knowledge that Dad was afflicted by MS.

Then again, with history as our guide, all I had to do to calm myself was remember what had happened with the worry that Michelle and I had about my parents' smoking. Back when I was almost nine and Miche was already seven, we had come home from school with the same message about how bad cigarettes were. It was no longer just a warning that they were harmful to your health. Now we were learning that "smoking kills." As we helped unpack the groceries and noticed Dad put away four cartons of cigarettes he had just purchased on sale, she and I exchanged fearful expressions.

In our room later that night, Michelle brought up the subject. The mere thought of losing our parents scared the living daylights out of both of us. But Miche, always full of bright ideas, had a plan.

We waited for the right opportunity when Mom and Dad went downstairs to visit Aunt Robbie and Uncle Terry, as they regularly did. They said they'd be back in ten to fifteen minutes. As soon as we heard the creak of the floorboards downstairs, we leapt into action to execute my sister's plan. The intention was to get both of our parents to quit smoking. To do that, the mission we had undertaken was to rid the Robinson household of any last vestige of a cigarette that could be smoked in any way, shape, or form.

We moved quickly and were back sitting in front of the television when our parents returned.

Mom, at the usual after-dinner hour when she liked to enjoy one of only a few cigarettes she had every day, checked in on us before heading into the kitchen, where we heard her rattling around. "Fraser," she called to Dad, "I thought you said those cigarettes were in the cabinet."

He confirmed that's where he had put the four cartons.

"I don't see them."

She kept looking around, and we were feeling proud, at least at first, as we listened from the other room. But as her search continued, our self-assured confidence that we had done the right thing started to fade.

Then we heard a shriek. "Fraser, come in here," Mom called to him, gasping in shock. Obviously she had found our handiwork. We had gone through the house and destroyed every cigarette, including every single one that was in the cartons, tearing them up by hand into bits and putting what was left of the shredded tobacco and paper into the trash can under the sink.

There was silence as my father shuffled into the kitchen.

Moments later we heard, "Craig! Michelle! Get in here!" as our parents called to us in unison. We were crying our eyes out by the time we got to the kitchen, both of us apologizing and explaining that we didn't want them to die from smoking.

Of the many extraordinary feats that I witnessed my father accomplish over the years, I always thought the decision he made to quit smoking—right then and there—was indicative of the different kind of octane that he ran on. Just about anyone else would have at least had a last smoke or would have cut back or enrolled in a smoking cessation program. But Fraser Robinson was someone who had made major decisions at various crossroads to change and alter the course of his life and had then acted upon those choices immediately. That's what he did in this case. He quit cold turkey. His rationale was that if his two children were as upset as we were about his smoking, then he wasn't going to keep doing it. It could not have been easy, since he had been smoking for many years, but he managed to quit on love and respect for our concern and with the discipline required for stopping a habit.

Let me add that we weren't told his thinking or reasoning for quitting at that time. Later Mom recalled that it was an emotional decision he made because he didn't want us to worry about him. When they discussed it, Mom, in her independent, moderate manner, told him that as for herself, she wasn't quitting. Mom didn't smoke much anyway; it was something that she enjoyed and could maintain in moderation, and would continue to do so. At the same time, from then on, Mom was much more conscious about not doing it in front of us or giving us any reason to fret over her health and stamina.

The lesson, as usual, would have lasting meaning and uses. It was important for us to see how habits, good and bad, require awareness and deliberate choices in order to improve those we want to build or to minimize those that aren't working for us—whether on the court, with our studies, in our household, or in our lifestyle. We also learned that everyone is different when it comes to those choices, just as everyone is motivated differently. There are times, I know, when my players see the level of discipline that building a strong team requires and may think that I'm the toughest coach they've ever encountered. But they also know that underneath the discipline is a foundation of caring and concern for them as individuals and as a team. They know, too, that I respect them; I believe I'm learning as much from what they're discovering about themselves on the court as they are from my efforts at instruction.

And the most effective strategy for winning is to develop the right habits early on. That's straight from the Fraser and Marian Robinson school of coaching. Or as I like to tell my players as often as I can: "First you do the work to build the habits; then, when it's game time, you let your habits win for you."

3

KNOW WHO YOU ARE AND LIVE YOUR LIFE WITH CONVICTION

On the court, as in life, one of the most valuable character traits of them all is the ability to make important decisions under pressure that may impact a lot of other people—to be the kind of go-to individual who can be trusted to think for himself and make the best possible choice in any given situation. As a coach and as a parent, I lean a lot on the example set by my parents as to how they were able to nurture a sense of trustworthiness in us, by giving us the freedom to think and act for ourselves while still providing safe boundaries. They tried not to hover too closely but they never cut us so loose that they weren't involved. In my book, that's never an easy balancing act—although, not surprisingly, Fraser and Marian Robinson made it seem so.

One strategy that worked wonders was making sure all channels of communication were kept open. That meant not only could we talk to them and they to us, but they would talk to coaches and teachers and others with whom we interacted.

These days I see parents generally much more involved in this sense. But back in the 1970s in our neighborhood, Dad and Mom were well ahead of the curve. In fact, I remember that most of the time the only parent at any of my basketball practices or at our team's away games was my father.

This was the case when I started playing at the local YMCA in the Biddy Basketball League, which used smaller-sized balls and lowered the hoop to eight and a half feet. With the skills that I had already developed on my own and the fact that I was tall for my age, I did well and ended up being chosen for an all-star YMCA team from the Southside that competed around Chicago. Transportation and chaperones were supposed to be provided, but because Dad and Mom didn't always know those people, they did their utmost to make sure that we were safe and in the care of responsible adults. In keeping with their policy of giving us freedom of movement within boundaries, we were raised as city kids, after all. And the watchwords were: Be careful.

When I was twelve years old, our team went to play in a tournament at the Martin Luther King Boys Club on the Westside. To us Southside kids, the Westside was the scariest part of town there was. Ironically, it turned out that the Westside kids felt the same way about coming over to the Southside. Between the black communities in the two areas, there weren't that many differences except by degree. The Southside was more working middle class, whereas the Westside was poorer, more blighted, and falling under the poverty line. It occurred to me later on that neither group had any idea that we were equally afraid of each other.

But judging from what I saw in the game that first day, as far as organized basketball, the Southside couldn't hold a candle to the Westside. We got stomped! Our coach was so embarrassed, he actually walked out and left a bunch of us kids at the gym. While he may have been correct that we didn't play as well as we could have and that we allowed ourselves to be psyched out by our opponents (who were clearly well-coached), abandoning young players in enemy territory was plain wrong.

As the rest of the guys and I huddled to figure out what to do, Dad made his way from the spectator section to the back of the gym where we were standing and assured all of us he would see that we got home safely. He didn't need to say a word to express what I could read on his face—that he was appalled by our coach's actions. Yet his main concern at the moment was to calm everyone down—especially me. In those days, it was becoming increasingly apparent to my folks that I tended to worry, a lot, about situations that threatened to be out of my control. Dad's mantra for keeping me on an even keel on the court was to remind me, as needed, "Not too high, not too low." No matter how resounding a victory, his position was that we could savor the moment, see it as a building block to further success, and celebrate—but not to excess. No matter how crushing a defeat, Dad's counsel was to acknowledge it, learn lessons from what didn't work on the court, and then move on. The Fraser Robinson emotional survival approach definitely helped me through big-time losses in the years to come. Even as a teenager, I wasn't prone to tears or prolonged regrets after a defeat.

So on the way home, keeping things normal and even-keel, the conversation was more about how we were going to have a better showing in our next games. Unbeknownst to me, however, Dad was troubled enough by the incident that he had decided to seek out some other options in terms of a team for me to play on. Actually, my father had been so impressed by the young guy who had coached the team that beat us, that he had gone up to him and introduced himself, saying,

"You're doing a great job with these kids." Then, in his direct way, Dad had explained, "I'm looking for a good team for my son to be on."

The young man's name was Johnnie Gage—"Not John, not Jonathan, just call me Johnnie"—who was no more than nineteen years old at the time, over six feet five, and a student at Wright Junior College, where he played on the basketball team. As it so happened, Johnnie Gage was open to the possibility of coaching some of us who were willing to make the trek to the Westside and who were able to keep up with a higher level of training than we might have known before.

With that, not only had a very influential basketball mentor entered my life, but so, too, had a person of exceptional character. Tough, strict, and often exacting, Johnnie was able to ask so much from us because—a) he was fair and treated everyone with the same level of respect and b) we knew how much he cared about us. We saw how hard he worked at coaching—at the same time that he was going to college and playing ball—and we were motivated to work harder as well. And what I came to value most about him was Johnnie's maturity, which was beyond his years. Whether it came from a difficult childhood or earlier challenges in life, I didn't know. All that was clear was that he knew who he was and didn't have to prove himself to anyone else. He lived his values and beliefs with conviction and, at the same time that he was furthering his education and experience on the court, had the desire and the commitment to further our education.

Bottom line, Dad could not have picked a better coach for me if he and Mom had conducted a nationwide search. The only hitch was that our practices and many of our games were at the Boys Club over on the Westside—a forty-five-minute drive from our neighborhood. In the beginning, Dad drove me there and back as often as he could. But it wasn't long before I needed to travel there on my own at least part of the time—not an easy route to navigate, as it involved taking the bus to the El, where I'd start out on one train before switching to a second one, all through some pretty rough areas.

When my friends on the Southside found out that I was playing basketball on the Westside, and sometimes traveling there and back by myself, they were scared for me. After all, the Westside was the territory of the Vice Lords, a violent street gang at that time, and some of the guys on the court had older brothers or cousins who were gangbanging. It was no best-kept secret that these were tough kids. I mean, even the twelve-year-olds had scars!

But, then again, the Southside had its share of gangs, and certain streets and corners you had to avoid too. Or so Dad pointed out, reminding me that I had developed some street smarts that would be as useful in an unfamiliar neighborhood as they were in my own. Over the years, he had taught me to carry myself with a knowledge of the streets, telling me, "If you walk with a purpose, you won't stick out. You don't want to be looking around, lost or afraid." Whenever I ran errands even a few blocks from home, I'd learned not to put all my money in the same place. Dad's advice was, "Put a few dollars in your pocket, then find a hiding spot for the rest." He also taught me not to carry cash in my wallet, telling me, "If you get pickpocketed or somebody wants to steal something from you, hand over your wallet, no questions asked." This developed into a lifelong habit of carrying enough money hidden on me somewhere to get me safely home from wherever I've traveled. Just in case.

Adjusting to the commute to a different neighborhood was not as difficult as I'd expected. Nor was it hard to adapt to Johnnie Gage's coaching style, which was much more intensive than I'd experienced before. Not that he was introducing new strategies or complicated screens that were foreign to me. On the contrary, Coach Johnnie was all about fundamentals—moving your feet on defense, using your weak hand to strengthen it, being able to drive to the basket left or right, shooting foul shots and just ball-handling in general. This was all stuff everyone knew but in some cases needed to learn all over again because of bad habits developed either under inattentive coaches or from picking up sloppy habits playing street basketball.

During one of our first practices, I had an opportunity to see what Johnnie Gage's pet peeves and priorities were. For him, what counted was attitude. Didn't matter how gifted a basketball prodigy you might be. If you were going through the motions halfheartedly just because this was only practice, or, worse, if you were mouthing off and acting put-upon because the drills were getting too repetitive, Johnnie would sit you down. He did something else that day, to one of the players who was in a surly mood, that got everyone's attention. Coach pulled his keys out of his pocket and started to jingle them right at the surly kid. No one knew what that was supposed to mean until he explained to the player, "Go to your locker and get your stuff." That was code for—*you're outta here!*

At the next practice, that same kid was back and working harder on the floor than anyone else.

Rarely did Coach kick players out when it was game time. But every now and then it was warranted. And we all felt terrible for the player who had made Johnnie Gage send him home. That had certainly been the case during a memorable instance when we were getting ready to leave town for a national championship and learned that one of our star players wouldn't be traveling with us to play.

As part of the AAU (Amateur Athletic Union) League the teams that came out of the MLK Boys Club were known for attracting some of the best young players in Chicago—kids who wanted to play competitive youth basketball and who had aspirations of going further, whether it was also playing on high school teams, continuing into the college leagues, or even into the NBA. One such player on our team was a teenager by the name of Isiah Thomas, a year older than me, who even at that age was phenomenal—and a fascinating player for the future coach in me to watch.

Shorter than a lot of us in those days, Isiah Thomas (who was just barely six feet tall when he later played in the NBA), made up for what he lacked in height by controlling every single part of the game. The only thing he had a problem controlling was Coach Johnnie Gage. It wasn't that Isiah was intentionally disrespectful or defiant. It was that he had an outsized fire inside. When that energy was channeled into the game, he was unstoppable. But when it came out in stubbornness or the attitude that nobody could tell him anything about how to play what he already knew better, well, that was trouble. No matter what he said or did after that, Johnnie refused to give him special treatment. And that was what happened when we found out that Isiah wasn't going to play in the national championship tournament game.

Dad was the one who observed that Johnnie did this to make a point to the rest of the team as well. Initially, when Dad was still driving me to practice fairly often, I couldn't help but feel somewhat embarrassed. Of course, not in a million years would I have ever complained about the fact he was there during practice and was the only father in the entire gym. But I was sure my teammates had to be thinking that I was not the coolest guy around.

This was where one of my mother's most important tenets held sway, one that I started hearing more frequently from her as adolescence and concerns about peer pressure set in, namely, "You do not care about what other people think

because you know what to think." And so, upon further reflection, what I really thought was that I was proud to have a
dad who not only sought out a team that allowed me to step
out of my comfort zone and grow as a player, but was willing
to make the sacrifice of getting me there and back. In fact, if
I really wanted to know what others thought, I had only to
pay attention and notice that instead of looking down on me,
most of my teammates seemed to wish they had a parent like
Dad. Some didn't have fathers that played any kind of role in
their lives, let alone have the time or inclination to be involved at the level my father was. What was more, every single
one of the guys knew Fraser Robinson and saw him as the
unofficial team dad. Before too much time went by, I felt silly
for having been embarrassed and worried at all.

But that doesn't mean my tendency to worry about a lot
of things had abated. During these preteen and early adolescent years, I solidified my role as the family worrier—which
would have become more problematic without the healthy
outlet that basketball and my other sports provided. Even so,
I think some of the ways that my worry manifested may have
caught Mom and Dad off guard.

These fears probably had to do with underlying concerns
about my father's disability. It was around this period when he
started to walk with a cane for support. When climbing the
stairs, he took to moving his better leg up first and then hoist-
ing the other leg up to meet it—one step at a time. As the
oldest child and only male, I saw these signs as urgent reasons
for me to figure out, in advance, what I was going to do in
the event of calamity, when I would have to protect and rescue my other family members. To complicate the worst-case
scenarios, some of the calamities that I was envisioning were
the kinds of things you imagine happening in the middle of
nightmares—like not being able to speak or see. Irrational

though it was, I decided to be prepared and came up with contingency plans.

The first major worry I confronted was the fear that I was going deaf. The solution? Learn sign language, of course. Over the next several weeks, by teaching myself from books checked out from the library, I became fluent in sign language. Though I was then much less scared of going deaf, I suddenly became deathly afraid of going blind. Preparing for the worst, I practiced walking through the entire house with my eyes closed and blindfolded until I could do it without falling over anything. In the event of a fire, my plan entailed having to open the window in my parents' room, climb out, and jump to the next roof. When Mom came home from an errand to find me out on the roof measuring the distance, all she could do was say, "Craig, stop worrying about stuff," as she often did.

Dad went along with my crisis-training exercises and fire drills for a while. At thirteen I was already a big kid but I still needed to know that I could carry him and get him out of the house to safety, especially if I went blind *and* there was a fire. Whenever I called a fire drill, I'd practice lifting Dad up under his arms and drag him around the house, testing myself to see if I was strong enough to handle it, and kept going until he would reach his limit and yell out, "That's enough, man, put me down!"

For reasons that I understand about as well as I know where the worries came from in the first place, I soon outgrew the extreme fears and went back to worrying about normal adolescent things—like grades, games, and, eventually, girls. The benefit of the period of irrational worrying was that it allowed me to process my fears in a reasonable way and come up with a game plan in those worst-case-scenario situations. Between that and my otherwise almost idyllic childhood, I had been given a great foundation for later on, when expecting the best outcome while planning for the unexpected would be a coaching survival skill.

Throughout this episode, Mom's refrain of "Stop worrying!" helped keep me grounded. My impression was that she assumed my fears of going deaf and blind and having to rescue everyone from a fire were only part of a phase and that I'd outgrow it. What she was also trying to do was to get me to think for myself and to be able to talk myself down off the ledge, as it were.

During this unusual interlude, none of my quirky worries seemed to show up on the basketball court. Johnnie Gage might have sensed that I was going through a nervous period in everyday life, but he never held back from putting me into clutch situations in the game. He didn't coddle or do too much pep-talking, but he projected a level of confidence in me that was contagious. Basketball became my safe haven, my anchor.

The other saving grace was the humor, teasing, fun, and games that flourished in our household. Our long-standing game of trying to creatively scare each other kept things lively. But we started to have second thoughts about it one day when I went into the room where Mom was looking for something in a drawer and, unintentionally, really scared her badly. I had spent so many hours teaching myself how to sneak up on family members by walking on the wooden floors without letting them squeak or creak that it was just my habit to walk soundlessly. But when Mom stood up and I was standing there, she screamed and said that I had overdone it this time.

"Oh, no, I wasn't trying to scare you," I explained. "It was a coincidence that I just walked in here when you stood up."

Mom gave me a look as if to suggest she didn't believe me and it was her turn to get me back. No matter how much I told her that it was wholly unintentional, nothing convinced her.

Then, a few days later, as I was stepping out of the shower, I looked down and there was Mom, sitting on the floor. Scared me to absolute death! I couldn't catch my breath and even started to cry.

My mother felt so horrible that then and there she called an end to our trying to scare each other. From that point on, it was her, me, and Miche versus Dad—partly because nothing really scared him and also because he wasn't that good at scaring us. Michelle was very inventive, coming up with practical jokes like putting shaving cream on his glasses when he fell asleep in front of the TV. Since she used to call him Daddy, at some point she changed it to Diddley (as in Bo Diddley) and then we all started calling him Diddy, Did, and Dit too.

The idea that we could cut up and be silly and even outrageous at home was to be balanced with being on our best or at least appropriate behavior in the classroom. Mom also encouraged me to speak up for myself when I thought something was unfair. In certain cases, she didn't hold back from speaking up for me too. There was the time in the sixth grade, for example, when a teacher gave me a B in a class where I'd been doing top-notch work. Confused, I asked the teacher why she'd given me a B instead of the A that I had expected, and not checking her notes, she went over this, that, and the other to show what had caused her to give me the lower grade. Since none of those things were true, I spoke up for myself, saying, "But I did each of those things and you can check my work again to see."

"Well," the teacher said, holding on to the power that her authority gave her, "you can't get A's all the time."

Upon hearing that comment, Mom made an appointment to see the teacher. Since she had volunteered in our classes from the time we started school and as both of our parents were familiar figures at school who often stopped by—known both to staff and the student body—this was nothing new. Being reasonable and direct, Mom spoke to the teacher and made a strong case for why a good student could most certainly make A's all the time.

That was Marian Robinson, not one to back down from a discussion when it was a matter of principle and when she believed that right was on her side. In another life, Mom would have made a formidable lawyer. As our mother, when she was acting on our behalf, she was unstoppable and fearless.

But I'm not sure that either she or Dad knew how to react when they received a phone call from school about how well I had scored on a test in sex education. Ironically, this was an area in which I was unsophisticated and clueless—if you had called me a complete square you would have been right. Many of my sixth-grade classmates were much hipper and more in the know about "where babies come from." But because of my knowledge of language and science fundamentals, when the teacher presented us with a quiz on our first day of sex education to gauge how much or how little we knew, I used the old-fashioned process of elimination to figure out the right answers. The quiz was nothing more than a list of words related to reproduction that we were asked to identify and put in one of three categories by answering whether the word had do with men, women, or both. Even though I really didn't know what the words meant, I guessed so well that every answer was correct except for one. Somehow it was a red flag to my teacher that Craig Robinson knew a lot more than he should have, and so she decided to alert my parents.

After dinner, with Dad seated at the table with us kids, and Mom getting up to start the dishes, they brought the subject up casually. Mom began, "So you had sex education today," and explained that the teacher called to say that I'd scored a 99 percent on it.

Dad continued, "That's impressive that you knew all those words, son. Which word did you miss?"

"Menstruation," I said, and went on to tell them that because of *men* in the word itself, I'd assumed it had to do with men. How my parents kept a straight face I do not know.

By this point, Michelle was no longer interested. Having finished helping clean up, she left the kitchen in time for me to ask my parents the big question: "Well, what is menstruation?"

Mom rejoined me and Dad at the table and answered in a very practical, no-nonsense way. Then he took over and gave me a quick overview of the facts of life that was much more down-to-earth than the course in sex education at school turned out to be. My parents didn't make sex a bad or shameful subject at all, at the same time they didn't mince words about why teenage pregnancy and sexually transmitted diseases were issues to understand and take precautions against.

Later on, when I'd learn that a friend had gotten a girl pregnant and that someone I knew had to drop out of school because she was having a baby, I'd wish they'd had the benefit of a talk with their parents like the one I had with mine. Granted, when I left the kitchen table that night I was still clueless about what the big deal over sex was. When I said as much to Mom and Dad, they basically said that I'd find out later on.

If my father was slightly taken aback at how square I was, he didn't show it. But it was around this time that he started bringing me along whenever he was heading over to the barbershop. The outing wasn't to get a haircut—he cut my hair at home—but for me to have exposure to cultural and social ways of getting along in the world. The guys at the barbershop were all characters, all different. Some were hip, some were squares too. Even in this setting Dad was always front and center. He walked in and lit up the place with his presence.

The barbershop was a feast and a show for the senses. The minute we arrived, I could discern the different smells—talc, shaving cream, menthol, and alcohol—along with the stranger chemical treatments for straightening and dyeing hair. All of the grooming equipment—combs, brushes, clippers, and razors— adorned the various stations in front of a full bank of mirrors, while a fan in the middle of that un-air-conditioned room blew clumps of hair every which way. Either there was a Cubs or other important game on the TV or the radio was tuned to a hip jazz station.

In the sixth grade, it was impossible not to feel cool walking into the barbershop and having all the guys look up and hear my dad quip, "Hey, I brought my bodyguard with me."

Somebody in a barber's chair would have to look up and say, "Craig, you done shot up, boy!" and someone else would say, "Yeah, and you still gettin' all them A's?"

Once we were done with the niceties, then they'd go back to their regular men talk—some sports, some politics, and mostly women. And of course there was a lot of cursing, and some very colorful jokes that probably taught me more about sex education than I ever would have learned at school—though not necessarily with words I'd want to repeat. After the punch lines and the laughter died down, someone would have to turn to me and, all polite and everything, say, "Uh, don't tell your mother."

Just to make sure he had covered all the bases, Dad also encouraged me to hang out with his two younger brothers, Andrew and Carlton, my uncles, who were the height of cool in the 1970s with their Super Fly pants and their Afros and their platform shoes. At one family outing, I traveled with the two of them and we were dressed formally in long raincoats and were carrying umbrellas and they were horrified by my stance as we were waiting for the bus.

Andrew asked, "Are you just gonna plant yourself there all flat-footed?"

Carlton added, "Well, Craig *is* flat-footed."

Andrew studied me for a few minutes before making some adjustments, telling me, "Nah, don't stand like that, separate your feet, turn your right foot like this," and he showed me how it needed to be pointed one way and the left foot another way. Then Carlton demonstrated how my hands had to be balanced on my umbrella so that I could lean back almost at a thirty-degree angle. I was instantly cooler! And to stay that way, I've stood like that ever since.

The kitchen-table talks, visits to the barbershop, and exposure to my young uncles—all of these instances were ways the line of communication stayed open with me. That was my parents' style—not to overwhelm us with too much information or insist that we embrace their line of thinking wholesale. If we raised questions, that was an effective way to generate a dialogue. Or they would create opportunities to expose us to different kinds of food for thought and conversation. Toward that end, one of my favorite all-time Robinson family traditions was our classic Sunday-afternoon drive.

These were always sort of impromptu, even though I had to suspect Dad and Mom had masterminded the perfect adventure and only made it seem spur-of-the-moment. But in any event, whenever Dad would say, "C'mon let's go for a drive," I knew there was adventure in store. There was no agenda other than to ride around different neighborhoods in Chicago, recall familiar places my parents had frequented in the past, and discover new ones. All of these drives provided me with some of my fondest memories—with no rush, no worry, not a care in the world for any of us. I loved watching the delight on my father's face as he came upon a landmark that reminded him of a great story we had never heard. I loved seeing my mother enjoying what a raconteur Dad, the keeper of the family folklore, was—and how she watched our reactions at the same time. She had a memorably relaxed, contented way of sitting on these drives that was not face-forward in the passenger seat but sideways, leaning against the door, so that she could see all three of us.

When I was twelve, toward the end of seventh grade, we went for a long Sunday drive that took us into a neighborhood full of lavish mansions. As we were comparing the different styles of architecture, I asked why so many of the older colonial-style houses had what looked like additional little houses in the back. My parents explained that those were carriage houses where black folks who took care of the family stayed. Thus began a conversation about racism and classism, integration and segregation, along with the history of slavery and Jim Crow.

Not all of these issues were new to me. When we started studying black history in school, and we were old enough to ask about Martin Luther King, my mother ordered an encyclopedia set that was written from the black perspective. I read each of those volumes from cover to cover. Now I could understand not only what the tragedy of Dr. King's killing meant but also what he represented in terms of the dream of equality that belonged to all races. I also learned about why "turn the other cheek" wasn't always easy to do and a little more about other civil rights leaders in 1960s like Malcolm X. As it so happened, in April of 1962 when Mom was expecting me, she read an article about his work and, as she was looking for a middle name for a boy if she should have one, decided Malcolm had a nice ring to it.

Interestingly enough, movies and TV had helped me to put racism into context—starting with a *Star Trek* episode in which there was a guy whose face was half-black and half-white and Captain Kirk couldn't figure out why two groups were fighting about him. And then there were the *Planet of the Apes* movies that showed how different apes formed groups and were biased against each other, just like human beings. Later, the miniseries *Roots* would definitely elevate my consciousness about the African American experience.

But in the meantime, in 1974 it was eye-opening to go for a drive with my family and see how the dividing lines between black and white manifested in the neighborhoods that weren't very far from ours, even though very different. By this era, most of the white folks had moved away from the Southside. And living in a mostly black neighborhood, I had been more or less protected from experiencing prejudice against me or my family members because of color. Actually, if I felt any prejudice in these earlier years, it was from some of my black classmates who gave me a hard time about my proper grammar and careful pronunciation and who accused me of "trying to sound white."

Whatever that meant! Being articulate didn't just come from Dandy's habit of barking at us to go look up words and increase our vocabulary. Dad was also fond of making sure we said "something" instead of "somethin'" and "isn't" instead of "ain't," and he didn't like "you know" thrown in every other sentence. He'd correct us all the time, and if we said "you know," he'd say, "No, I don't."

When, on our drive, I brought up the comments that the kids had been making, that opened the door for my mom to say she was happy that I knew well enough to just ignore them. Again, the point was to think for yourself and make your own decisions. But that still left the question of why people were judgmental and even mean, whether they were black or white or whatever, something that both Michelle and I wanted to know.

Dad shook his head and turned the wheel to head back home, stressing that when people acted ignorant, rather than write them off, put yourself in their shoes and try to understand them.

"A lot of people are just insecure," my mother noted.

And the moral of the story they both used to conclude our drive, just as Diddley parked the car so that we could top off our day with a visit to Tastee Freez and cones for all: "No one can make you feel bad if you feel good about yourself."

It wasn't more than a couple weeks later that I had a chance to test that theory when I had my first real brush with racism—but of a different stripe than I might have expected. With my newfound independence and self-confidence, earned, in part, from playing basketball on the Westside, Mom and Diddy began to give me a wider range of motion. That meant on a Saturday after chores that I could ride my bike over to Rainbow Beach on Lake Michigan and cruise around to my heart's content. Not just on any bike. This was the bike that had recently gone on sale at Goldblatt's Department Store so that suddenly it seemed that every kid in Chicago, including me, had the exact same bike—a yellow ten-speed with curved handlebars and wires going down to the brakes.

And there I was, proud of my new pair of wheels, basking in a beautiful day at Rainbow Beach as I rode along the lakefront, when a policeman stopped me and gruffly accused me of stealing the bike. Not just any cop. This fellow was on his regular beat in the Southside and he was black.

Me steal anything? I spoke up for myself on the spot, saying, "Oh, no, I didn't steal it. This is a brand-new bike. My parents bought it on sale at Goldblatt's. It belongs to me."

The policeman barely let me get my words out before he shook his head and said, "Nope, I know you stole this bike."

Since he was black, and in my neighborhood, I wasn't worried. Obviously, there was some misunderstanding and I needed to clear up whatever was causing the confusion. Again, I let him know that it was mine and while I could see that maybe somebody else had had a bike stolen, this bike was not that one. Pretty sensible for a twelve-year-old, I figured.

Apparently, he didn't buy it. Instead of taking me at my word, he insisted on loading the bike into the back of his cruiser and driving me home so he could speak to my parents. That was not the worst of it. What really got to me was that on the drive back to our house, he continued to interrogate me about why I had stolen the bike. By the time we pulled up to our curb, I was fuming inside.

From downstairs I called up to Mom that the policeman had accused me of stealing a bike, and when she came outside, I saw a look on her face that I'd never seen before. "Go on inside, Craig," she said, barely glancing at me but steeling her eyes on the officer, preparing to read him the riot act.

I stood watching from the front screened-in porch, and she must have talked to that policeman for forty-five minutes. Then he pulled the bike out of the trunk, set it on the curb, and drove off.

"Come on out here and get your bike," Mom called to me as she watched the patrol car drive off down Euclid Avenue.

But that wasn't the end of it. The next day, Marian Robinson paid a visit to the station house. And the day after that, the policeman came to our home and apologized to me.

As soon as he left, Mom observed, "You know, there's all different kinds of races, and you're going to see prejudice even from people who are just like you. That's why he assumed you stole the bike." Then she said, "He didn't treat you well. But rest assured, he will never do that to anyone else again."

That's my mother—a force to be reckoned with.

Mom was so much in our corner that the mere thought of letting her down or not living up to what she had taught us was hard to bear.

But I was a normal adolescent, after all. And when early in the eighth grade a cute girl in my class invited me over to her house—at a time when her mother wasn't going to be there—I was tempted. Yes, even though the Robinson family rule was that we didn't go over to anybody else's house unless that person's parents were home, I was tempted. Our arrangement was that she was going to swing by the house and when I saw her walk by, I would casually announce that I was going to the playground. But my nerves started to kick in after several attempts at being casual every time I walked over to the window and looked outside to see if she was walking by yet.

Mom, seeing me so agitated, finally asked, "All right, what's wrong?"

I denied that anything was bothering me and she let it go. But a few minutes later, I fessed up and told Mom that a cute girl had invited me over and her mother wasn't going to be home.

My mom didn't bat an eyelash other than to ask, "Well, do you think you should go over there if her mother's not home?"

"No."

Then she just sighed and said, "Well, do what you think is best."

And that was that. She didn't have to worry whatsoever. The trustworthiness I valued about myself was not something worth jeopardizing.

The situations and conflicts may have changed as the years have gone by. But the lessons still hold. My players know that I trust them on the court to make the right choices that will impact the whole team. And we work on what happens off the court too. Whenever we win and celebrations are in order, I say, "Have fun!" But then I also remind them that "nothing good happens after midnight." In my experience, even when something is feeling good in the moment, that doesn't mean it will in the long run. I like the saying, "Morality is what feels good after," and I like even better that I can trust my guys to make the best decision for themselves about what that's going to be.

4

BE RELENTLESS:
YOU HAVE TO WIN TO
STAY ON THE COURT

If I had to choose one NBA player who most epitomizes someone who showed remarkable character both on and off the court, that would easily be my first and most lasting sports hero, Bob Love. Who knows, if it weren't for Bob Love—who played for the Chicago Bulls from 1969 to 1976 and who remains to this day the team's second highest all-time scorer (after Michael Jordan)—I might not have chosen basketball as my top sport and would be telling you a very different story about myself today.

Six-eight, long and sinewy, Bob Love had a style all his own and could make shots from out of nowhere that were impossible to block. Watching him from the time I was seven years old up until I was fourteen—when a back injury forced Love into retirement—I studied him, rooted for him, and idolized him. This wasn't only because I loved how he played the game. What inspired me was how he transcended his disability, a horrendous speech impediment. Love stuttered so badly that he wasn't able to give interviews. After scoring forty-some points in a game, instead of Bob Love stepping to the mics and in front of the press corps for the glory, others would have to stand in for him. He would later admit to praying nightly for the miracle of speech to be granted to him. He dreamed of being able to speak in front of massive crowds and even imagined their faces.

If Bob Love was suffering in silence, I would have never known it because in no way did his inability to speak deter him from giving what he himself would later describe as 110 percent, no matter what. I'm sure that I did see something of my father in Bob Love, given that both had a disability. But the most important quality that stood out for me, back when I was a kid, was how he never tired, never gave up, and never gave in. Bob Love was relentless!

Back then, I didn't even know the half of it. The story of what came later was even more inspiring. After leaving basketball, Love would fall into obscurity. Unable to support himself in a sports-related capacity or anything involving communication, he would wind up doing things like busing tables. From time to time, he would be recognized and would overhear people saying what a shame it was to see a legend brought so low. But he wasn't done. At some point, he learned that speech therapy could help cure him of his stutter and over the next several painstaking years, he worked so relentlessly and was so successful that in the 1990s he returned to work for the Chicago Bulls—in the communications office, no less! Before long, he would find his calling as one of the most in-demand public speakers in the world.

While none of that had yet happened back in the days when I was growing up and following Bob Love's career, there was already something about his humble origins that said to me—hey, if he can overcome so much to play the game, what's stopping me?

And just to reinforce that idea, playing in the AAU league with the Boys Club, under Coach Johnnie Gage, continued to help me build the skills that went along with my growing confidence. But no experience either watching my hero in the NBA or playing in league competition taught me relentlessness like the education that I received from learning the rules of street basketball.

On the Southside, like a lot of places where there are unwritten but strict laws of survival in street pickup games, there was one rule that stood above the rest: The team that wins stays on the court. Some courts I've heard about might be more genteel and require a team to sit down after its second win. Not in our neighborhood. It was a battle for supremacy—absolutely Darwinian—with the winning team staying on the court, game after game, as long as they kept winning, until they were too tired or another team was able to beat them. If you wanted to stay on the court and continue playing, you had to win and nothing would determine the outcome except making sure you were better than the other teams. Even to get on the court in the first place, you needed to be good enough so that someone would pick you.

The court nearest our house was known far and wide for attracting some of the stiffest local competition. It was a weeding-out process for a lot of players. Many a future NBA star played on that court—including Tim Hardaway and Rickey Green, among others, back in their early days. Nobody showed up, however, with their credits from elsewhere or their basketball pedigree in hand. By the rules of the street, if didn't matter what other league you played in or how well you had done the day before; you were judged by what you could do today, and by what you brought to the game and left on the court, nothing else. Then again, if you could deliver in the game, it might help your credibility off the court.

At age ten, when I first started getting in on the pickup

games, I might wait all day to be picked. By the time I was in the eighth grade, I regularly held my own on teams nobody could beat. The feeling that you and your team were unbeatable and could play on to midnight—if your mother would have allowed it—was one of those experiences that, once you've tasted it, you were always looking for again.

Street basketball teaches many things that structured competition doesn't. It definitely keeps a player real and helps you be in the zone of "not too high, not too low." Being badly beaten in pickup only means that you have to go to the back of the line and wait your turn to challenge the winners; conversely, winning gives you few bragging rights, since it only grants you the right to play on. That said, nothing gives a player the edge that growing up in the school of street basketball does.

In my case, really finding that edge as a player wouldn't come until my last years of high school. But as for the future coach in me, pickup games in the park provided me with a knowledge of the game that would later earn me the nickname "The Edge" when I first became an assistant coach. And it's something that I'm always interested to discover in players and figure out how to tap on behalf of the team. Coaches who haven't had to survive the law of having to win to stay on the court sometimes tend to run their strategies "by the book." Similarly, players who've never had to swim with the sharks in neighborhood pickup games can be disadvantaged, even when they've been well-coached.

One aspect of that edge needed in the survival of the fittest comes from what I refer to as "guile"—not in a negative sense at all but rather in terms of being clever and wily on your feet. There is no guile in old-hat moves like trying to pump-fake before actually taking a shot. The street-schooled player learns to read the opponent, know what he is about to do, and then throw him off his game. Having guile also means that if someone sees what you're doing and anticipates your next move, you have to change up your game on the fly. Many of the skills that go into bluffing in card games can be useful in the development of a pretty crafty basketball player.

Between everything that I learned competing in games of strategy in our household and the fundamentals that Johnnie Gage was helping me master, once I got into my teens I could hold my own playing street ball. This didn't mean that my relentless mom and dad were leaving me out there without rules that were also designed for my survival.

If I was going to the park and wasn't going to be on the court, the message delivered repeatedly so that it was drummed into my head was, "Don't stand out on the corner. Even if you're with your friends and you're not doing anything, don't stand on the corner. Go to someone's house, find another activity at the park, or come home." In the mid- and late 1970s, corners were about to become hot spots for trouble— where drugs were starting to exchange hands, with gangs looking to control turf, and where police were beginning to scout for suspected troublemakers. After my run-in with the cop who accused me of stealing a bike, I understood the reason for avoiding corners. But Mom was still strict even when she knew that I'd be on the court playing and insisted I check in with her in between games. Luckily, the breaks were long enough for me to run down the alley, jump two fences, and then yell up, "Mom, I'm back!"

As soon as I'd hear her "Okay!" I'd return to the park and continue playing. I was crafty enough not to announce to anyone that I had to check in periodically with my mother. That wouldn't have played well on the court. But because I saw this as my way of giving her peace of mind, the dash home and back never really bothered me. And when I did encounter the rougher element on the streets, they didn't

My paternal grandparents, LaVaughn and Fraser Robinson II.

Me and my maternal grandfather, Purnell Shields, a.k.a. Southside.

My father, Fraser Robinson III.
My hero, a cool cat even in his thirties!

Mom, Marian Shields Robinson,
from the early 1960s—
she has barely aged since!

My parents, Marian Shields
and Fraser Robinson III,
at their wedding.

Here I am on my father's knee—probably talking about basketball already!

Mom with baby Michelle in early 1964—my great-aunt Robbie looks on approvingly.

Here I am with Mom soon after learning that I was going to skip third grade.

A Robinson family portrait, 1964. Fraser and Marian Robinson, baby Michelle, and me at age two.

On Christmas, even when we were toddlers, the best part for me was seeing what Santa Claus brought my baby sister. She felt the same about what I received too.

Summer fun at Dukes Happy Holiday Resort with "Diddley" (our nickname for Dad), Miche, and me, circa 1967.

Early on, Michelle was proud of being known as Craig Robinson's little sister, just as I'm proud today of being known as Michelle Obama's big brother.

Michelle and I were so close, both in age and temperament, we were almost like twins.

Our Buick Electra 225—the first car I ever drove, including the night of my Honest John outing.

Every outing with our family was an adventure—whether it was to the drive-in or on a trip like this memorable excursion to Indiana Dunes.

Before heading out to play some pickup basketball, I show off my shooting form at home.

I'm number 44, standing next to Coach Johnnie Gage, and with my teammates at the Martin Luther King Boys Club on the Westside of Chicago.

Sophomore year at Mount Carmel, where I attended high school just as the game of basketball began to click for me.

Early in my college playing time I began to understand the Princeton offense, not only as a strategy but as a mindset.

At Princeton. By the intensity of my expression, you can bet it's toward the end of the season.

The first time, when I tied for Ivy League Player of the Year, Coach Carril said he didn't vote for me. The next year I won it outright. He didn't say anything, but I think he was proud.

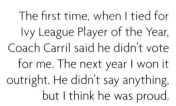

mess with any of us who played basketball—provided we didn't get cocky.

For the most part, I managed to avoid any off-the-court confrontations in these years—with the exception of an incident that took place back in the sixth grade when a scary behemoth in the eighth grade took a dislike to me. Raised to put myself in his shoes, I analyzed the situation and came to the conclusion that he was used to being picked on for not being very good in school. So naturally he was going to go after someone who was a top student—and someone like me who was not aggressive or confrontational.

"I don't want to fight him!" I told Dad flat-out, knowing that I would get crushed.

In his own relentless fashion, my father heard me and my fears out before coming up with a strategy for dealing with someone who obviously knew how afraid I was. His recommendation? That I learn to fight. But he was very crafty in his approach. Instead of telling me to go put on my boxing gloves and prepare for battle, Dad announced that everyone should learn to defend themselves—just in case. And he bought Michelle boxing gloves too. Since he had fought in the ring, he was able to draw from his experience to tell us how to stand, how to jab with one hand and protect ourselves from incoming with the other. But Dad wouldn't box with us—probably because he was afraid to really hit us. He did, however, urge me and Michelle to go at it. Since I wasn't going to hit my little sister, she got to wale on me with all her might. Man, did I learn how to protect myself from her well-paced hits!

Once Dad saw that I could defend myself from my sister— thank you very much—he decided that I was ready to hit back and then enlisted Uncle Andrew to work with me. Ninety percent of the time he had me back on my flat-footed heels— hitting me so hard that a few times I saw stars. But ten percent of the time, I was able to use my basketball guile to sneak in some good jabs and catch Andrew off guard. The training gave me enough confidence to know that if the eighth-grade Godzilla came after me and wanted to fight, at least I'd be able to get some punches in.

The moment of truth came outside on the playground one day as I was happily minding my own business, when he lumbered menacingly toward me, expecting, no doubt, that I was going to turn and flee. Rather than running the other way, I took a deep breath and walked in his direction, stopping him in his tracks. "Hold it right there," I said, my voice sounding oddly loud and clear. "You wanna fight? Let's fight. Let's get it over with."

What I saw next has lived with me ever since. It was as if all the wind went out of his sails and he crumbled in front of me, all of his rage and bullying ire evaporating in the air of the school playground. Needless to say, there was no fight. He simply backed down because I had stood up to him.

The postscript on that story was that neither Dad nor Mom said, "I told you so," or tried to take credit for all the years of encouraging me to stand up for myself. They didn't overdo the praise either. Yet I knew they were proud of me.

And I really knew how proud they were when eighth-grade graduation was fast approaching and it was announced that I was the valedictorian. This was the end of the ride at Bryn Mawr, which Michelle would continue attending for another two years—and where she would actually be chosen as salutatorian for her eighth-grade graduation. Little did I know that we wouldn't go to school on the same campus again—until college. But I did feel that change and challenge were in the wind when I sat down to write my speech, starting out with words that came to me easily at first—"Ladies and gentlemen, I stand before you with pride and humility. . . ." After that, I was stumped and ended up sitting there worried about how to top such a strong opening. Eventually, I wrote a speech about gratitude to our teachers and, of course, to our parents.

Up until a week before starting high school, I had always assumed that I'd be attending one of the two public schools in our area. But when Mom and Dad had a chance to visit them just before school started, they came to the conclusion that I wouldn't be challenged academically and that I needed to break out of the comfort zone of the Southside. True, competing in AAU league under Johnnie Gage on the Westside was giving me some of that. But Mom and Dad believed that I could get a much better education in a different environment. Two years later we would have access to Whitney Young, a public magnet school outside of our district but inside the city limits, where Miche would go, that offered accelerated and honors classes. Though the commute there and back added as much as three hours to her long day, it would be worth it. But the opportunity to attend Whitney Young wasn't available when I was getting ready to start high school.

My reaction to switching to a private school or possibly going away to boarding school was not too different from my reaction to hearing the news at age three that we were moving to Euclid Avenue. Why rock the boat? After all, everyone knew who I was. At age thirteen, I had made something of a name for myself.

In spite of some misgivings, I trusted my parents so completely that if they felt this was important, I had to be willing to look at the options. What this would cost didn't enter the conversation. The next thing I knew, we were bound for Wisconsin; we had friends who attended a prep school there that I distinctly disliked. When I took the entrance exam—although I usually tested very well—I had a mediocre score. If it had anything to do with the fact that I didn't want to go there, my mother would not have been surprised. Then I attended an open house at Mount Carmel, a parochial school in Chicago. Although I had finished playing football and baseball, making basketball my main sport, Mount Carmel didn't recruit me for basketball or any other sports. Acceptance and the choice to go there would thus be solely academic decisions, and, considering the substantial tuition they would be paying, not an inexpensive one for my parents. But they didn't want that to be an issue. This time, when I took the exam, I did extremely well, qualifying for the honors program. So Mount Carmel it was.

Three days later, in my pressed slacks, collared shirt and tie, and leather shoes—attire that conformed with Mount Carmel's dress code—I walked up the steps to the high school I would attend for the next four years, preparing myself to enter a whole new universe.

The enrollment at Mount Carmel was 85 percent white, just for starters. Plus, it was an all–boys' school—a big change from the coed education at Bryn Mawr. Then there was my religious upbringing as a Protestant—which had included attending church and Sunday school at the Methodist church where Mom's family belonged, along with occasional visits to the Baptist church where most of the Robinson side of the family went. None of that had exposed me to the teachings of Catholicism, nor had I ever heard of different Catholic orders like the Carmelite brothers, who were administrators and teachers at Mount Carmel. In their long brown robes, with their austere way of life, and the main focus they put on faith and service, the brethren definitely seemed different from other educators I'd encountered. *Culture shock* seems too mild of a term to describe what I knew was in store for me.

Was I nervous? The answer might be a rhetorical and fitting "Is the pope Catholic?" But I tried to convince myself otherwise. After all, I told myself, it was not so different from being picked for a new team playing street basketball. And I suspected that the lessons of being relentless, of not forgetting that your turn will come and until then you have to be patient and persistent, and that you have to win to stay on the court, would serve me well—in the classroom and otherwise.

Relentlessness, of course, is taught in many settings. My parents were the Rhodes scholars of being relentless, never losing stamina, always rising above their own level of achievement, never limiting their beliefs or aspirations, a constant energy source. In our teen years, it seemed that the busier Michelle and I became, instead of Mom and Dad taking it easier, they became more involved not just in our lives but in being there for our extended family and for anyone else who needed them. The diagnosis of MS my father had been given didn't change that in the least. No matter what, if Uncle Terry or Aunt Robbie needed something downstairs, it might be in the middle of the night, Mom or Dad would head down there.

Initially, it was Uncle Terry who began to decline rapidly. There were certain needs—like bathing him or helping him to the toilet or giving him a shave—that my father insisted he be the one to offer. Dad was soon going to use a kind of crutch that wrapped around his bicep for support; later it would be two crutches. But if Uncle Terry needed him, he wouldn't hear of anyone else giving that care. Before leaving for his shift, Dad would always check to see if Uncle Terry was all right and he'd check on him again as soon as he arrived home. It was relentless compassion. I went downstairs one day to ask my father a question before he left. Walking into the bathroom, I came upon the unforgettable sight of Fraser Robinson III standing propped against the sink while he gave his older in-law a trim and a shave. The sight of my great-uncle's gratitude and Dad's incredible patience humbled me for the rest of my life. It was almost too much to process at the time.

Not too long after Uncle Terry passed away, Aunt Robbie's health began to deteriorate. My mother was on call constantly and my aunt's illness went on for ages. When Aunt Robbie needed something, she would ring the bell at her bedside so urgently that we would all jump out of bed as if it were a fire alarm. Mom was always up and already down the stairs. For years, my mother didn't get a good night's sleep.

But the joy and the pleasure we shared as a family continued full force. They were relentless about that too! Dad was never too tired when he came home from work to play with us, talk with us, joke with us, or be anything less than 110 percent engaged—as Bob Love might have said—in our lives. Mom never slowed down either. She was right there in the trenches, not just keeping pace but usually about three moves ahead of us. My parents, like Johnnie Gage, were not afraid to enforce the rules. They knew that kids want to play and that if they're not behaving, just sit them down or send them home.

My parents also understood one of the toughest lessons for those of us parents and coaches who want to do everything for our kids and players to make their lives safe, happy, and fulfilling. Mom and Dad understood that in providing the foundation for learning, there will come a time when you have to stand back and know you've covered the fundamentals.

You can lead others up the steps to where they need to go and maybe help open the door. But it's up to the individual to walk through it. Or not.

5

DON'T BE AFRAID TO BE SMART *AND* COOL

Just as every game has a distinct beginning, a middle, and an end, so, too, does an athletic season. In my high school years, I started to have a stronger sense of how momentum builds over the course of the season and why you should never count yourself out in the early stages—even when you're not winning many games. I also tried to take a longer view about how and when I was ever going to feel like I really fit in at Mount Carmel. Not that I had such a hard time. The fact was that my jump to a new school happened to coincide with a growth spurt and the onset of a mild case of teenage angst. All of sudden, I was tall and gangly, still pretty square and unsophisticated, all in addition to being identified as one of the smarter kids. If it hadn't been for basketball, I would have been doomed to a life of uncoolness.

So it definitely helped when I made the freshman basketball team and then was moved up to play as a starter on the sophomore team. Even more important was that I had a new mentor, Father Mike, my first coach at Mount Carmel, and a role model for me as a person and a coach in training. At a time when I was concerned that others might stereotype or prejudge me, Father Mike provided me with an updated version of my parents' admonitions not to care what others thought. Father Mike defied all the conventional wisdom of what a priest was supposed to be. Far from the gentle, ethereal figure dressed in flowing robes that fit the stereotype, Father Mike dressed in sweats along with his collar, and ran up and down the court, yelling and screaming. He could be gentle, but he also could be tough as nails, and he had a piercing gaze that made me suspect he saw more in me than I was allowing to come to the surface and he was trying to coax it out.

Between Dad lighting the competitive flame, Johnnie Gage grounding me in fundamentals, and street ball teaching me how to be crafty, I really had all the elements going for me. It was Father Mike who was going to push me to the next place—where I could hopefully put it all together.

In the meantime, adjusting to a higher level of scholarship in the honors program at Mount Carmel wasn't very challenging, though most of my classes were interesting and well-taught. Religion was a required subject and I had the pleasure of studying with Father Carroll, a middle-aged priest with thin blond hair and round wire-rimmed glasses. Reminiscent of an Ivy League professor, Father Carroll was brilliant, thoughtful, and tempered serious ideas with great humor. We covered a range of religions and a good deal of philosophy—everyone from Aristotle to Camus. While I might have expected more dogma, Father Carroll proved to be very tolerant of other faiths and other people's opinions. He was more interested in generating curiosity and critical thinking than in having us appropriate his point of view and regurgitate what we'd been fed. His approach was not unlike how we talked about religion in the Robinson household, where we were encouraged, as always, to explore and find our own basis for faith by thinking for ourselves.

But this is not to say that it was all smooth sailing. For all the encouragement that I felt from Fathers Mike and Carroll, I wasn't universally welcomed. No one said anything outright. But there was a certain scrutinizing look some students and teachers gave me that was as if to say—"Why are you here?" Others would make thinly veiled comments to the effect that I couldn't possibly be smart and must have only gotten in because of some kind of minority quota. Naturally, raised as I was not to let those petty looks and remarks get to me, I mostly ignored them. But not when I encountered a lay teacher of history and American government who was almost villainous in his contempt for me. I was really shaken.

In hindsight, I have to feel a little sorry for him and the fact that this history teacher missed an opportunity to face his own bias against a kid who bothered him so much because he happened to be black. And I can also feel thankful that his attitude helped me develop a tougher skin and gave me a preview of his kind of prejudice—not as overt as what I'd heard about before but just as insidious. It was something I'd face later on when trying to get through the door in the financial industry. Looking back, I can appreciate the history lesson that this teacher gave me, even if it was unintended—that though the days of marching and confronting police dogs and fire hoses were over, our generation's struggle for equality was going to be in classrooms and corporate offices. The preview I was shown, however, made me think that, even when given a chance to compete, it's not enough that we do very well and make ourselves stand out; there still will be those who resent us all the more for our efforts.

As the saying goes—forewarned is forearmed. But at the time, I convinced myself that on some level it was my fault, that I had done something wrong to offend him, and if I could only right it, he would let up and cut me some slack. Initially I decided that if he could just get to know the real Craig Robinson—nice, smart, friendly, conscientious, a team player, and all the other reasons that others seemed to like me—he would see that his animosity was ill-founded. When working harder to prove myself on these merits didn't move him, I went the other direction and downplayed my intelligence and did as little to call attention to myself as possible. Since we had so few black students at Mount Carmel and I was in the handful who made it into the honors program, I assumed after a while that it was my smarts that bugged him. But playing dumb, as it were, didn't make a bit of difference. It was like trying to befriend a pit bull. At a certain point you realize that you're just going to get bit!

Eventually, it was my basketball education that helped me survive my history teacher. It occurred to me, the more frustrated and potentially angry that I was becoming, that this teacher was no different from a punk on an opposing team who was trying to get under my skin and psych me out on the court. True, the teacher had the authority and the power to cause trouble for me. But that wouldn't happen as long as I kept my cool.

Big revelation! For the first time in my life I was able to tell myself that it was possible to be both smart and cool. And by *cool,* I mean in the sense of not becoming overly heated or frustrated, as well as being cool in the hip sense. My question then became—how?

Out of the blue, I recalled a day back in the fourth grade when Mom was in our class as a volunteer, helping a classmate with his arithmetic. He kept insisting, "Mrs. Robinson, I can't count."

Mom said, "Try counting on your fingers." After all, that was how I was taught to count.

My classmate refused. Finally he admitted that he was too embarrassed to have to do that.

My mother said, "Well, shoot, if you don't want anyone to know, here's what you do . . ." and she demonstrated how he could put his fingers on the desk and count on them by pressing each one down subtly as he counted to himself. By the end of class, he'd mastered the approach and soon could do advanced math.

The takeaway for me was slightly different from that student's. What I realized was that you can be smart and nobody has to know. In high school, rediscovering that lesson was like coming up with lost treasure. Besides, I knew from the bluffing and strategy of street basketball and board games that you never want your opponent to know everything you've got up your sleeve. That was another way that I could be cool.

In this fashion, I processed my teenage angst and had a much different attitude walking the halls of Mount Carmel. Before long, I'd made a name for myself and stopped second-guessing whether the move to the new school had been a good idea. Yes, at Mount Carmel, I was the outsider, the racial minority, and the brainy athlete I had always been. But that was starting to be sort of cool.

When I confided in Michelle about my new attitude, she couldn't have done more to cheer me on. But in her honest, direct way, she did mention, "There's only one problem. . . ." Her voice wavered as she considered the best way to explain where I was still really lacking in the coolness department. In typical Robinson fashion, she was able to turn her concern into affectionate teasing when she broke it to me that until I improved my dance moves, I was going to be at a loss in getting girls.

Now, I didn't think my dancing was all that awful. But because I didn't go to school with any girls, local dances at various community and church functions were about the only place I could socialize with the opposite sex. So when my little sis offered to give me dance lessons to improve my chances, I wasn't opposed to the idea. Was she a good dancer? No, she wasn't. She was a great dancer!

By this time, my parents had refinished the back porch and turned it into a bedroom for me. Then Michelle had taken over their bedroom while Mom and Dad moved into our old bedroom. We tried dance lessons in a couple of places before settling on the kitchen—where Dad and Mom decided to get in on the teasing by suggesting that Michelle really had her work cut out for her.

"Hey, I'm a good dancer," I finally defended myself one day. "Miche is just getting me caught up on some new moves."

Michelle not only agreed but went on to admit that part of her motivation to teach me was to make sure I didn't go to the dances—which she attended as well—and wind up embarrassing her! You'd think my parents would have been appalled, but they laughed uproariously and agreed that dancing was not my calling in life.

Joking aside, my parents were relieved that I had decided that being smart and being cool weren't mutually exclusive. And Michelle was head of my fan club in just about every other respect. Being known as "Craig Robinson's little sister" was a badge of honor that she wore well into our college years. Of course, later on the tables would turn and I would have the honor of being known as "Michelle Obama's big brother"!

Early in my days of playing competitive basketball the whole family attended all the games as much as possible. Sometimes Dad's swing shift conflicted with a game and he might not be able to come, but Mom and Michelle did their best to make it when he couldn't. The farther up the food chain my teams went—either in high school or in the highly competitive summer league that many of my fellow players from Johnnie Gage's team and from Mount Carmel played in—the tougher it was for my mother and sister to watch from start to finish. If a game was neck-and-neck, or we started to lose with little time left on the clock, it was not uncommon for the two of them to shield their eyes or even to step outside. Whenever I looked up in the stands and noticed that the two Robinson women weren't there, I knew it was not for lack of love or support.

Fortunately, all of the Robinsons were able to enjoy watching our team score some significant wins over the course of my first two years at Mount Carmel—thanks to the coaching and team-building of Father Mike. In the summer after sophomore year, several of us were on a killer summer league team and had even beaten players from the team that had just won the state high school championship. We had also scrimmaged and won against our teammates who were going to be seniors, so we figured that as juniors, we'd move up and get to be starters on Varsity. We were ready to go all the way and emerge victorious in the Chicago Catholic League—and beyond.

Unfortunately, a new head coach who was brought in to oversee the juniors and seniors disrupted the momentum. The new coach, Ed McQuillan, only played the older guys, whether they were the better-skilled players or not. As a player I disagreed then and as a coach today I still disagree with that tactic. But I will also add that my hero Bob Love became the giant that he was in part from *listening* to his coaches—one of his rules for success. So we could only sit on the bench and respect that Coach McQuillan was the boss. When the season was over and we had won only one game and had lost twenty-two, my fellow juniors and I did our best to keep our cool. We knew that the following year the slate would be wiped clean and we would have the chance to prove ourselves.

That long, frustrating junior-year season wouldn't have been bearable without the tight-knit group of guys my team-mates and I were by then. We had come to Mount Carmel from a mix of backgrounds: from well-to-do households, from working-class homes, and some from very poor families; we had players who were black and white; and we were even a diverse religious group. We also competed in everything—grades and sports, summer jobs, whatever. The ongoing com-petition was a sophisticated form of the dozens that involved teasing each other incessantly and calling one another by our mother's first name. So if you could manage it, you tried to keep your mother's name to yourself. But no such luck for me—they all called me Marian. One of the guys might say, "Yeah, I was over at Marian's last night," and someone else would pipe up, "Oh, hey, Marian, what time is practice?"

Nobody did this to me more often than my best friend, Julius Rhodes. Julius was and is larger than life, extremely intelligent, an all-around free spirit, and one of the most out-going people I've ever met. At Mount Carmel he was the king of smart and cool.

Slightly taller than me at the time (when I was only six four), Julius had one leg that was a good deal shorter than the other. But he used it to his advantage, somehow managing to bend it down lower before going up to the basket and achiev-ing so much liftoff that he was the first in our group to really dunk the ball. Sometimes there were shades of my dad in Julius—especially during practice when I was tired of the boring repetition of drills and would look over to see Julius with his stutter-skipping step and his beaming smile, and real-ize I had nothing to complain about. Besides basketball, we also shared the status, more or less, as the only two African American students in the honors classes for our grade. Later, after graduating from Beloit University, where he played, Julius would go on to become a prominent entrepreneur and social figure in Chicago—with a graduate degree or two he'd pick up along the way too.

Ironically, the idea of one day maybe playing college basketball only seriously entered my mind senior year. In those days college basketball wasn't on everyone's radar, partly because it wasn't shown as much on television—with the exception of the games during March Madness. Whenever anyone talked about college basketball, most everyone knew about the Final Four and then the final face-off for the championship.

While those games were incredibly exciting, of course, the true promised land for me and my guys back in high school was the NBA. I might not have admitted that at the time—because I was enough of a realist to know what the odds really were and because it wouldn't have been either smart or cool to admit it. Still, around about my junior year, I suddenly became much more serious about excelling in ways that I hadn't before. It wasn't that I was preparing to shoot for the NBA. But I wanted to have the satisfaction of knowing that I'd pushed myself enough that if the opportunity to get that far ever arose, I'd be ready.

This was easier envisioned than put into action. As Father Mike seemed to have noticed, I did hold back from being the all-out, no-holds-barred driver on offense. On defense and rebounding, I had found my groove earlier. Without strong defense, as I knew all too well from sitting on the bench for a season, teams can't win. But like Dad had said early in my development, basketball is a game where the object is putting the ball through the hoop. And that's what I really wanted to do—to put points on the board.

The confidence that I could do that at a high level received a major boost during the summer before senior year. In Chicago's summer leagues—a kind of honors program for local basketball—NBA stars, along with top college players and qualified high school players, played together on the same teams and competed in what was a thrilling blend of exhibition basketball, inner-city street ball, and just serious competition.

Getting ready for these games I was a nervous wreck, not only because I was almost always the youngest kid on the floor—out there playing against the likes of Sonny Parker from the Golden State Warriors, and Maurice Cheeks from the Philadelphia 76ers—but also because of other concerns on my mind. In the summers I co-ran a hot dog concession at the lakefront that was a huge moneymaking opportunity and a big responsibility. That meant juggling hot dog duties with practice and games. It also required figuring out the logistics of getting to the game with plenty of time to warm up and find my footing.

Earlier in high school, Michelle had come up with a solution to nerves when I had trouble sleeping the night before an important game. Seeing me tossing and turning on the sofa where I was trying to rest, Miche had said, "Craig, how about some music to relax you?"

She promptly sat down at the small upright that we kept in the adjacent alcove and began to play the cheery theme from the Charlie Brown specials on television. The tune worked its magic within minutes. When I opened my eyes I was rested and confident. From then on, this was our pregame ritual for getting me to zone out either with a nap or a full night's sleep. Miche had a terrific repertoire that worked—jazz, classical, Stevie Wonder, even Broadway show tunes.

The most memorable of these summer league games was the day that I played on a team with Reggie Theus, David Greenwood, and Quintin Dailey, all from the Bulls. In that game, we faced a team that touted some other big names—among them Michael Jordan. Even before the pros arrived, the arena was packed to overflowing—with fans, family, and friends, along with talent scouts, coaches, and assorted hangers-on. The games were free and every sector of society was represented—including the high-rolling drug dealers, pimps, and hustlers who'd show up decked out in so much bling that you knew who they were and were happy this was just a friendly family affair so nobody was going to be shooting one another.

Apparently nobody but me was raised in the Fraser Robinson school of being on time, and on this occasion, as the other ones, I was the only player out on the floor warming up because I had arrived early—which was actually the appointed time when we were supposed to be there. As the other players straggled in, with the NBA stars arriving fashionably late to screams and cheers from the fans, music blared from loudspeakers and the whole place started to cook. Literally. Down on the court it was 115 degrees before the game had even started! As a remedy—such as it was— the arena staff brought out industrial-sized fans to keep the floor from becoming too slippery with everyone's sweat.

And then it was game time. For a lot of folks in the crowd who could never have afforded tickets to see an NBA game, this was an opportunity to see the famous basketball players live and in person. For younger players like me, it was a showcase for being seen, and where being seen could actually lead to something. What that was, I didn't really know, but the heightened stakes revved me up enough that I was able to draft off of all the energy and excitement in the arena and do pretty well. I had a hard time believing that, but the stats confirmed a surprising fact: In the game, Michael Jordan scored twenty-eight points and I scored twenty-one! But the best compliment came from Dad, who nodded proudly when he said, "You were doing everything out there in that game! Not everybody can do everything, but you might just be someone who can."

Praise like that, coming from my father, replaced every

coolest feeling that had preceded it. But before I allowed myself to become too bigheaded about it, there was an incident
a short while later (having nothing to do with basketball) that
brought me right back down to the ground.

As I'd turned sixteen a few months earlier and had recently gotten my license, Dad decided that he could trust me
with the car to run a short errand over to a shop in the neighborhood that served hand-packed ice cream. When he asked
if I wanted to go, handing me ten bucks and the keys to the
car, I practically sprinted out the door. This was a simple route
to navigate—by driving down to the end of our block, then
turning left and keeping straight until I pulled up to the ice
cream joint. Coming home, all I had to do was drive around
the block and return to Euclid Avenue. There was nothing to
worry about in terms of a complicated order either. We always ordered chocolate, black cherry, and butter pecan, as if
those were the only three flavors in the world.

The man who ran the ice cream store was not the friend-
liest guy in the world, so much so that I used to wonder why
he was in this kind of business. And this occasion was no different. He didn't smile or say a word when I came in. And as
he was filling the order, he did so with the same impassive
expression he always wore. At the register, he rang everything
up, gave me the total in a monotone, and waited impatiently
for the money.

Hoping to get out of there as fast as possible, I handed
him the ten dollars and when he returned the change to me,
perhaps because I was preoccupied with the thought of driving home, I stuffed what he handed me in my pocket and
took off. Suddenly, after a block or so, I realized that I hadn't
counted my change—a no-no in the Robinson household.

Well, I reassured myself, he wouldn't have tried to short-
change me. But just to be sure, I pulled the money out of my

pocket and spread it out on the seat beside me. Horrors! The unfriendly guy at the ice cream store had given me change for a twenty—which I realized was the case, since the change included some singles and a ten-dollar bill. Now I had a dilemma. Should I allow the ice cream to melt while I turned around to go back and give him the money that wasn't mine? Or should I let it be his fault, and get my family their ice cream? There was only one course of action, I decided, and that was to go back to the store. When I ran in and handed the man back the ten dollars, he didn't react at all. He looked at the money, at me, then back at the money, and didn't say a word.

As soon as I arrived at home, before I could explain the melted ice cream, everyone asked in unison, "What happened?" They had begun to wonder if I'd gotten lost or in an accident.

As I relayed the details of my ordeal, they may have been tempted to laugh, but I was so earnest, they all seemed to think that I'd done the right thing. But Michelle couldn't resist an opportunity to tease me mercilessly about what a Goody Two-shoes I was. Actually, she came up with another nickname for me that must have come from a story we had read as children.

"Craig," she said, "I can't believe that you could be that honest and the guy didn't even appreciate it! You know, we're going to have to call you 'Honest John' from here on out."

And for the rest of the night she stayed with it. Michelle even came up with other scenarios, asking what I would do if I found one million dollars on the street. Honest John would have to give it back, she'd point out. As the days went by, I still didn't hear the end of it. Eventually she shortened my nickname to "H.J."

We all had fun with it, but the real joke was that she was

making fun of herself just as much as she was me, because, all teasing aside, Michelle would have done exactly the same thing.

And the bottom line was that I didn't mind being Honest John. It might not have been smart or cool to do what I had done, but that's who I was—and it wasn't such a bad guy to be.

That summer marked a turning point in my life. Something powerful was stirring up inside me—what would be a real breakthrough in my development as a basketball player and in my connection to the game. I didn't know what exactly it was or how it would manifest. It was just that a new season would be starting soon and I had high expectations for the team and for me. Anything was possible. And that was cool!

6

THE CORRECT CHOICE MAY NOT BE THE RIGHT CHOICE

Whenever I think of individuals whom I see as exemplary, I often find that it is through their choices made at different turning points that their true character can be revealed. It's a point of view that I've brought to the way that I coach and how I assess my players and the decision-making process they use at important turning points in the game. Certain players, not all, will usually reveal their capacity for leadership by how they balance the need to be unselfish during the game with the need to take control when the opening is there. These are the players who know, without being told, that sometimes the correct play at a key moment may not be the right play. That awareness requires the leader on the court to take the risk to go against the conventional wisdom and to take the shot—in one form or another.

In life this understanding has many applications as well, which is something that my father used to talk about and point out to me as a child. But it was only going into my last year of high school that I started to get what he meant—both basketball-wise and as it pertained to all the pressing personal decisions that loomed up ahead. The first glimmers came to me at the end of the summer of 1978, right before school started, when I attended Athletes for Better Education in Wisconsin, a one-week basketball camp that was the precursor of the Nike All-American Camps. There were classes in the daytime, basketball games in the afternoon and evening, and as we were being introduced to the fundamentals of what playing college basketball was all about, coaches from an array of universities would come to see who could do what.

Maybe it was the fact that the competition was so good or that we were there on our own, not with the loyalty to team as was usually in my thinking, but I was aware of kicking into a higher gear—one that I didn't even know that I had. It was an aggressive, high-powered side of me that was almost primal and that seemed to take over instinctually. The next thing I knew, I was in the air readying to dunk on an opponent who was about four inches taller than me. Totally out of character. I was a correct kind of player, a nice guy who passed the ball to the open teammate, and who, frankly, preferred a passive or less aggressive style on the court. But in the heat of the game, I went with my gut, even though it was not correct, and dunked the ball. Something clicked in my brain. Ah, it was all coming clear. Dad was right: Sometimes the correct play wasn't always the right play.

What good timing to make that discovery. Unbeknownst to me at the time, watching me in that game were individuals who would have a hand in determining my future choices and whose attention I'd definitely just commanded.

For the rest of the camp, I played well and correctly, sending the more primitive side of me back to its cage. But once basketball season began and we started to win again as a team, now that Coach McQuillan was playing us as seniors, I suspected that it would come out again at the time and place of its choosing. Sure enough, in one of the first games when Mount Carmel hosted a team from a school that, ironically, was closer to my neighborhood, everything clicked again, only more powerfully than the last time. My confidence was soaring because I knew that there had been a lot of improvement since the year before, not to mention a strong summer in league play, plus the fact that I was still getting taller, and then a good showing at camp with that dunk that had seemed to come from out of nowhere.

Suddenly in this game I get the ball and take off, going for a dunk that's going to make the first one look like child's play, and before you know it, I have entered another realm where everything goes into slow motion and I'm up above the rim so high it's like wearing antigravity boots! It was like being on top of the world and I could see forever—including our gym's upper tier that had a track for running around the court, which was so short that, in order to run a mile, you had to go around it twenty-two times. I could see every inch of that and behind the basket I could see the dangling feet of people who were sitting on the track. That's how high I dunked it. The crowd went crazy! And before the game was over, I ended up getting two more dunks—after blocking shots like a madman, stealing the ball right and left, and making plenty more incorrect but right plays.

It was not that I was suddenly someone else. I still had a lot to learn about how to harness this heretofore underused force. But it was a rite of passage to the next leg of the basketball journey. This was the first time I could honestly say to myself, "Now I'm a player!"

The rest of the season made up for the previous year's dismal showing when we claimed a final record of 19 and 8. Riding high on what was a lot of overachieving, we went into the state play-offs as real contenders. Everything hinged on whether we could beat one of the higher-ranked teams at the regional championship game. With that win in our pocket. we would then advance to sectionals and then on to the state championship. In spite of the knowledge that the team we were playing had some big-time recruits, we were so confident that in the closing minutes we had them on the ropes. Then, just as it was crunch time, our coach made a strategic decision to pull one of our players with whom he didn't exactly see eye-to-eye. Because this player wasn't someone known always to make the correct play—though he was a senior and our coach had previously had a preference for playing those of us with seniority—Coach pulled him and put in a younger, greener player who wasn't able to handle the pressure. We had a couple of turnovers as the clock wound down and we ended up losing.

Because we had come so close to going all the way, and we really could have won, that was one of the most disappointing losses in my high school career. But I didn't blame the coach, even if I disagreed with some of his strategies. At the same time, I kept a mental inventory of how I might have done things differently—useful material for down the road, even if those days were a long ways off.

The more immediate decision was for what road I was going to take after high school graduation. The process for making that choice had actually begun the previous summer when I attended the Athletes for a Better Education Camp in Wisconsin. It was run, as it so happened, by a Princeton grad who arranged for Tony Relvas, Princeton's Men's Basketball assistant coach, to come watch me play.

Though I didn't know much about elite colleges versus good state schools versus schools that were basically basketball factories, I knew that Princeton carried a level of prestige that impressed people when the name came up. One of my reference points for the Ivy League was from watching *The Flint-stones* and how in Bedrock the top-notch schools were "Princestone" and "Shale."

On the one hand, I was flattered and intrigued at being recruited by the Ivy League. On the other hand, the University of Washington and the University of Texas at Arlington were each interested in me and they both had terrific basketball programs and also touted strong academic options. It turned out that at the camp, the Princeton people put the word out that they had me locked up. If I had known about it then, it would have been news to me.

Then, that fall, the Princeton athletic department paid for me to fly out and visit the campus. Oh, they knew what they were doing. Through basketball, I had traveled before to places like Kansas City for a Boys Club tournament with Johnnie Gage and had been to South Carolina as a kid with my family. But a plane ride on my own to the wilds of New Jersey was pretty exciting. And then, when the head coach, Pete Carril, came to meet me at Newark, I was duly impressed that they were going all out. It was as if I'd stepped into a movie and a Burgess Meredith–type guy (Sylvester Stallone's manager in *Rocky*) wanted to take me under his wing. A scrappy fellow who could have come from central casting under "classic college basketball coach," Coach Carril was dressed in an orange Princeton polo shirt under a gray Princeton sweatshirt, and I noticed on the ride to campus that he smoked cheap White Owl cigars that left ash all over the place. It didn't take me long to pick up on some of the reasons why he was also one of the most successful college basketball coaches in the history of the game.

When we arrived at Princeton, it was dark and I couldn't make out much except that the buildings were old and had a lot of character. Daylight confirmed the impression. For the duration of my visit, which was focused almost exclusively on the basketball program, it really felt like an unbelievable dream. And yet when I left to go back to Chicago, it felt like a dream that I could grow to be at home in.

Now that I was a viable potential recruit, there were more hoops to jump through—so to speak. First of all, there are no athletic scholarships in the Ivy League and for athletes who are recruited, there are no lowered academic standards for admission. So I was fully prepared for the Princeton possibility to be just a dream that wasn't realistic.

But then, increasing the possibility that they were serious, Pete Carril came to Chicago to see me play and to talk to my parents. Coach Carril came to our neighborhood, recognized the Robinson family values when he visited our small apartment, saw the devotion my mother had to raising her kids, and witnessed my dad limping around while supporting his family and investing everything and then some into giving his children opportunities that he hadn't had. I think Coach Carril recognized my parents' character from that visit and knew that it was by no accident that they had produced two honor students under not the easiest of circumstances.

After that visit, once I made the official decision to apply to Princeton, I had the pleasure of meeting Dennis Bonebreak, an alum, for my admissions interview. Dennis was the opposite of every stereotype I'd ever heard of the typical stuffy Princeton Man. He didn't talk like a country club snob or like the Professor on *Gilligan's Island* or have any airs about him. After his Ivy education, Dennis had come back to Chicago, where he was from, and had made the choice to pursue a career as a social worker. Besides his day job, he volunteered as a coach of Little League and high school baseball, while also working with minority kids to try to improve their educational prospects. He walked me through the admissions process, advising me every step of the way. I really had no idea what was at stake, or what a long shot it would be for me—or anyone else, for that matter—to be accepted. Since the two other big state schools that had shown interest had come after me already with scholarships, Princeton was actually the only college to which I formally applied.

How naïve could I have been? But sometimes ignorance is bliss. Or at least in this case, my assumption that I would be accepted was right on.

My former history teacher was apparently stunned—first, that I'd even apply to an Ivy League school and second, that I got in when our class valedictorian didn't. Maybe the reality hadn't settled in with me yet, but I found it funny that everyone was so amazed that I'd been accepted to Princeton. But as word got out, and people reacted as if I were Neil Armstrong just come back from the moon, I started to pinch myself too. Everyone also assumed that based on prestige alone, there was no choice but to go there.

Still, when the dust settled a bit, I had to come to grips with the financial reality. Years before, Dad had opened my eyes to the fact that we weren't rich. True, Princeton was offering a financial aid package based on my family's income, but after you took the scholarship and set it down alongside tuition and fees and living expenses, he would have to come up with at least an additional three thousand a year. This was in contrast to the full free ride being offered to me by both the University of Washington and the University of Texas at Arlington. How could I even think of putting my parents into the poorhouse?

The decision weighed heavily on my brain and my heart until one day in April 1979, when Dad and I sat down at the kitchen table so he could ask me, "Well, what do you think? You've got these three offers . . . which one of them appeals to you?"

"You know," I said, "I think I've pretty well got it figured out. I think I'd really like to go to the University of Washington."

"Oh, really?" Dad looked puzzled but wanted to hear me out, asking, "Now, why is that?"

"Well," I said, "it's a great school, and I really liked the coach, and I think they've got a really strong program. . . ."

My dad raised his eyebrow, looked at me, and said, "Is there any other reason . . . ?"

"Well," I said, "they're giving me a free ride, and if I went to Princeton, for instance, that'd be another three thousand dollars we have to come up with every year. So it seems to me that Washington makes a lot more sense."

Dad nodded thoughtfully, stroking his chin, as if not sure how to convey his concern without making a decision for me. Then finally he said to me, "Well, son, you know I'd be awfully disappointed if I thought you were making a decision this important on the basis of what we could afford."

I looked at him across that kitchen table, and even though I couldn't say anything right away, or perhaps even process the emotion, it felt like the weight of the world was being lifted off my shoulders—like I could soar across the playing field of life and not hold back.

Of course, going to Princeton was not the correct choice by any stretch of practical thinking. But it was an opportunity that, if I turned it down, I might always regret not having taken. The gift Dad gave to me in that discussion couldn't have made me love him more than I already did. It did reveal to me yet one more aspect of his character—which was a degree of generosity greater than I have ever witnessed in any other human being before or since.

We left it at that and agreed that I'd think about it and let him know what I'd decided the next day.

Close to twenty-four hours later we sat down again and Dad smiled as he asked what I'd decided.

"Well," I said, pausing to take a deep breath, "I guess going to Princeton really would be pretty cool."

"Then Princeton it is," he said, as if he knew that's what I was going to say. Or at least he really looked happy that it's what I did say.

It wasn't until years later that I learned how he pulled it off but it was something, like his pain and his disability, that he didn't want us to know. But after he died and it was time to sort through family finances, I found out that he and Mom had managed to put both of their kids through college in the Ivy League by taking out loans and putting a large portion of the tuition on credit cards. They'd saddled themselves with debt so that we could get the education they thought we deserved.

Though I never had a chance to directly acknowledge to him what that sacrifice meant to me, Dad knew how I felt— which I know with all my heart. And I also know that not for a minute did he or Mom ever regret how they chose to prepare us and support us before sending us out into the world.

Of course, it wasn't like I was being sent off to Siberia on my own. I was going to Princeton University, after all, a dream come true. But believe it or not, there were some cold realities coming up for me just the same.

PART II

ON THE ROAD

7

FROM THE SOUTHSIDE OF CHICAGO TO PRINCETON

One of the least comforting truisms tossed at me plenty of times over the years is the idea that nothing builds character like being pushed out of your comfort zone, really challenged, and even knocked on your ass. While I've never liked hearing it—especially in those moments when I've just been thrown off balance and am struggling to get back onto my feet—I know it's not a truism for nothing. In fact, I believe that in the game of character that is both life and basketball and any other field of endeavor you want to name, it's those out-of-your-comfort-zone lessons you learn on the road—often when you don't have home court advantage—that can be your most enriching.

None of that was in my thinking when the date rolled around for me to report to orientation at Princeton University in August 1979. Ironically, though it might have been like me to be nervous about departing from the comfort of our close family and the familiar neighborhood where I'd grown up for most of my seventeen years, when my parents and sister came to see me off at Chicago's O'Hare Airport, I was actually pretty cavalier about leaving home for the first time. The future beckoned. I was confident, sure of myself and of what I had to offer, and ready, or so I thought, to be in a different, challenging environment.

That confidence didn't change even when Mom, Dad, and Michelle gave me a last round of hugs before I boarded the plane. There were absolutely no tears. For all of us this was a time to rejoice and celebrate a new beginning and a new experience that wasn't only for me but for our entire extended family. Or if there were any tears shed over this first-time separation, I never knew about them.

None of that celebratory and adventurous spirit had diminished when I landed in Newark, nor when I grabbed my one big suitcase and oversized gym bag from the baggage carousel and went to find the direct bus that would deposit me at the doorstep of Princeton's Nassau Hall, right in the center of campus.

Watching the scenery fly by outside the bus window, I remembered some of the landmarks from the previous fall when Pete Carril had picked me up at the airport and had driven me to campus—the oil storage towers that pockmarked the skyline, the industrial stockyards scattered along the New Jersey Turnpike, the exit ramps leading off to sleepy commuter suburbs, and the stretches of woods and fields mixed in with corporate office parks.

As I replayed that visit, it only now occurred to me that it had really been a kind of tryout—not just to entice me to want to play at Princeton but also to see me in action. But as I recalled some of the things that Coach Carril had said during the ride, I wondered if he was also trying to rough me up a bit with criticism to see how I could take it. For a recruiting tactic, it could have been a bit of reverse psychology that he didn't shower me with a lot of praise—come to think of it—or tell me why I would be a strong addition to the team. Rather, one of the first things he had said was, "You know, you're not that fast."

To which I had only nodded, even if I didn't completely agree.

"And you don't shoot that well," Coach Carril went on.

Somehow that didn't intimidate me either. Maybe it was because the coaches at the bigger state schools (who were much more intimidating) had been impressed by my shooting.

That evening Pete Carril did, however, pay me a kind of compliment when he took a puff of his cigar and acknowledged, "You can stand a lot of improvement, but one thing I do think is that you really like to play the game."

Coach Carril was a character! He was like a cross between my scowling grandpa Dandy and my gregarious grandpa Southside, with his own inscrutable traits thrown in. Asking me little about myself, and volunteering even less about himself, Coach drove me straight to the athletic offices, where he showed me around Jadwin Gym—which may have sold me on Princeton on sight. Still state of the art in the Ivy League today as it was then, Jadwin to me was so spectacular and unparalleled as a facility, it was as if I'd died and gone to heaven. Dug out of a hill, with multiple levels and over two hundred thousand square feet, it housed three full basketball courts, three thousand–plus permanent seats, and a separate area for track and field. When we walked into one of the darkened basketball courts and he flipped on the lights that came on row by row across the domed arena ceiling, it was like we were blasting off to another galaxy. Pete Carril saw me gazing up at the lights and just grinned.

That evening a dinner had been arranged with a group of players—mainly upperclassmen—at the County Line Inn, a quaint local favorite, where pitchers of beer were brought to the table along with huge platters of chicken, steak, shrimp, crab, and other seafood. I'd never seen a spread that big for a group our size. And I'd never even had beer before in my life.

When I asked the waitress if I could have a Coke, Coach Carril waved her off, telling me, "Coke makes you weak. Have some beer." At what must have been my surprised expression, he observed, "Beer's good for you! Replenishes your fluids."

Again, in hindsight I wondered if that wasn't just to test me. At the time, there was no way that I was going to argue, especially when one of the upperclassmen, John Rogers, shot me a protective look that encouraged me to have the beer. Not bad!

John, then a junior, had been assigned as one of my tour guides during the recruiting trip. Whether this was fate or a lucky coincidence, I can't say, as we were destined to become lifelong friends. But I do know from the moment I met John Rogers, I felt as if we'd known each other forever. No, it wasn't because he was black, or that he also happened to be from Chicago. Actually, our backgrounds were very different. He was from an upper-middle-class family, his mother an attorney and his father a judge, and he had a level of sophistication that I certainly didn't. But I could relate to his enthusiasm. You could tell, just talking to John, that he had big plans and was going somewhere in life. Or that was my conclusion when he mentioned, with great confidence, that at Princeton he was majoring in economics.

Whatever that was—and I really had no idea at the time—I was impressed. But as for being intimidated, the only flash of nerves had come the next morning when I was invited to attend practice and scrimmage with the team. Without a doubt, these guys played with skills that were at the next level from where I'd been playing. Nonetheless, once I was on the floor in the competition, contributing quite nicely, I thought, there was nothing to be nervous about. But since my focus was less on proving myself to them and more on deciding if this was where I wanted to play, I must have overlooked how closely my skills were being scrutinized. My own evaluation was that when it came to pure athleticism, I was at an advantage. But in terms of the level of expert execution that the Princeton players demonstrated, I had some work to do. According to Pete Carril, who came over at the end of the scrimmage and wasted no time telling me how bad I looked that morning, I had a lot of work to do.

Now, almost a year later, as the bus veered onto Route 1, and I saw the tall office building with bold green letters spelling out HESS OIL—a landmark indicating to anyone traveling to Princeton University that arrival at campus is twenty minutes away—I suddenly remembered some of those details that hadn't seemed to bother me at the time. Of course, I had to remind myself, I was reading too much into Coach's comments. That was just his style, right? After all, here I was returning to New Jersey, as a member of the freshman class. But as soon as the bus pulled up to the guard gate and I realized that we were leaving civilization as I knew it behind and entering a world that existed practically in its own time-and-space continuum—with two-hundred-plus–year-old ivy-covered towers now coming into view—it finally hit me that I had no frame of reference whatsoever to adjust to any of this. Now I was officially nervous!

"Nassau Street," the overly cheerful bus driver announced, as I made my way down the aisle, and stepped out onto the curb into the muggy August afternoon. With suitcase and gym bag in hand, I paused to breathe in the rarefied air of Princeton, the fourth-oldest university in the United States, founded in 1746, before we were even a nation. But instead of being awed by a feeling of "Wow, I'm at Princeton," it was more "Wow, I'm really on my own." Nobody would know who I was or have any reason to care. For the first time in my life, there would be no Southside Family Robinson there for me at home. It was all entirely up to me. For an instant, a wave of uncertainty descended over me and I couldn't help but wonder if maybe I had made a mistake.

So, what were my options? There was nothing to do but walk up the hill toward Nassau Hall, the oldest building on campus—which in early days had comprised the entire college and now housed the administrative offices—and make the first orientation session on time. Just looking at the building and thinking of the history it had seen, I could feel my trepidation turn back to excitement. I was really here—standing in front of the building where, in the days when Princeton had become the first capital of the United States, Congress had convened on its second floor. It was reassuring to consider that I was now joining the ranks of more than two centuries of incoming freshman classes who had come before me. Somehow that was enough to persuade me to give this place a try.

As it turned out, the orientation program for minority students that I was attending was designed in part to calm similar nerves. The purpose was to give us a feel for going to classes and living on campus before all the other students showed up. Many of the students I had a chance to meet in this program were from a mix of minority backgrounds— African American, Hispanic, Asian, Native American, immigrant and foreign students, and so on. Many were the first in their families to go to college, and many, but not all, had come from middle- and lower-income backgrounds. There were other minority athletes in our program, like myself, but none that I got to meet who were playing basketball. As it so happened, I was about to learn that I was the only black player recruited among the six or so freshman recruits. I also heard that Coach Carril apparently had much higher expectations for the other five recruits.

If that really were the case, I'd have my work cut out for me even more than I already did with him. But in the meantime, a more daunting challenge loomed when the full freshman class arrived and I went to register for classes. The problem for me was that I had no idea what I wanted to study.

In retrospect, it was very naïve of me not to have given a great deal of thought to what subjects I was passionate about or that I might want to major in. Then again, basketball had long been front and center—nothing out of the ordinary for many student athletes even in the Ivy League. However, it seemed to me that everyone I met was intensely devoted to a course of study and knew exactly what classes would be right for them. And everyone had arrived with remarkable scholastic, creative, and athletic achievement already under their belts. There were science and engineering students who allegedly had come up with patents to cure diseases when they were in grammar school and liberal arts students who were already published. Or if they hadn't already done something to make headlines, they intended to do so in the near future. True, many of them had come from privilege and famous prep schools where they were encouraged to plan their college journey ahead of time. Not that Mount Carmel hadn't provided me with a strong academic foundation. Still, I was at a loss.

When I sought guidance, the young man at the desk, who would become my freshman counselor, asked, "Well, what are you good at?"

The first thing that came to me were the courses that I'd aced without much effort over the years and scored very high in. So I shrugged and said, "Math and science." But compared to the Albert Einsteins who came to this school, I was not in that boat at all. If I had thought back to high school, I would have said philosophy or social studies; or, with the exception of the bad experience with the one teacher, history.

"Have you thought about engineering?" he said. If the counselor had reviewed my transcript, he would have seen that I'd never taken calculus or physics, which would have revealed that this was not where I needed to be my freshman year.

But wanting to be agreeable—not always a helpful character trait—I politely said, "Engineering? Sounds good," and he signed me up.

Today I can laugh thinking back to that moment when I picked up my class schedule and stood there as a kid from the Southside of Chicago now at Princeton University, the first time away from home, the first in my family to go to college, and looked at my textbook list for calculus, physics, chemistry, and economics. Talk about being Greek to me! I can laugh today, but it wasn't funny back then.

An even ruder awakening was that though basketball should have been a breeze by comparison, it wasn't. To my horror, when October came around and practice began, Coach Carril had me down on the third string. So, I now knew, those criticisms weren't just part of his caustic style. I was as mystified as I was disappointed. But something deep down told me that being relegated to the third string wasn't a permanent sentence. If I could stay cool, bide my time, and keep working, I had to believe that my shot would come.

My beacon of hope during this period was John Rogers— a senior when I arrived as a freshman who was the captain of our basketball team, and a prime example of a player and a person of tremendous character. After being one of my tour guides and hosts when I'd come out for my recruiting trip, John was also someone whom I already knew—so much so that I quickly let go of any notions that his more sophisticated background made us significantly different from one another or that he was more advantaged because of his family lineage. Just like me, John still had to deal with assumptions made by others on the basis of skin color—even at Princeton. While I don't know if he heard some of the questions that I did when others found out I was from the Southside of Chicago—like, "Oh, do you carry a gun?"—it was evident that John Rogers had been through his own culture shock when he arrived, and clearly, he had lived to tell the tale.

At one of the first practices, I picked up on some of the reasons that Coach Carril and his coaching staff had selected John as the team captain—starting with John's irrepressible energy level and enthusiasm. Watching him bound down the court during drills, I did a double take when it struck me that he was inches shorter than most of the rest of the guys on the team. Later, I learned that he was just about six foot even, give or take. But you would never have known it because of his personal stature and high confidence level. He was the definitive unselfish player, continually looking to set up his teammates to be playmakers, not trying to grab the glory for himself.

Later, when our official season got under way, John started that first game but rarely did for the rest of the season. In fact, he wasn't off the bench very much. Didn't mar his enthusiasm or readiness one iota! Whether on the floor or on the bench, he was still the captain, still a team leader. Eye-opening! And when he did get playing time, he hustled as if the game was for the championship and he had an NBA contract hanging on the outcome.

That was the John Rogers I first encountered in my preseason practices in the fall of '79—same guy, hustling every minute, diving for the ball, and never complaining or bridling about the barrage of criticism he endured from Coach Carril. Whatever the method to the madness was, I couldn't figure it out. After all, if Coach could berate the team captain for not being able to pass the ball or shoot it decently—and had been doing so for four years—all I could think as a freshman was, "Oh God, how much worse can he throw at me?"

But it was the prep school guys who really caught hell. In the first couple of weeks, Coach Carril didn't go after them as much but like a faucet, the zingers started to fly about the third week in, when I recall him singling out one of the preppiest freshmen on the team.

"Oh, Worthington!" Pete Carril sang out with a bad attempt at a British accent. "Time for tea!"

That wasn't the end of the mockery for that player or for the rest of the fellows who had attended schools like Andover or Exeter—and who had to put up with Coach Carril's familiar snarl, "Whadya think this is, the argyle sock league?"

Of course, I started to see that this was how he was toughening all of us up by calling us out in front of one another. Some of these tactics weren't totally new; Johnnie Gage and Father Mike also would put the spotlight on you if your effort wasn't up to par or if you were screwing around. Pete Carril also had some innovative tricks up his sleeve. Once, when he thought a player was losing weight, he sent a case of beer to his dorm room.

Some would later describe Pete Carril as the kind of coach most people hate playing for but love later after they're done playing. That may be true for others. But for me, even coming in at third string (which would change once the season got under way—I'd end the year as a starter), that's not the case. Maybe it was his biting humor that was an extreme version of Robinson family–style teasing. Maybe it was the respect that I held for him that allowed me to see how much I really could learn. Whatever it was, my happiest memories from my entire time at Princeton were of being part of the men's basketball family headed by Pete Carril.

Meanwhile, as I was trying to find my footing under his tough mentorship, scrambling just to keep up with a course load that hadn't been well planned, I was also attempting to navigate new experiences with girlfriends and have a semblance of a social life. Pretty much of a normal freshman year. To make matters slightly more challenging, however, after about a month, I had decided to leave the dorm where I was staying and move into what was then called the Third World Center, where I received a free room in return for custodial work. The Third World Center was along the lines of a student union—a place where international students and minority students could congregate and interact with one other. With a busy schedule of parties and classes, a few caretakers were needed to keep the place clean, make sure the garbage was taken out, the lights were off, and everything was locked up at the end of the day.

One of the first thoughts that crossed my mind when I settled into my routine of cleaning up was that having to do all those chores back at home had definitely paid off! Not only that, but I was happy to do my part to save money and cut down on what Mom and Dad would owe. Another perk was that when a deejay was needed for parties at the Third World Center, I was the go-to guy. Being the grandson of Southside had taught me a thing or two about spinning some records, not to mention that I was getting paid for it!

The good news was that the two other caretakers and I were given leeway as to when we did our chores. The bad news was that between classes, basketball, and classwork, there weren't enough hours in the day. Then again, as I thought of Dad, who still worked the swing shift and adapted to the needs of the city's water department, I wondered why I couldn't come up with a swing shift Princeton schedule on my own.

All of my classes were in the morning or early afternoon,

with enough time to catch a decent nap, get to the gym by three thirty P.M., and be on the court warming up early for practice that started at four thirty P.M. Three to four hours later I'd grab dinner, then get back to the Third World Center, do my custodial duties, and then go to sleep. At one A.M., I woke to study in the wee hours of the night, usually getting a lot done without any distractions. By four A.M., I was back in bed for more sleep. That gave me enough time to have breakfast and make it to my first class by nine A.M. That was the daily drill, from October 15 through sometime in the spring, depending on how far we went in the postseason play.

Midway through my first semester, just as I came up with my own swing shift schedule and started to think that I was maybe getting a hang of college life, I was totally thrown for a loop by midterm grades. So far for the semester I had a C, two Ds, and an F.

All of a sudden, the dream come true of attending Princeton was turning into a nightmare! Somewhere in the recesses of memory, I had to remember some precedent that had prepared me for falling down and failing to this extent. The only things that came to mind were those fears about calamity happening—that I was going deaf and blind and wouldn't be able to rescue my family in the event of a fire. This was reminiscent of that same feeling of not having any control over my normal faculties.

Instead of reporting early to basketball, I made a beeline across the middle of the leaf-strewn campus for the nearest pay phone as a blizzard of worries came at me from every direction. I had never gotten grades like these. Maybe I needed to find someplace I could handle before I slid any further into a complete disaster.

And before I had the chance beat myself up even worse by thinking about how let-down my family was going to be, I got to the phone booth, picked up the receiver, and deposited enough coins to make the call. It was like being sent to bad-grade jail, and I was being given my only phone call.

The minute Dad answered, I told him about the disastrous grades, forcing myself not to start crying, and then went on, "Maybe I'm in over my head. Maybe I shouldn't be here. Maybe coming here I reached too far—"

"Calm down, son. Calm down," he interrupted me in a reassuring voice. I took a breath or two, and listened as my father reminded me, "First of all, this is just the midterm. The game's far from over."

Of course, I listened because he was my dad and the wisest person I knew. But there was another side of me that questioned—*Hey, what does he know, he never went to college.*

Then Dad asked me a question that I didn't expect. "Listen, Cat, tell me something. How many students attend Princeton University?"

I told him that there were about four thousand undergraduates, give or take.

"Okay," Dad said, and then continued, "So out of those four thousand, there's probably about a thousand students in your class?"

"Right," I answered, but then asked, "So?"

"So," my father explained, "you are not going to be number one in your class at Princeton. That's just the nature of the beast. But that's one of the reasons you went there."

That was true. After being valedictorian at Bryn Mawr and being close to the top of my class at Mount Carmel, I had wanted more of an academic challenge. I supposed that making the best grades didn't have to define me. Still.

Dad wasn't finished. Finally, he let me see where he was going when he went on to say, "Now we've accepted that you're not going to be number one in your class. But I guarantee you, you're not going to be number one thousand either."

I thought about that for a minute, and the logic of it settled in, and then the reassurance. It was so simple that I started laughing. "Right," I said. "There's gotta be somebody even dumber than me."

By helping me put it into perspective, Dad enabled me to regain all of the fundamentals that were much more part of who I was—self-esteem, enthusiasm, conviction, relentlessness, diligence, and the belief that I had made the right choice in stepping out of my comfort zone. Now it was a matter of picking myself up off the floor and doing some extra legwork to optimize the skills that I already had and work on some of my weaknesses.

Once again Dad brought it back to basketball, recalling some pretty ugly scores from high school games that had taken place earlier in the season. You never wanted to count yourself out. He was right there too. This was early in the game.

Before we hung up, my father gave me more food for thought by telling me, "Craig, you picked a great school. By the time you graduate and have a degree from Princeton, you think people will care what your grade was in freshman calculus?" He also wanted me to know that Princeton had picked me not because I was just like everybody or anybody else who was going to fit a mold and make straight A's. Rather, he believed, it was because of what made me distinctive and because of the contribution that I could make to the school.

The lightbulb went on after that. Thanks to the rude awakening that the awful midterm grades had given me, I had to face the honest truth that it was time to go and ask for guidance from someone in the know. A woman in the administrative office of one of the departments heard me out and then asked, "Have you tried office hours?"

"What are office hours?"

Lo and behold, unbeknownst to me all this time, all of

the professors had office hours, and they made themselves available to provide direction and clarification for classwork and tests, along with teaching assistants who were there to help as well. Instead of shaming me for needing the direction, everyone was excited when I started using this wonderful resource called office hours—as if I were the person they'd been waiting for all along!

With this support system that I discovered and tapped, I pulled myself out of the gutter, with improvement in every course. What I had learned was something only adversity could have taught me—which is that Princeton University, like most every other institution of higher learning, isn't in the business of wanting to flunk students out. In fact, quite the opposite, programs are designed and resources are available to give everyone enrolled the tools for success.

One of those tools, in my case, was the opportunity to revise my academic program and to switch to liberal arts—where I was soon thriving beyond my own expectations. Part of that had to do with my newfound skill of asking professors for direction when something was unclear and to take advantage of office hours, not only improving weaknesses but also building strengths.

As you might imagine, I have gotten great mileage out of the story of how I almost counted myself out at Princeton. The fact is, as I tell my players frequently, there is a formula to getting a college degree. It's very straightforward—whether it's Princeton or Oregon State University. First, and this is key, go to class. Every class. You need to take off your hat, remove your earphones, sit up straight, in the front row, and pay attention to what your professor has spent his or her whole life learning about and then ask a question or two to show that you care. Those steps alone that show your respect will get you a C. And then, if you do enough of the reading so that you can answer a few questions in class, your grade might be even better. What I don't usually tell my players—because they need to discover it for themselves—is that beyond the grades, if you do all these things, you end up learning something. And that is really what college and this character lesson of stepping out of your comfort zone is all about.

8

LEARN THE GAME, NOT JUST YOUR POSITION

What is the Princeton offense?

Well, without giving away too many of Pete Carril's trade secrets—or, for that matter, tipping my hand as to what extent my own coaching does or does not borrow from the Princeton offense—I must answer this frequently asked question by at least noting that it is as much a mind-set as it is a set of strategies designed for winning the game of basketball. Let me also add that just as Marian Robinson once told me that she and Dad weren't magic but were only trying to find what worked in child rearing, Pete Carril likewise never set out to discover the basketball Holy Grail; he, too, instead, was only trying to find what worked.

Once he found what worked, he developed a framework for his strategies that could be adapted and improvised upon—depending on all the different circumstances that a team encounters in any given game. Now, as to what that basic framework is, many expert observers would say that it is a slow-down offense that is deliberate and methodical, requiring both patience and skill, and tends to result in lower-scoring games that are the opposite of run-and-gun or "showtime" basketball. Such descriptions miss the mark—but neither Pete Carril, who started coaching at Princeton in 1967 (and who sometimes credits his predecessor, Butch van Breda Kolff, with coming up with the underpinnings of the Princeton offense) nor any of his coaching protégés would bother disagreeing. In fact, if anyone is responsible for the myth that the Princeton offense slows down the game rhythm, it's probably Carril himself. Many an opponent walked into that trap because their coaches read the wrong scouting reports that perpetuated a limited understanding of what was in store for them.

Others will talk about the Princeton offense as being good use of fundamentals—passing, moving without the ball, and backdoor cuts. Yes, those are some of the strategies. In the Ivy League, when no one could figure out how Princeton managed to kill allegedly much stronger teams, the saying to describe the unrelenting offense was "death by a thousand cuts."

All of that obscures what the real Princeton offense is. Bottom line, it comes down to playing unselfishly, passing and cutting until you get open for a shot—as a team. It is a way of thinking. You not only need very skilled players with a level of precision required for making that perfect shot, but they also need to be patient—hence what may parade as slow isn't necessarily. Parts of this approach became second nature to me as a player and certainly became a foundation for my coaching philosophy—especially the unselfishness and the emphasis on passing and cutting while giving yourself up for the other guy. In other respects, my approach differs and is my own, including my preference for a decidedly up-tempo athletic rhythm and for cultivating players who can score under pressure even when it isn't the perfect shot—who are confident enough to make plays that might not be correct but are right. But to cultivate that level of confidence requires doing big-time player development and a focus on teamwork—both Pete Carril mainstays.

It was January—a month into the season freshman year—that some of these principles started to make sense to me. During the fall preseason, when I'd found myself on the third string and shared my concerns with Dad, he encouraged me to keep my nose to the grindstone in practice and not to let Coach's use of character assassination as a means of motivating players get to me. When I worried about the fact that I'd come in with five other recruits that Coach Carril seemed to have higher expectations for, Dad predicted that was going to change.

Much as my father might have tried to downplay how proud he was of both Michelle and me, he couldn't help himself sometimes. Freshman year the family didn't travel to visit me at Princeton, but the following years they came to see me play every season. And there was no better feeling in the world than looking up and seeing a smile of joy and amazement on Fraser Robinson's face on those occasions. Mom and Miche were just as proud, of course, but they weren't demonstrative the way Dad was. Mom never bragged but Dad would. And sometimes he went overboard.

But having Dad give me a rave review in the form of a pep talk early on was just what the doctor ordered. He had always believed that you never know what you're going to be asked to do, so it was best to be ready to do it all. How? By following the teachings of whoever the wise person was who first said, "Don't learn to play a position, learn to play the game." Mom backed that approach up with her familiar refrain that knowledge acquired can never be taken away.

Their input was well-timed. Though I would leave Princeton at almost six feet seven inches, in those days when I arrived as a freshman I was still right at six-five. As a late bloomer—something that may explain why Coach Carril didn't know what to do with me at first—it actually worked to my advantage to develop expertise in everything. The conventional wisdom is that bigger guys need to work on their dribbling and speed while the small, quick guys have to overcome their height disadvantage by learning how to block out under the basket and rebound. None of that was below or above me, even if those were fundamentals I'd been taught early on.

And as it so happened, being well-rounded was the best fit possible for running the Princeton offense, as well as the Carril and coaching staff complementary defensive strategy that could alternate from zone (where you protect a particular zone on the court) to "man" (where you guard a particular player) and all combinations in between. That was where I finally started to understand the method to the madness, when it dawned on me that Pete Carril wasn't training us to run particular plays drawn on a blackboard. Rather, he was just a genius at player development, which most people don't talk about. Relentless, with evaluations, drills, repetition, and his cantankerous wit—whether it was finessing the backdoor cut or working on left-handed dribbling—he simply made you a better player. He almost never coached from the bench in the middle of the game. His goal was to develop communication as a team, almost like a vibe between jazz musicians jamming together.

Right before a home game we were playing against Yale, Coach Carril finally acknowledged my work ethic. Instead of saying anything to me whenever he came into the gym early and found me there working on my shooting—getting in as many as two hundred shots before practice—he would only grunt in greeting and vanish until a half hour later when practice officially began. That was until the middle of practice that freezing cold January night, when I went up for a jump shot and sank it as though effortlessly.

Coach stopped the scrimmage. "Didya see that?" he barked to everyone. "You know why Craig made that shot? Because he was in here [insert expletive] thirty minutes early practicing!"

That was the nicest and possibly only compliment he ever gave me. But it worked! Next day, I was at practice even earlier.

As the season forged on, I soon advanced from third-string center to playing second-string forward. There were fifteen of us on the team, and Coach Carril typically played six or seven guys. By February, I had graduated to being one of the six or seven who were on the court during the game.

During preseason the games were on Tuesday and Saturday, and then during the regular Ivy League season we had them on the weekends so that we didn't miss class. If we were the home team one weekend, we'd play both Harvard and Dartmouth, say, for one game on Friday night and then on Saturday night. When we were traveling, we would take a bus up to Harvard for a game on Friday, and then head up to Hanover, New Hampshire, later that night for a Saturday game at Dartmouth. Similarly, when we traveled to faraway venues like Hawaii and California for preseason nonconference games, they would try to arrange it so we didn't have to miss too many classes and we could return to campus to study on Sunday.

It was a whirlwind and I loved every minute of it. Interestingly enough, my grades were better during basketball season because the focus and discipline from one area flowed naturally into the other. With classes in such subjects as sociology, philosophy, English, and history that I was much more interested in, when midterm grades came out second semester I had reclaimed my mantle of doing well academically.

When spring rolled around, it had sunk in that the idea of learning the game rather than just one position could be applied to my Princeton experience in general. I remember jogging past one of the many pairs of tiger statues that guarded several of the older buildings on campus and slowing down for a moment to absorb the distance that I'd traveled and how much I'd grown since getting off the bus nine months and a seeming lifetime earlier. With great pride, I thought about how wonderful it felt to have played for a year with the Princeton Tigers—to wear the school colors of orange and black, as a student and an athlete, and to feel the good fortune that was mine to be part of something so special. The fact that long before coming to Princeton orange had always been one of my favorite colors—one I felt was underused—made it that much more special.

Those were feelings that I shared with a member of our extended family who—by coincidence—happened to live in downtown Princeton. Ernestine Jones—Aunt Sis, as we called her—was our great-aunt on the Robinson side of the family and had graciously invited me to dinner on a few other occasions that my schedule had prevented me from accepting. The minute that I sat down and took a bite of the feast she set out for me at her dining table in her very small house—even smaller than the place we'd grown up in—I started telling Aunt Sis about the whole year and my high hopes for improving the next year.

"Oh, yes," Aunt Sis said, "you will! We're just so proud of you." For all Aunt Sis's life she had lived in Princeton and worked as a housemaid. Now a member of her family was there as a student.

By my junior year, Aunt Sis could say that not one but two of her family members were students at Princeton. That was when Michelle arrived as a freshman, having decided that out of all the options available to her—and they were many—this was where she was meant to be. Everyone assumed that it was during visits to campus with my parents that she came to love what she saw and had decided to follow me to Princeton.

Michelle has corrected that version a few times. For her, it took the guesswork out of applying to lots of other places. After all, she figured, if Craig could get into Princeton, then she was a shoo-in!

Up until Miche's arrival, my college experience mostly revolved around basketball. Socially my life was hanging out with teammates and sometimes our dates, deejaying parties at the Third World Center, and mixing in at the Princeton Inn College, where most of the minority students lived and ate. In spite of the camaraderie and school spirit, it wasn't until Michelle got there in the fall of 1981 that I felt really anchored and normal.

Usually I could stop by her dorm on the way to the gym or leave a message if she wasn't there. Not so different from Euclid Avenue, we were there for each other unconditionally. She was my little sister, making sure that I was up on the latest dance moves, and I was her big brother, keeping a protective eye out for her at all times even if she didn't need it.

It would be fair to say that my grades improved even more during the last two years when Michelle happened to be at Princeton. Maybe it was only a coincidence, but possibly that added bit of sibling competition helped me raise my game studywise.

During this period, my most memorable professor relationship was with Marvin Bressler. Bald and pipe-smoking, he was the head of the sociology department and a faculty representative for the basketball team. Bressler was one of the few professors that Coach Carril allowed in his presence. Marvin Bressler was a huge fan of basketball and of the Princeton Tigers as well as a brilliant man who recounted stories of past players and games with an eloquence that was unmatched.

While I loved history and African American studies, the classes that truly left their mark were in philosophy and religion. Both challenging and interesting, they built nicely upon the foundation that Father Carroll had given me at Mount Carmel. The workload was heavy, with lots of discussions and papers. But when I was sitting in the middle of a provocative lecture presented by a professor who, sometimes, was one of the world's foremost authorities in that subject, it really didn't feel like class. It felt like therapy.

Basketball-wise, my growth spurt had kicked in during sophomore year and mentally everything that Coach Carril had been trying to get me to think about differently started to click. By junior year, I was on fire. So much so that I was named Ivy League Co-Player of the Year.

After my teammates finished a round of congratulations and our assistant coaches were done high-fiving me, in classic Carril fashion he shrugged and told me, "I didn't vote for you. I didn't think you were the player of the year."

What could I say or do but allow him to explain what he thought was required of the best player that I couldn't do? Inside I was thinking—*Geez, you can't win with this guy!* But I listened nonetheless, reminding myself that even as he was withholding approval, he had a crazy-like-a-fox plan up his sleeve for pushing me further.

To wit—the following year, yours truly, Craig Robinson, won Ivy League Player of the Year outright. Coach Carril didn't say a word, but that year I suspect he did vote for me.

As the years have gone by, and my applications of everything that he taught me have multiplied many times over, I am increasingly indebted to the huge role Pete Carril played in my development as a player and a coach. He helped me look at basketball from a different perspective, one that I hadn't experienced or even known was out there. This new perspective led to my becoming a very good player. This, in turn, gave me confidence, which then led to me becoming a better student and more confident person. All connected.

One of my truly happiest days as a player took place in my next–to-last game under Pete Carril. Auspiciously, it was played at Gill Coliseum, Oregon State University, where I am now a head coach. On March 18, 1983, the Princeton Tigers had advanced to the first round of the NCAA championship play-offs held at OSU in Corvallis, Oregon, and were pitted against Oklahoma State—a team that was ranked fourteenth in the country overall. We were not just underdogs, as the Ivy League team not picked to win, but weren't even ranked. Coach Carril, poker-faced yet combusting internally for most of the game, didn't even appear to think we could pull it off. Assistant Coach Bill Carmody, later to take over at Princeton as head coach before moving to Northwestern, was more animated, reminding us of everyone's responsibility to get the open shots and score.

Whenever I looked into the stands, all there was to be seen was a sea of orange and black. Ironically, Oregon State colors are orange and black, the same as Princeton's. And since they were there to root for us as the underdog, the energy and support were electrifying. The first half we slugged it out and were surprised ourselves that Oklahoma didn't start to pull away. That fed us to keep up the pressure and by half-time, we began to think maybe we could pull off this upset and win it. The key, we decided, was that we stick with our game plan. As tempting as it was to play their game, we knew that was dangerous and that we had to be careful with the ball not to turn it over.

Coach Carril and Bill Carmody were very stoic when we began the second half. They didn't want to upset the applecart or act overly amazed that we were apparently doing something we couldn't possibly have been doing. And they wanted us to keep doing it. Almost to the end the game was close, with the lead trading back and forth, until there were only two minutes left and we had the lead. To close the game down, all we had to do was make our final shot and then take care of the ball without any turnovers. After we had our last possession and scored, we were up by five points. They came down and scored, but it wasn't enough, and we won by three points. The final score was 56–53. I scored 20 points and grabbed 14 rebounds. In the second round of the NCAA play-offs we lost to Boston College, but our win two days earlier over Oklahoma State was an unforgettable way to finish my last season—as one of the biggest wins in my career at Princeton and one of the bigger wins in Princeton history.

Emotionally, little could have topped that experience except graduation a few short months later. Mom and Dad flew out and were part of the unforgettable festivities held over the next week. Not surprisingly, Coach Carril and Dad had gotten on famously since the first time they'd met. That gave my father special privileges to come to practices during the visits he and Mom had made to campus. When my folks arrived at commencement exercises with Michelle, they knew all of my teammates and many of the graduating seniors.

Just as I was feeling very impressed at all the fans my parents had at my school, I received a memorable acknowledgment myself from none other than Senator Bill Bradley—who was being given an honorary degree as part of our commencement exercises. A former Princeton player who had led the Tigers to the Final Four in 1965, Bill Bradley had been a Rhodes Scholar and an Olympic athlete, and had then gone on to play with the Knicks before turning to politics and public service.

As Bradley walked past me in the procession with President Bill Bowen, the provost, and all those getting their honorary degrees, I happened to look in his direction from my seat on the aisle. Just at that moment, he stopped right in front of me, stuck out his hand, and said, "Hi, Craig, how are you doing? Good to meet you," before walking on. I almost fainted.

Then I turned back to see if my family had noticed how Bill Bradley had acknowledged me. But no, they were too busy basking in the happiness of the occasion to have seen the exchange. In that moment, I felt as if this was a graduation for all of us. The hard work and sacrifices on everyone's part had brought us to this day.

Mom and Dad wanted me to savor every second. They also emphasized the reality that just because I had a Princeton degree, things weren't going to get easier—in fact, they would get harder. Expectations were going to be greater and obstacles tougher. And the stakes of the game were going to change.

9

LUCK IS JUST ANOTHER WORD FOR HARD WORK

In the tradition of Fraser Robinson III, it is now time for some brutal honesty. That happens to be one more of my father's exceptional character traits, which he could employ when it was crunch time—when he had this special gift for turning to another person and baring unpleasant but needed truths, though always in a loving way and solely in that person's best interests.

So here it comes, from me to you, under the heading of "if only I'd known then what I know now," and that is the cold, cruel fact that no matter how much we may love to compare basketball to life as a game of character—this maxim does not apply to the NBA.

Of course, for anyone who has diligently, passionately pursued the skills for excelling at the highest level of the sport, this may come as a letdown. My point is not to discourage anyone who has ever dreamed of winning what seems to be the ultimate prize of landing a spot on one of the thirty professional teams that make up the National Basketball Association's current slate. Not at all. The point is that whether or not you have what it takes to make it, and whether or not you make it—the two may have little to do with each other—there isn't much about the experience that correlates reasonably to real life. Everything about the NBA is a world apart—one that can be as shattering as it is glorious and as grueling as it glamorous; and though it can provide an E-ticket ride to fame and fortune, with rare exceptions the time in the sun is short-lived. The example that comes to mind was how Bob Love plunged into obscurity as soon as he was injured and could no longer play.

All of that said, to be even more brutally honest, whenever I encounter serious, hardworking, talented players who have the drive and daring to take their shot at the NBA, the first person in line to offer assistance is me. Other than offering an anecdote or two about what I learned in the process, my number-one piece of advice to contenders is to remember, no matter what— "Don't let basketball use you, instead you use it." And one of the best ways of doing that, as the ever-realistic Marian Robinson might have counseled, is to figure out ahead of time what success will mean to you in your own terms, not in anyone else's.

In some ways, I was going to have to learn that the hard way—starting with my aspirations for playing in the NBA. In June 1983, when I returned to Chicago from Princeton and moved back into our upstairs apartment on Euclid Avenue, outwardly I was being cool and more or less playing down my chances of being drafted. Inwardly was another story! Who me, worry? But rather than sit around and wait by the phone, I got busy and came up with a contingency plan in the event that I didn't get the call. In real-world terms, it was the smartest thing that I could have done. But in the way that the chips would fall, this move would be the worst thing that I could have done.

Yet how could I have known when I lined up a job complete with a sales training program at Proctor & Gamble, the same company that had employed me in the two previous summers, that this would in any way impact my NBA prospects? My arrangement with P&G, I thought, was ideal. They were willing to wait to see if I was drafted, and if not, then I could enter corporate life and the real world in August. Meanwhile, until there was a verdict, I was in training—working out and playing hoops every day, competing in the summer league, and keeping on my toes with pickup games at the park. At first, I was glued to sports news in every form, hanging on every word of speculation from newscasters about who looked likely to be in the first round. When my name wasn't mentioned, I didn't put much stock in that, but when the first-round draft picks were announced and I wasn't in that group, my anxiety was overwhelming. Better to tune it all out, I decided, and develop a more wait-and-see attitude.

Then one muggy June afternoon—everything outside in full bloom and hay fever symptoms kicking in—the telephone rang with a distinctly optimistic ring.

As fate and possibly magic would have it, I was at home, picked up the phone, and answered congenially, "Hello?"

"Is Craig Robinson there?" The voice sounded business-like and important.

"Yep, this is Craig."

Whatever the person said next—which involved identifying himself as being a representative from the Philadelphia 76ers—I have no idea. The only part that is emblazoned in my memory was when he went on to inform me, "We drafted you in the fourth round."

Stop the press! Hold your horses! This wasn't just any fourth-round draft pick. This was the Philadelphia 76ers, my second-favorite team in the country after the Bulls. So what if it wasn't a million-dollar contract? Considering the odds—

the fact that if there were twenty to twenty-five players per round, which made me somewhere around the eightieth pick overall—this was thrilling. Not bad for an Ivy Leaguer. Not bad at all.

Dad, Mom, and Michelle were just as thrilled but understood when I cautiously explained why I couldn't get ahead of myself. Unless you were a first-round draft pick, being drafted was really just a glorified tryout. Still, for the next several weeks, until it was time to report to free-agent camp in July, I walked around at about ten feet off the ground—just floating toward the clouds—with all thoughts of a career in sales drifting away into the hot summer air. Whenever my name was announced before a summer league game, I had to pinch myself. In past years, I'd been announced as "Craig Robinson, from Princeton University." But this summer it was ". . . and now, property of the Philadelphia 76ers, Craig Robinson!" Incredible!

As the Sixers had just won the championship the year before, and weren't rebuilding the team, I knew that spots on their roster were going to be few and far between. The July free-agent camp that was held at Saint Joseph's University in Philadelphia would begin the winnowing process. Out of approximately twenty-five players, more than half would be quickly eliminated and the remaining twelve would continue on to play in the professionals' summer league games, which would take place in August.

For lack of a better phrase, camp that week was like a whole new ball game. On and off the court, there was a lot of jockeying for position, anything to show that you were bringing something different to the game and that you knew your stuff. For the first time in four years, nobody appeared to be impressed that I'd grown up on Chicago's Southside and had made it to the top of the Ivy League as player of the year. As a matter of fact, most of the other players didn't know the difference between Princeton and Podunk. But I tried to use that to my advantage and decided to show them where I was from on the court. It felt as if I had held my own, but there was no playbook to say what the coaching staff was really looking for.

After the last scrimmage at the end of the week, we were told, "Shower up, go eat." We all knew that when we came back from the meal, the list would be posted saying who was going to make it to the summer league and who was going to have to start rethinking his future. For some, this would be "the last supper," for others, a chance to play on.

When I came back from the dining hall, I watched other players take turns looking for their name on the list. Some of their faces were euphoric, others looked heartbroken. Trying to steel myself, no matter what, I walked up to the paper, scanned the list, and saw my name, clear as day. I'd made the cut! Phew! And—hallelujah!

It felt as if I'd just crested the top of a climb on a giant roller coaster and had descended into that thrilling first big drop. I would have danced and hollered for joy if I hadn't been standing next to guys whose lifelong dreams were coming to a screeching halt.

"Craig, got a minute?" one of the trainers beckoned me toward the coaching office, looking grim.

My first thought was that there had been a mistake and I hadn't made the cut after all.

Instead, I was told that a message had been left for me from home. As it turned out, the news wasn't good. My beloved grandfather, Southside, had passed away. In disbelief, I had a hard time accepting that Purnell Shields could be gone. In my mind, even at twenty-one years of age, I saw him as immune to disease and aging. For a moment I just stood there remembering his barbecue and homemade malteds, all the spur-of-the-moment visits and Charlie Parker on the stereo and the time Aunt Carolyn had made him liver on his birthday.

After composing myself, I went to a nearby phone booth and called Mom. We were both in tears, as she told me about the funeral arrangements. Selfishly, I was even sadder that I wouldn't have a chance to tell Southside that I had made it through the first round and was on my way to officially becoming a Philadelphia 76er. He would have been over the moon!

Not long after the funeral, I was notified that the next round of the selection process was going to be held at none other than Princeton's Jadwin Gymnasium. Was this kismet or maybe Southside pulling some strings for me? In any event, it could only give me some kind of home court advantage. This summer league consisted of games between the 76ers, the New York Knicks, the New Jersey Nets, and the Washington Bullets, each team with a makeup similar to ours—draft picks, free agents, and first- and second-year players. Out of the twelve players who were still in contention, nine of us played a lot of minutes. That was a good sign for me. I wasn't sure if it helped or hurt that I had my own cheering section on hand from the Princeton community. Slightly embarrassing though it was, it helped me calm some big-time nerves that were building as the week came to an end.

I knew that only one or two guys would be asked to come back for veterans' camp in October. I also knew that the Sixers' first-round draft pick, who happened to play the same position I did, would be one of them. His contract was already guaranteed. But I held out the hope that I would be one of the two still standing at the end. As one of the very few who could immediately run every play, I had made my shots and had delivered what they had asked us to do (which was nowhere near as tough as what I had done at Princeton), so it seemed that I would be the natural choice.

But what I didn't understand until years later—when I could be brutally honest with myself—was that being an unselfish contributor to the team, making plays to win on everyone's behalf, as I'd been trained, was not what was needed to put me over the top. What was needed, and other players brought it, was more of a Machiavellian edge, more of a fire in the belly to be the superstar, superhero. If ever there was a time to say, "Look at me," and showcase your talent—this was it. It wasn't that I hadn't pushed myself to play at full capacity, nor was I lacking in confidence. But this was a situation where I could have been cocky too.

When Matt Guokas, the assistant coach, called me over to give me the bad news, because I knew the odds, I was prepared. What I wasn't prepared for was what he said next. Somehow, he'd learned that I had the position lined up in the sales training program if all else failed. "Well, anyway," Matt concluded, "you've got the job with P&G, so you don't need to worry about this."

!@#%★(@$★ (Insert expletive).

I was livid. Two questions I wanted to ask were: a) Would the decision have been different if I hadn't gone to Princeton? and b) Given a choice, you think I'd really want to sell toothpaste instead of playing for the Sixers?

Now, this was an instance when I could have learned that I needed to define success on my own terms. It might have been as simple as realizing that just because the NBA hadn't worked out didn't mean that I was through with basketball. But before I could do that, I needed to mourn what I thought was the passing of a dream. Mom and Dad understood that and didn't try to make my discoveries for me. Michelle (who two years later would graduate cum laude from Princeton and then move on to Harvard Law School) did think the process was entirely unfair and wanted to know what recourse I might have in addressing the 76ers' lack of vision. Even though I had to tell her it didn't work that way, she cheered me up enough to consider that maybe getting as far as I had was a kind of success. After all, I had dressed out in the uniform of my second-favorite team and forevermore could say that I'd had a stint in the NBA.

Shortly after coming to this epiphany, I happened to be at home thinking about what I was going to do now that basketball was out of the picture when the phone rang with what was yet again a decidedly optimistic ring.

As fate and possibly magic would have it this time, the phone call was from my sports agent, who informed me that thanks to how far I'd gone in the tryout with the 76ers, I'd been showcased in front of other scouts who were impressed. One scout had called him to say that a team in the European league urgently needed to replace an American in their lineup. The season had already started, so there was not too much time to decide. He had seen me deliver and knew that I could handle it.

And the next thing I knew, I was heading to Manchester, England. Was this a stroke of luck? Well, partly. But this was an opportunity to really see why my parents always emphasized that luck is actually just a word for hard work.

My efforts on the court had paid off after all. For the next two years, I continued my love affair with the game of basketball and not only had the chance to see it from a perspective that was nothing like anything I could have experienced in the United States, but I also had an all-expense-paid two-year European vacation. How 'bout that for a rebound?

Okay, so I wasn't staying in five-star hotels, eating caviar, and drinking champagne. That wasn't me anyway. But I must say when I first caught sight of Manchester—with smokestacks dotting the skyline and the gray, gritty industrial look of it under the steady falling rain—I had a few second thoughts. That was until the smaller cobblestone streets and charming old buildings came into view and England reminded me of Princeton.

Before my contracts were signed, there was one hitch—another tryout in the form of an intense scrimmage with the Manchester team. I pulled out the stops and watched as the coach and the team owner, a Lebanese businessman named Amir Midani, commented under their breath to one another. After we finished playing, Amir said to me, "You are our gift from America." Then he signed my contract.

The English arenas were used for every kind of sport, so on the floor you had lines painted for volleyball, basketball, badminton, soccer—even team handball, whatever that is. It was all confusing enough for the players, but for television it was a nightmare. Consequently, when our games were tele-vised we played on thin, indoor-outdoor carpeting that was only for basketball. Without the familiar sounds of balls bouncing on the floor or hearing shoes squeak on the hard-wood, it was a whole other rhythm. Then there was the thick layer of smoke that came from the pubs that were housed above every gym. The first game we played I was amused by the crowd above us in the bar who were watching the game and smoking like chimneys. It did get old.

Just about every big city in Great Britain had a team. We'd start up north, traveling around by bus, playing Glasgow, Ed-inburgh, Sunderland; and then to shorter destinations, like Liverpool, we drove our cars.

The owners were still experimenting, trying to market basketball as a family event. British football—what is soccer to us—was much too rough-and-tumble for younger spectators at the time. For me, the activities planned with kids were wonderful—autograph signings, raffles, half-time contests where a fan would come out try to make a shot for a prize. Our schedule afforded me the time to go exploring on my own or with teammates, stopping into pubs and taking in the lush green countryside. Learning to drive on the left side of the road—with a left-handed stick shift, no less—added to the adventure. The Brits I encountered were courteous through and through. Shockingly, they believed in stopping their cars when you tried to cross the street as a pedestrian.

Had it not been for the major culture shock that I had experienced while adjusting to Princeton, it would have been harder to adapt to England. What really helped throughout my two years was recalling what I had learned from Professor Bressler's sociology lectures—that we are all biologically primed to be fearful of differences, but we also have an almost infinite capacity to expand our definition of "a person like me." To many of the folks I was meeting, I was something of a celebrity and a novelty. The young women in England, for example, made a fuss over how I talked.

One of the girls I dated actually made the first move after a game, coming over and saying, "Just say something, say anything!"

"Hello . . ." I grinned. "How are you?"

And she cracked up laughing, and said, "That's so great! I love your accent!"

"What accent?"

Then we both cracked up.

There was an assumption by most Europeans I met that if you were playing professional basketball and were an American you had to be rich. Often I would have to clarify that the difference between what the NBA paid and what we were making was night and day. And usually this conversation would eventually lead to the big question about what I really wanted to do with the rest of my life. The first inkling of the answer came as the result of a favor our coach had asked of me one day when he said, somewhat offhandedly, "Craig, would you mind helping me run some of the plays you learned at Princeton, maybe teach some of that Princeton offense to the rest of the team?"

My answer was along the lines of—why hadn't he asked sooner? Showing the team even a few plays was almost as much fun as playing myself. The fact is that I had been coached and taught so well, it came to me all at once that there wasn't anything I wanted to do more than become a basketball coach. So, fine, I was going to be Peter Pan, never grow up, and coach lost boys as to the best way to put a ball through a hoop. Not just to avoid growing up but to teach and help kids develop and grasp the fundamentals of character. Why not?

Well, according to Coach Carril, whom I went to visit at Princeton when I returned from England after playing for two seasons, because it was a dead-end, no-win, thankless job.

What he also said was, "YOU DON'T WANT TO BE A [insert expletive] COACH!"

A little projection on his part? In his defense, I understood that he saw me as being someone who had managed to come from behind to acquire a really first-rate education, and that, as a result, I should be doing something "more" with it.

What really needed to happen was that I should have a brutally honest conversation with myself in which I would have recognized that coaching was the path that was calling to me. Instead, I came up with a practical compromise to pursue a career in business, put some savings in the bank, and then be able to afford to go after my low-paying dream. Once I made the decision to throw myself totally into something new, to try a completely new game, it was kind of liberating. True, I was going to be playing someone else's game. But oddly enough, there was not a question in my mind about whether or not I could make it. If I was going to take anything away from everything I'd achieved on the court and in the classroom at Princeton, from my brief moment in the sun with the NBA, and from my European adventure as a professional basketball player, it was that I wasn't afraid to hustle and work hard.

I knew that by itself would give me luck.

10

CHARACTER IS SHAPED BY CHOICES MADE EVERY STEP OF THE WAY

It is no secret that one of the keys to building a highly successful basketball team all comes down to a superior recruiting process. You could say the same about the keys to building a successful business, large or small, or a community organizing effort, or a transformational political campaign. Recruiting! You may be the most visionary coach in the world with the edgiest strategies for winning ever developed, but without the right players on your team to adapt and run those plays on the hardwood, you will just use up a lot of chalk on the blackboard and face a constant uphill battle.

So, what makes an effective recruiter? Well, to be as general as possible so as not to completely show my hand to the competition, it comes down first to recruiting fundamentals—reading the reports and having a command of the stats, retaining info about player histories and establishing relationships with players earlier rather than later in the process, being enough of a student of psychology to see how players will help or harm the team's direction. But really successful recruiting, I believe, also requires an understanding of the intangibles, and a curiosity into the character that a player will bring to the team—with qualities like courage, integrity, discipline, enthusiasm, and that dual capacity for unselfishness and leadership.

Of course, if it was always easy to discern those traits, none of us who compete in the recruitment game would have jobs! That said, I do think one of the best ways to gather insights about character is to look at the choices an individual has made throughout his or her life. Not so much as to whether the choice was right or wrong, successful or unsuccessful, but what that person took from the experience to further develop himself or herself. Though others may disagree, my feeling is that character is not a static commodity. It is shaped by choices made every step of the way.

Interestingly enough, a lot of what I learned about effective recruiting didn't come from the world of basketball. Where I really earned an advanced degree in team building was during my fifteen-year career in the financial world. And it wasn't only from lessons about my own choices that seemed to send me onto a detour far afield from what I wanted to do. I also had a chance to value how other people made different kinds of choices and to see how that played out for them.

Take, for example, my former teammate and captain of the Princeton Tigers, John Rogers, who, two years out of Princeton, had founded his own Chicago investment firm, Ariel Capital Management, that was having dramatic success. Not that I was surprised, recalling John's habit back at Princeton of reading stock reports and *The Wall Street Journal* in the locker room and calling his stockbroker after a game to get in on early-morning trading.

"Send your résumé to Phil Purcell" were the first words out of John's mouth when he learned that I was back from

Europe and looking to be recruited by the right financial firm. To refer me to none other than Phil Purcell, the head of Sears—which had recently purchased Dean Witter, the retail brokerage firm—gives you an idea of the generosity and loyalty of John Rogers.

By the time I went in for my interview at Dean Witter, the good news was that I'd already started to make the Chicago rounds of other investment firms and had been brushing up on my Wall Street x's and o's. During my first visit to a trading floor, the whole fuel-injected energy completely captivated me. It was like a crazy nonstop street pickup game—except most of the players were white and wore ties. But the gamesmanship, teamwork, strategy, and, of course, competition were all familiar. And whatever terms and phrases sounded unfamiliar, well, thank God for Grandpa Dandy and how he'd drilled looking up information in the dictionary and encyclopedia: All I had to do was get my hands on business-related resources. So when I arrived at my Dean Witter interview, I was very prepared to be articulate and knowledgeable on everything from price-earnings ratios to current monetary exchange and interest rates—you name it.

Much to my surprise, the fellow conducting the interview wasn't interested in my knowledge of the business. First question out of his mouth was, "How much money do you want to make?"

I almost spat out my coffee. Then I repeated his question (what you always should do when you don't know the answer). "How much do I *want* to make," I began with an air of mystery, and then paused to think fast.

It was not at all in my training to think about money as an objective, in and of itself. But right there and then, before I gave an answer, I made up mind—hey, having some money would be nice; there is nothing wrong with making some serious money. Besides, I reminded myself, the whole point of going into business was to achieve some financial security so that I could afford to coach down the line, and hopefully to make my parents' lives more comfortable. Dad was still going to the job every day, working as hard as ever, now with the use of two crutches. And Mom was employed by a bank, after returning to the workplace around the time that Michelle had gone off to college. There would soon be a need to have a special van for Dad and then a wheelchair, and all those things would cost some big bucks.

So with all of that in my thinking, after my long pause, I smiled and blurted out the healthiest request I could utter: "A hundred thousand dollars!"

"Oh," he murmured, with a look that said—*Is that all?* "You'll be making three times that much by your second year out of the training program."

I don't think I heard another word he said. But because that's what he had said was possible, I believed. And because I believed, after the six months' training, once I passed the next hurdle of becoming a licensed broker, when the really tough stretch came to build my portfolio of clients—from cold-calling—I was an ace. Making those calls was just like practicing free throws: the more shots on basket, the more shots made—the more deals closed. On schedule, give or take a year or so, I was on my way to making the kind of money first predicted. Did I love what I was doing? If I was being brutally honest with myself, the answer was no.

But I was Craig Robinson, firstborn child of Fraser and Marian, responsible, dutiful, an unselfish guy, who worried—yes, that's me—about living up to expectations. Maybe that was to a fault. But still, I wanted to make the most of everything that my parents had taught us. I had never forgotten how Dad gave up the life of a young man-about-town to settle down and devote himself to his family. I had never forgotten how Mom was his total partner, best friend, and lover, and how their marriage infused our lives with joy and learning.

That's what was in my thinking when, in 1988, I married a lovely young woman I'd been seeing for a few years, and why continuing to climb the Wall Street business ladder seemed important for the stability and security of the family that we were building.

Early on, when I was getting started at Dean Witter, I had been urged by my much-trusted mentor from Princeton, Professor Marvin Bressler, not to wait forever to marry my girlfriend. At the time, I had said, "Well, I'm waiting until I get established."

He made the wise observation that too often men want to make their life and then find the right woman who can be brought into it. Ideally, he pointed out, "You're supposed to build it together."

It was great advice, but instead of finding the right person to marry who was compatible with me and with whom I shared similar goals and values, I committed to a marriage that wasn't right for either of us in the long run. In the beginning, of course, none of this was readily apparent. We had dated off and on before the time I left for England and it didn't seem rushed for that reason. My wife was loving, smart, well-educated, from an upper-middle-class black family, level-headed, and proficient at her job. But I didn't know what made her tick, what she was most passionate about, how she dealt with some of the challenges she had faced—or really to what extent she had faced them. And I think she married the guy on his way up in the business world, not someone who had a lower-paying dream on the back burner.

Not long after the wedding, the phone rang at my office with a decidedly different kind of ring than usual. The call was from Jan van Breda Kolff, one of Coach Carril's former assistants, who had just become head coach at Cornell University. Without so much as a how-do-you-do, he offered me an assistant coaching job at Cornell!

The timing was perfect, as far as I was concerned. We hadn't gotten into an expensive lifestyle, we were young, no kids yet. Why not?

My wife was adamant about why not. "I'm not moving to Ithaca," she said. Besides, she had talked it over with members of her family, who couldn't understand why anyone would want to be a coach. Their logic, she explained, was based on the fact that coaches don't make any money.

In hindsight, I see that should have been a clue that we needed to spend some time talking about what our values and priorities were. But instead I did what seemed like the correct thing to do, which was to stay with the game I was learning in the business world—even if I was playing someone else's game—and put the full-time-coaching dream on hold. In the meantime, for my sanity and to remind myself what really mattered, I signed up as a volunteer to coach classes at the Y and then landed a side job as an assistant coach at Illinois Institute of Technology.

Working with kids put me in my element. It wasn't just that I had the capacity to teach. I was also learning. When I saw them on the court, many of them pushing themselves and choosing not to give up when I pushed them some more, I was inspired to excel even more in my day job. What had become abundantly clear in that respect was that the exciting investment action was in the institutional side of the business—investing large sums of money for such entities as union pension funds, insurance companies, university endowments, and government employee groups. But the players controlling the ball in this business were pretty much in the all-white-boys' club. With some exceptions. There were a handful of women breaking the glass ceiling. The top firms seemed to have one or two blacks playing at this higher level, all of whom had M.B.A.s from the top business schools in the country. There was something of a double standard in that there were plenty of white "masters of the universe" who had just worked their way up without M.B.A.s; some had no degrees at all. But if getting my master's degree was the price of admission for a black professional in my field to ascend the ladder, then so be it.

In fact, getting an advanced degree gave me an opportunity to focus on studies in a way that hadn't been possible when I was juggling all my course work with the rigors of playing basketball. Not only that, but with real-world experience under my belt, I could make sense out of subjects like economics and actually excel at them. Man, could I hear Dad's voice ringing in my ear about how that first awful semester at Princeton wasn't going to haunt me forever.

When it came to choosing where to go for my M.B.A., depending on where I was accepted, it was logical that we would have to consider moving. When I learned that I'd been accepted at my top three choices—Wharton School of Business at the University of Pennsylvania in Philadelphia, Harvard Business School in Cambridge, Massachusetts, and the University of Chicago—before I talked to my wife or to any of my business associates, I hopped in the car and headed to Euclid Avenue to see what my parents had to say.

"Well, Cat, what are your thoughts?" was Dad's immediate response. Mom echoed that question.

Ah, the music of home that never changed!

When I explained that it would be cool to go to the University of Chicago—which had an M.B.A. program that was at the top of a lot of the lists and wouldn't cause me to have to uproot us to another city—Dad wanted to make sure that I wasn't basing my decision on not wanting to rock the boat.

"That's part of it," I sighed. But then I told them about the job opportunity that I had with Exchange Bank—a firm that offered a tuition reimbursement program. While I studied for my M.B.A., I would work as a trust officer at the bank and continue my volunteer coaching.

"Craig," Mom said, "it sounds like a plan."

Dad just gave me a big bear hug and then sized me up, shaking his head proudly. "University of Chicago, M.B.A.!" His eyes misted over with pride.

What I didn't say is that one of the reasons that I'd really decided not to leave town was that some strange flickers of worry, irrational though they were, had started back up. Mom wouldn't have admitted that she needed me, even if she did. My father was only fifty-four years old, going strong as always, working full-time, serving as an unofficial counselor to family, friends, and strangers all around Chicago. But still, the insidious toll that MS could take was unpredictable.

While we never had an in-depth discussion at home about the frightening course that MS was known to take, I had by this point in my adulthood done enough research on my own about the disease to understand the reality of what Dad was up against. I knew that MS was an autoimmune disease, meaning that my father's immune system—part of what battles the foreign intrusion of infections and other diseases—was, by mistake, attacking healthy, normal tissues. In the case of MS, the immune system attacks the brain and spinal cord, destroying the myelin that protects and insulates nerves and wreaking havoc in the communication network between the brain and the rest of the body. The multiple scarring (sclerosis) or build-up of scar tissue on the myelin causes the communication breakdown and the resulting symptoms of MS—from tingling, numbness, fatigue, and chronic pain, to problems walking, moving, and even standing, to a range of other debilitating symptoms like vision impairment. Although medications and other possible treatments were being developed in these years, none of them were yet available for MS sufferers. Of course, given the nature of the beast, every case is different—with disability progressing at a terrifying pace for some or very slowly and subtly for others. While I hoped Dad would be more in the latter category, I worried about him. However, airing such concerns wasn't encouraged in the Robinson household. So I kept the conversation about my plans for the future, announcing that the way I had it figured, by 1992, or in about three years or so, I'd have my master's and could catch up with my high-achieving sister!

Mom and Dad laughed but it was no joke. After earning her degree from Harvard Law in 1988, Michelle LaVaughn Robinson hadn't missed a beat in landing a job as an associate at the prestigious Chicago law firm of Sidley Austin. It was there, the following summer, when she was in charge of a group of interns, that one of them, twenty-eight-year-old Barack Obama, first crossed her path.

Barack, a year older than me, had received his undergraduate degree during the same time frame that I did. He spent his first two years at Occidental College in California before transferring to Columbia University in New York City, where he graduated in 1983. After spending the next couple of years in New York working in both business and public-interest capacities, he had taken a detour from pursuing his law degree and had come to Chicago to work for three years in the poorest sections of the Southside as a community organizer—focusing on issues such as literacy, education, and job training. Then, in 1988, three months after Michelle graduated from Harvard Law, Barack enrolled there. If fate was trying to get them together, it wasn't doing a very good job of it!

But then the stars aligned. After Barack became an editor of the *Harvard Law Review* at the end of his first year, the first African American ever so named, during the summer of 1989—there he was interning at Sidley Austin.

Not that we knew about any of this at the time. Miche

was—let me clear my throat—decidedly not interested in becoming involved romantically with anyone. A rising star at the law firm, she knew herself well enough that it was going to take someone really special just to keep up with her—and then some. And it wasn't only about how many hours she was putting in, but also it was nearly impossible for any man to keep up with her and, more important, to measure up to the larger-than-life Fraser Robinson. Yes, of course, Michelle dated. But no beau had ever been brought over to the house for the prospective son-in-law treatment.

Then along came Barack Obama.

But before that evening when we first met him, apparently Barack almost blew it by asking her out that first summer when he worked for her as an intern.

Big mistake! When I heard about that, I had little hope for the guy.

Michelle turned him down, adamantly. While I didn't get the transcript of what she said, I can assure you that when my sister is adamant about something, there is no negotiating to follow. She apparently pointed out a) you don't ask your boss out, and b) as two of the few blacks working in the firm, it would be a distraction for the two of them to become an item.

Not to be undone, Barack kept his cool and backed off. But when he returned the following summer, he made the excellent choice to intern at another law firm. This time when he asked my sister out, she accepted. The two started dating then and before too long, Miche casually mentioned that she was going to be bringing him by to meet Mom and Dad and for me to be there just in case. As I understood it, he knew that we'd be there, so it wasn't entirely an ambush.

What I later learned about my future brother-in-law and the person of character he is—when Michelle asked me to set up the basketball pickup game and check him out—was really just a confirmation of everything that we had all seen in him on earlier occasions. Barack's choices, like my sister's, were inspiring—especially how they viewed public service not as duty but as opportunity to positively impact others. It was also impressive to see how unrushed their courtship was and what a team they became even before they were engaged.

Those are the types of choices that reveal character to me whenever I'm in the midst of the recruiting process. By 1991, even though I was not yet coaching full-time, I was starting to become aware of how individuals in our extended family had made extraordinary choices in their lives and how they impacted others—stories that I was determined to collect from my dad, the keeper of family folklore.

Tragically, that would never happen, due to an unexpected turn of events.

11

EXPECT THE BEST BUT PREPARE FOR THE UNEXPECTED

Every team that I've ever coached has had at least one, if not a few, real head cases whose tendency to worry gets on everybody else's last nerve. But not mine—that is, as long as I can work with them and help provide some guidance as to how to channel their energy in a productive direction. After all, this is something I have personal experience in.

My penchant for worrying turned out to be an asset once I'd gained a foothold in the arena of bond trading. Even with the M.B.A. I'd earned in a shorter amount of time than originally planned, I still faced resistance at several firms where I interviewed. Education aside, the attitude was—what could someone who grew up on the Southside with basketball in his blood know about the risk involved in investing huge amounts of other people's money?

That was until I met with Greg McLaughlin, who managed Morgan Stanley's offices in Chicago and San Francisco.

A tough Irish kid who had been a helicopter pilot in Vietnam, Greg was eager to have me on board. Anyone who had played against Michael Jordan as a teenager, in his mind, had to know what risk really was. The point, and he got it, is that if you are a worrier, you can anticipate circumstances going awry and be prepared for how to respond. Obviously, if you're going to risk investing large sums of capital, you want to expect the best in terms of the return on your investment while still preparing for the unexpected. Same principles apply when you're coaching as in investing, when you're in charge of the game plan in the short and the long run.

Greg was so convinced of my potential that he waived the normal dues-paying period that most new investment bankers in the Morgan Stanley program usually went through. To introduce me to the right clients, he accompanied me on the rounds in both Chicago and New York, opening doors to income streams that were pretty dazzling. It didn't take long at all, with money coming in, to start spending at similarly high levels—and to start feeling that the more expensive suits, jewelry, cars, vacations, and, soon, the big new home, were all necessary expenditures to keep up with the competition. To be sure, my wife and I were enjoying the perks and the newfound social whirl. But for all the luxury, there wasn't any leisure. Even lavish resort getaways were just fancy settings for amped-up wheeling and dealing. Everyone was "on" all the time, everyone masking professional worrying with bravado and designer clothes.

Every now and then, I'd catch myself thinking that I'd much rather be kicking it in sweats, shooting hoops at Dukes Happy Holiday Resort, or jumping in the car to take off for a Sunday drive—destination to be determined on the ride.

Hanging with the high rollers, I sometimes felt as if I were performing a role in some kind of play and that eventually the curtain would fall and I could go back to that other

story about basketball that was the real me. Wall Street, cul-
turewise, was more alien to me than England. And to some of
my coworkers and clients, I may have been the first black
person they had ever known. During one of my first forays
to the New York Morgan Stanley office, I looked around
and realized that the only brothers in the office besides me
were among the shoeshine crew who showed up daily to pol-
ish the shoes of the white guys while they were at the trading
desk.

I was embarrassed for the shoeshine guys but understood
this was their livelihood. The first week I was there every
day, one or more of the guys would say, "You need a shine,
boss?" and I'd say, "No, thanks, but I appreciate it." The idea
of servitude, of them bending down to put themselves at a
lower station than I, was too much. I wondered sometimes
what their stories were, if they had kids, whether any of them
played basketball. I wanted to tell them about the possibilities
to come, about how my parents had raised me and my sister
from working-class beginnings. But that "recruiting," genuinely curious part of me who might have once asked them
about themselves was not much in evidence at this time.

After one of my first trips to New York, in the spring of
1991, I returned to Chicago with a lot of mixed feelings
about where my life seemed to be going. But the last thing
that I wanted to do was complain about an opportunity to
excel in a field that I'd chosen to pursue and in which I could
earn substantial wealth. All I could do was think of Dad—
never complaining all these years, and maybe, at the most,
missing four days of work ever.

Then, without a word of complaint that symptoms were
coming on, he suddenly began to have trouble breathing.

A few nights after he finally told anyone, Mom woke up
to find him struggling to breathe. Without warning, the next
thing she knew, he passed out. My mother called an ambulance.

At the hospital the doctors found that he had a mass in his airway, some kind of growth, but once they went in to operate they also found out he had a bleeding ulcer. The ulcer was what they listed on the death certificate—though we knew that compounding these causes were the complications of MS.

It felt as if the world had come to an end. Nothing made any sense. There had been no clues, no change in the momentum of joy and enthusiasm with which he embraced life. Less than a week before he died, Michelle was probably over having fun with him, like always, exchanging witty banter, sitting on fifty-six-year-old Diddley's lap, telling him all the latest news. At twenty-seven years old, she was a grown woman already, and a couple of inches taller than he was—but nothing had changed from how she would sit on his lap and lay her head on his shoulder, and all he would do was laugh like crazy, trapped underneath her!

That's how it had continued right up to the end. Not one complaint or indication of symptoms that were killing him. He had obviously masked his own worries for ages, if he had acknowledged them to himself at all.

In my heartbroken state, I couldn't help but be upset that he had never told us. If he had, I wondered, maybe we could have addressed the problems earlier. But to tear ourselves up over what could have or should have happened wasn't the way to honor Fraser Robinson or to respect my mother's mourning process. That was something that came up when Michelle and I had a serious argument about the wording of his obituary. As far as I could recall, the last time we had seriously argued was back in our childhood when I was mad that she had more money in her piggy bank than I did. Mom had intervened at that time, and wouldn't you know it, she did this time again.

"Would you two just stop it?" Mom finally insisted. "Do

you know why you're arguing? You're arguing because you miss your father!" And we all started crying.

The three of us then huddled, as we would have if Dad were right there with us, and talked about how we could bear the loss more easily because we had not waited to express our love for him and we had no unfinished business.

Mom gently pointed out that though we all would have wanted him to stay with us longer, he had packed lifetimes into his fifty-six years and that we were the center of his world. "You're both so lucky," she went on, through her tears, "that you got to know Fraser Robinson, to be his kids, to know that he loved you, and let me tell you, he knew how much you loved him."

We held together throughout the funeral proceedings, aware that we were not the only ones who were shocked and deeply saddened that he would no longer be in our midst. During the simple service presided over by one of my dad's favorite ministers, Betty Reid, the eulogy was less about how Fraser Robinson had gone on to a better place—which would have been counter to his belief that life is what it is, here on earth—but more a celebration of who he was and how many of our lives he had impacted, inspired, and changed.

The real emotional challenge for me and Michelle came during the graveside ceremony. It was everything we could do to speak, as planned. Afterward, during the large gathering that followed, I would no sooner compose myself and wipe away the tears than I'd look over and spot friends from the barbershop or from basketball or from Dad's work or any member of the multiple sides of our family tree, and as they choked up, I would, too, all over again. Everyone was so sad for me. They knew that I'd lost my dad and my best friend in the world.

"Francesca," I confided in my father's younger sister,

holding back a sob, "I can't look at anybody else," and then I laughed in the middle of tears. My aunt burst out laughing and crying at the same time—because that was the kind of thing my father would laugh at. So I put my sunglasses on, and I started looking up over everybody's head, and we had a nice laugh before the next bout of crying.

Throughout this period, my mother was a study in grace and determination to go on and live every day to the fullest even after losing the love of her life, constant companion, and her soul mate. Whenever I checked in on her to make sure she was holding up, Mom was much more concerned that Michelle and I were okay.

In fact, I was just that—okay. When Dad died, I had some brutally honest moments of soul-searching and made a decision to stop worrying or needing to control everything, to keep everyone safe, make sure everyone was happy, and to stop expecting that we would always have smooth sailing. True, most of my life, all things considered, had been fairly charmed. So why worry? Besides, it was unfair to expect it to always be that way, not only because that's just unrealistic, but because it's much more productive to spend time planning for the unexpected and then dealing with it when it happened.

And, again, I could channel all those worrying what-ifs into my work and become the best investment banker on the block. Of course, if I wanted, I could fret over the possibility that the business world wasn't really where I wanted to be or that I was almost thirty years old and before long it might be too hard to get back to the full-time coaching game that I really wanted to be in. If I needed even more to worry about, I could run myself into the ground questioning whether my wife and I were really prepared to be parents. But that wasn't how I wanted to welcome our children into the world. I wanted to give them what Dad had given us—security, love, attention, and stability.

For the first time in my life, just in time, I decided to have some faith that everything would work out and that when it didn't, I was a grown-up and would know what to do. Not only because of how I was raised, but because of the support system I had around me and because I actually felt that my father's presence had never left me.

With that, I cast off for the next leg of a pretty tumultuous journey that spanned the years between 1991 and 2000. Out of the high points, I must start with Avery, the son born to me and my wife in 1992. Wow! Nothing could have prepared me for the incredible joy that becoming a father brought me. And in ways that were downright uncanny, Avery turned out to be a mini-Fraser—from the twinkle in his eyes, to the tenor of his voice, to the old soul-deep emotional intelligence that came from him. Four years later, our daughter, Leslie, was born, and when I first held this most beautiful baby girl in my arms, I knew that she was going to be a lot like her aunt Michelle.

Workwise, I was torn between wanting to really go the distance with the opportunities unfolding for me at Morgan Stanley—which meant a lot of travel and even the possibility of a move to New York—and knowing that I needed to be close to home as a father to my young children.

While I had made a promise to myself not to worry about what I couldn't control, I hadn't stopped thinking that it was up to me to fix everything that was broken and make it all fine again. That's what was happening with my marriage. Rather than acknowledge the growing chasm between me and my wife, with the lines of communication almost nonexistent, I avoided the subject altogether. Not only was the idea of divorce foreign to me—given my family background—but I knew from seeing what divorced friends and colleagues experienced that the pain felt by everyone involved takes a lasting toll.

What I should have done, but didn't, was to talk to someone, anyone, about my concerns. Later, my mother and Michelle would take me to task for not having said something sooner. They'd had no idea.

While hoping and trying to have faith that we would get through what I convinced myself was common in early marriages, there were a couple of bright spots in my decision that I needed to be closer to home. One of these was a shot at coaching the high school team at the University of Chicago Lab School when the regular coach had to take time off due to illness in the family.

"I'm in!" I accepted, gratefully. Even though this modest-paying job wouldn't let me quit my day gig, it was a bona fide coaching job and I was delighted.

Next thing I know, turns out I have just stepped into a high school hornet's nest of resentment from the black JV basketball coach who wanted the job and the raise that came with it, along with outrage from parents and community who couldn't understand how a Princeton grad with an M.B.A. and a day job at Morgan Stanley was being hired over the longtime employee. But the powers that be stuck with their decision to bring me in.

When I arrived at practice the first time, rushing to get there in time, I realized it might not be a good idea to pull into the parking lot in my Porsche and try to convince the kids that I knew anything about basketball standing there in my fancy suit. Actually, inside the gym nobody knew who I was. From everything they'd heard, they just assumed I was white.

After our first six games, we were 0–6, but then we turned it around. We went undefeated in league play and won the Independent School League championship for the first time in twenty-five years—when John Rogers had played on the high school team! The icing on the cake was learning that I had won coach of the year—as selected by coaches across our league.

Talk about a shot in the arm! It was a chance to begin to hone my coaching fundamentals and to remind myself that, hey, maybe I knew my stuff and that there was more to come.

Well, if there was more to come, it wasn't going to be happening there. After an unrelenting effort to get the job he felt was due him, the JV coach raised an issue of union regulations. Had it not been for other demands, I would have been much more riled than I was.

An opportunity had arisen after I met with my good friend Jim Reynolds, who was starting up a minority-owned investment company called Loop Capital Markets. Jim and his partner, Al Grace—both a little older than me—had been part of the first group of blacks to get into the sales and trading side at Smith Barney. Jim and I played basketball together, our kids were friends, he knew I was in the business, and we got along. I also knew that I could trust him.

As Jim and Al were on the municipal side of the business, and I was a corporate bond guy, I proposed that my skill set and area of expertise could nicely complement what they were doing. They agreed.

Thus began an entrepreneurial team-building adventure that would serve me in good stead. The whole company was no more than seven people, but we were able to demonstrate a skillful African American presence in this part of the financial industry—while also offering internships to minority and lower-income trainees. There was even a family-like atmosphere in the office.

Hoping for the best but planning for the unexpected, I threw myself into my new partnership at Loop with great zeal and began to contemplate practical solutions for dealing with what wasn't going well at home. But even hinting at our problems created pushback and resentment from my spouse, to the point that when I traveled, my phone calls went unanswered and I'd be left to worry whether everybody was okay or not.

Everything came to a head when I returned early from a trip out of state, arriving home at about five thirty A.M., and tiptoed through the house to find everyone gone. The beds were all made. They obviously hadn't been slept it.

The living daylights were scared out of me. Panic set in. Every possible scenario crossed my mind—car accident, kids hurt, lost, even abducted. After a half hour of frantically dialing and redialing my wife's cell phone, I located her and learned that she and the kids were fine. When they returned a short while later from having stayed at a friend's, she and I barely spoke. But neither one of us could ignore that it was the beginning of the end.

Angry as I was with her and knowing how angry she was with me, still I felt that I'd failed her. But brutal honesty set in right about then. Much as I wanted it to be otherwise, I was Craig—not Fraser—Robinson. My wife wasn't Marian and we weren't living in the upstairs Shangri-la bungalow on Euclid Avenue. My wife and I could acknowledge that we had come together to bring two amazing children into the world and nothing would ever change that. But we were falling down on the job of being parents to our kids by not working on our marriage.

After a short-lived effort to come up with solutions, it was obvious that our differences were irreconcilable. We went through a very painful period when we began living separately in the same house. When the divorce proceedings began, they were no less excruciating on all of us than I had expected. The financial agreement for me was terrible. Still, it was the right thing to do.

Meanwhile, I was just getting the bond business at Loop

off the ground and had next to no income. Mom knew that I wouldn't complain or ask for help, so she made the suggestion that I move back home.

Ever since Great-Aunt Robbie had died, Mom had owned the house outright and was living downstairs. This left the upstairs apartment—our old place—available for me. So I moved back into that very small space where I had grown up, and began a new life there, with Avery and Leslie staying over twice a week and then on alternate weekends. We managed to squeeze in daily visits—what with the various activities and sports of theirs that I was coaching—that also allowed me to keep tabs on their well-being.

"Listen," my partner Jim Reynolds announced one day as he walked into my office, "I know what you're going through and I want to give you something." Jim was a prince of a human being who had been through the divorce mill already and wanted me to know that I'd come out the other side. Then he handed me a check for five thousand dollars.

"Wh— Oh . . . my . . . th-th-thank . . .," I stammered, trying to thank him profusely, but the correct words wouldn't come out. How could he have known how much I needed that right then?

"Don't say anything," he told me. "This is not a loan. Please don't even try to pay me back. If you want, you can do the same for somebody else somewhere down the road."

For the rest of my life, I would never forget that incredibly generous gift that could not have come at a more lean time in my journey as a single father. Some years later, I had the pleasure of doing the same for someone else, and when I did, I let that person know, "This is from Jim Reynolds."

In a hopeful, happy mood over the next few weeks, I became aware of a rumor passing along the basketball grapevine— one that had me fantasizing about tossing in the high-finance towel and going back to the idea of being a coach full-time. As it so happened, the men's basketball head coaching job at Northwestern was open, and there was word that Bill Carmody, one of Coach Carril's assistants at Princeton, who continued on to be head coach there, might land the position. Whenever openings for head coach happen—especially with a top-flight program like Northwestern—a lot of names are thrown around as everyone in the know plays the speculation game. Fatefully, however, the recently installed president of Northwestern, Henry Bienen, had been provost at Princeton and that boded well for Bill Carmody.

Excited as I was for Bill, the question that was really on my mind was this: If he indeed was hired on at Northwestern, what were the chances he'd hire me?

The more I contemplated the possibilities, how he could use my expert knowledge of the Chicago and Illinois players, and how I'd run the recruiting process in the area for him, the more I avoided asking myself if—given all the current circumstances—this was what I could afford to do.

On the day after Labor Day—in fact, within Carmody's first hours at Northwestern—my cell phone rang with one of the most promising rings I'd ever heard.

Though I had a feeling it was him, I listened as he said, "Craig, this is Bill Carmody."

"Coach! How're you doing?"

Before I could get very far with my congratulations or my "Let me know if there's anything I can do to help," Bill interrupted, saying, "Hold on, hold on. You know I wouldn't be calling unless I wanted to offer you the job."

Pause. Taking a deep breath, I replied, "Let me call you right back."

On the trading floor at the moment, I knew that it was too noisy and distracting for us to have this conversation, so I went downstairs to stand outside on the street. But then, seeing as I was at the curb, and unsure what else to do, I hailed a cab and had the guy drive while I dialed the number back at Northwestern.

I was shaking like a leaf, trying not to be too eager.

And Bill Carmody, wouldn't you know, began with several disclaimers, clearly trying to talk me out of it. "I want to offer you the job," he said and then sighed, "but you should know what it really entails." He then went on to describe the less glamorous aspects of coaching that include errand running, travel coordinating, sometimes playing bad cop to the head coach's good cop. Bill continued, "You've been making pretty big money these last few years. Being an assistant coach doesn't pay much, you know. Are you sure you want to do it?"

It was a hilarious negotiation. For the next thirty minutes we went back and forth as I tried to convince him why I wanted it and would be great at it, and Bill listing all the reasons I'd be out of my mind to take it.

"Before you decide anything," he said finally, "why don't you come up here and take a look, and then we can talk a little bit more?"

Even as he said that, I knew it wasn't going to be necessary. The only question was whether it was realistic to expect that I could eventually move up from this position to a head coaching job. For the worrier/planner in me, I needed to know that this gamble—crazy as it was—had some upsides. Not a rookie, I was thirty-eight years old; I would be turning away from partnership in a business that was on its way to being very profitable; and I was accustomed to being the boss. Was it worth it to give up everything in the business for basically a low-paying coaching apprenticeship—knowing that there were only a little over three hundred Division 1 head coaching jobs in the whole country?

Bill's only assurance was, "If we do well at Northwestern, there will be opportunities."

That was enough for me.

Back at the office, I couldn't restrain my excitement when I stopped in to tell Jim Reynolds what had just transpired. He nodded and took a deep breath, as if he had seen this day coming for some time. Investment banking and corporate bond trading were character- and skill-building. But they weren't really my game, even though the opportunity to be there at the beginning of Loop was something that would make me a better coach of my game in the long run.

"Basketball?" Jim said, as if to himself. Then he had to ask, "So, how much money you going to make?"

Wow. I hadn't even talked to Bill Carmody about that. With a shrug, I answered, "I don't know."

Jim just looked at me for a minute, shook his head, and then cracked a smile, saying, "Man, you must really love this game."

This is me before my first wedding—with Julius Rhodes, my best friend from high school basketball at Mount Carmel.

Me here with longtime pickup basketball friends: John Rogers, Arne Duncan, and Kit Mueller (another great player from Princeton University). We competed in three-on-three tourneys together well into our thirties.

At my second wedding, the Princeton University crew was well represented. From left: John Rogers, Gordon Enderle, Kit Mueller, me, Dennis Clark (my first roommate and best friend from Princeton), Howie Levy, and Coach Bill Carmody. Kneeling: Mitch Henderson (assistant coach at Northwestern) and Roger Schmitt. All are former Princeton basketball players except Carmody and Clark.

Here I am with Avery at about age two. Just like my parents, I can't hold back from showing how proud I am of my children!

With Leslie, age two, in my arms. There is no role in life more important to me than parenthood.

Here I am with Avery and Leslie on the ferry to Newport, Rhode Island, back during my two seasons as head coach of Brown University.

With Michelle and Mom, honoring all that she taught us—not only how to be successful in life, but how to become parents in our own right.

At the wedding of Kelly and me. During Michelle's emotional toast, Barack steps in to help.

With my sister, after a tribute to our late father, whose presence is always with us.

The mother of the groom beams happily.

With my beautiful bride, surrounded by loving family and friends—
an unforgettable occasion.

Our wedding party from all sides of our family tree. Top row, from left:
Leslie Robinson, Malia Obama, Heidi Cook (maid of honor), me, Kelly, and Avery
Robinson. Foreground: Autumn McCrum and Maya McCrum (Kelly's nieces),
Sarah Hipwell and Caroline Hipwell (Kelly's cousins), Sasha Obama, and Jordan
and William McCrum (Kelly's nephews).

With Michelle and presumptive Vice President Joe Biden, during the convention while waiting for the official nomination to be announced.

Enjoying the moment, savoring history.

Michelle and I are officially introduced to President Jimmy Carter by Joe Biden, a thrill.

The First Family comes out to lend their *serious* support for me as head coach of Oregon State University's men's basketball team.

Coach Pete Carril, still going strong, still keeping me on my toes.

With coaching staff and players after we won the 2009 CBI Championship.
Go Beavers!

With Kelly, Leslie, and Avery at the inauguration of the 44th President of the United States of America, Barack Obama.

Inauguration night, witness to a new chapter in our nation's history.

PART III

A NEW SEASON

12

BUILDING A STRONG FAMILY IS LIKE BUILDING A STRONG TEAM

By the authority vested in me as the firstborn son of Fraser Robinson III, who always went overboard in showing how proud he was of me and my sister, I must pause for some unapologetic bragging about my two kids. Remember how much I hated change and resisted any moves that might rock the boat? From the time that I was three, the idea of pulling up stakes and going somewhere else or doing things in a new way would scare me until, of course, I gave it a try and, lo and behold, I'd wonder why we hadn't done it earlier.

Avery and Leslie, at this writing, are seventeen and thirteen respectively, and have experienced more moves and changes in their short lives than I have in my forty-seven years. Throughout, the two have exhibited so much resilience and courage that I think of them already as leading players in the game of character. They have helped me to become a better father and a better coach—and to know that everyone on the team contributes to the outcome. Not only that, but when it comes to motivating players—when you're trying to turn around a team in trouble or are in transition or just working on player development—engaging everyone in the effort is the ideal way to marshal forces and accomplish big things.

This is why I sat down eight-year-old Avery and four-year-old Leslie so they could voice their feelings about the coming changes.

"Daddy's thinking about taking a different job," I began.

They knew by now that their mother and I were splitting up for good, and this news made both of them ask, with concern, if I'd be moving away.

"No," I said, "but it's going to be a little different. I'm going to be a coach at a college here in town, but I won't be making nearly as much money."

I let the idea settle in with them for a moment, and then Avery asked me, "Does this mean your office is gonna be a gym?"

"Well, sort of. My office won't be a gym, but there'll be one right next door."

He said, "Cool."

Then Leslie picked it up. "Do they have a pool there?"

"Yes, they do."

"Great," she said.

Next, I had to let them know that on the nights when they would be staying with me, we would be upstairs in the little apartment on Euclid Avenue where Grandma lived. We'd sort of been camping out up until now, but it had been my plan to get an apartment of my own. But with my new job, of course, that wasn't going to be financially possible—even though my kids didn't need to know the details of my hugely reduced salary, or the cost of the divorce, the lawyers, and the decision by a judge that my child-support payments should be based on my former earnings in the financial industry rather than on my upcoming earnings as a college coach.

Avery and Leslie looked at me as if I was being silly. Why on earth would they want to live anywhere else but right upstairs from Grandma? Ever since they were small, I had been telling them about the Southside Family Robinson home and how we played board games and practical jokes and competed at everything. They were ready to re-create "back in the day" 2000-style. Mom was happy to oblige except when we stayed up too late or when the kids got into video games. Not her cup of tea. But I was right there with the controls, trying to keep up with the two of them. When we all wanted to get outside, the park was still right by the house, where we could watch the basketball or softball games or play ourselves, and it was déjà vu all over again.

Somehow, unbeknownst to me, Avery and Leslie persuaded Mom to tell them about how we all used to hide and scare each other. So the tradition was brought back and my kids were really ingenious at scaring the living daylights out of me especially. This went on for years, just as it had for us. That was, until Leslie was about eight and tiptoed up to scare Mom, who whirled around and scared Leslie first—who, in turn, ran screaming smack dab into a wooden door and scared us all really badly when we had to go to the emergency room. Thus came to a final end that particular game. The fun had gotten out of hand!

Trying to re-create some of the other strategies that my parents had employed for our entertainment, I definitely got a lot of mileage from the spur-of-the-moment suggestion to go drop by relatives'—including my sister and her family. Just as my life had been highly eventful, Michelle and Barack had not been idle in their careers or in their ongoing involvement in public affairs. After working for some years as a professor of constitutional law at the University of Chicago, Barack had entered politics in 1997 when he was elected to the Illinois State Senate, where he would serve for the next seven years. Meanwhile, Michelle's legal career had blossomed, before she went on to prestigious posts in public service and then became an associate dean of student services at the University of Chicago, where she was in this era. Malia, born in 1998, was two years younger than Leslie, and, in late 2000, as my first season got underway at Northwestern, Miche became pregnant with Sasha.

We were definitely a busy family! Michelle commented, whenever she saw me, about how happy I looked to be back in the game of basketball, though she was aware of the financial struggle. Her main concern, however, was whether I was dating someone. Between her and Mom, it was almost a daily question, whether it was a simple "Seeing anyone?" or a more direct "Oh, Craig, there is a great gal you really should meet."

Not saying a word, I would offer a hand gesture that they both understood as well as any of my players on the court—a pronounced "time-out."

Not interested, not ready.

Dating was not in the budget. I didn't have the wherewithal or the inclination. Family expenses were cut to the bone. No takeout, no vacations, no splurging. The last thing I wanted to do was ask a woman on a date and not have the means to pay for it!

Not long after I'd taken the assistant coaching job, a great friend, Andrew Rankowitz, who I knew from my Morgan Stanley days, told me I was nuts for leaving Loop and then insisted on writing me a check to help me get by during the transition. Another godsend. But it wasn't for dating. My focus was on my kids, and my job. And now that things were finally settling into a routine in both areas, why rock the boat?

The reason for rocking the boat became apparent not long after a trip to Minneapolis for the NCAA Final Four championships in March 2001, where college coaches hold an annual meeting. That year, it was also where fate finally decided to throw something wonderful and unexpected my way.

By now I'd finished up my first season at Northwestern as assistant coach under Bill Carmody and had been fortunate to be able to learn from the masterful way he had come in and motivated players to want to change. That in itself was an education. But there was so much more. Beyond running practices and the games, and the never-ending job of recruiting, a head coach oversees fund-raising, reviews film, handles media relations, and undertakes a range of responsibilities related to player development and welfare, not to mention travel logistics and every other administrative chore known to man.

Besides the team on the floor, a head coach at a Big Ten program like Northwestern also had another team to run that consisted of staff, including assistant coaches—like myself and Paul Lee, a veteran assistant coach (though younger than me), who had played for Columbia University and began his assistant coaching career there, and who was a great teacher and inspiration.

Unlike Coach Carril, Bill Carmody didn't go for the jugular in motivating players and recruits to work on what they needed to improve. Yet he was just as effective. But to turn around a program that was coming off a season like the preceding one was going to be a serious challenge. In the 1999–2000 season, the Northwestern Wildcats had finished 5-25 overall. All five of the wins were on home court and none were conference games. Bottom line, if Coach Carmody had come in and overplayed the role of tough taskmaster, it wouldn't have engaged the powers of courage and resilience that the players needed to bring to the team. The motivation to change doesn't really come from feeling worse about yourself than you already do, rather it comes from having hope of improvement, and firing up self-esteem and enthusiasm!

With those basics, the 2000–2001 season took us to a much improved 11-19 record overall—including a win on the road and three conference game wins. We didn't win a championship, but Bill Carmody had turned a basement program into a competitor. In the ensuing years, he would become the most successful coach in Northwestern's history—not only by importing his version of the Princeton offense to Evanston, but also by sticking to that strategy in the face of all his critics.

In addition to the fact that this first season as an assistant coach at Northwestern had set me back onto the path where, I felt, I was meant to be, I was able to hone my insights into the ways basketball can serve as a metaphor for life. Indeed, to instill confidence in our players during a time of transition, I made use of the same methods by which I had reassured my own children that we really were going to get through the divorce together and be all right. Building a strong family really was like building a strong team. And vice versa.

That's probably why in these years, I drew from the Marian Robinson playbook—her advocacy on behalf of her children inspired my advocacy on behalf of our players, earning me the nickname "The Edge." If that meant using tough love with starters who weren't conscientious students and didn't think they had to be, I had no problem playing the baddest bad cop you ever saw—in front of the whole team. Now, on the other hand, when a player was wrongfully accused of not giving his all in a class or was penalized unfairly with a bad grade because of excused travel absences, I didn't have any qualms about having a frank and pointed discussion with that professor. But before matters got to that point, my approach, just like Mom's, was to get to know everyone in the faculty and administration—so they could expect to see plenty of me whenever there was an issue.

So I was feeling pretty good about myself and my contribution during the annual coaches' conference when Final Four came around in March 2001. A man on a mission, I knew this was an opportunity to expand my horizons and was meeting everyone I could, attending every seminar and workshop, picking up every brochure, and taking notes like a graduate student. Being my old "Honest John" superdiligent self, I thought that was the purpose of the meeting, really, not to party and have a good time—although that was what everybody else seemed more interested in.

Rick Giles, a friend since high school who had graduated the same year I did from Princeton (and is now my sports agent), was determined to loosen me up.

"C'mon, Craig," Rick said after corralling me into a group of fifteen of us to head out for the evening, "let's go to the *USA Today* party." That was the hot place to be—for head coaches only.

"I'm not going to crash some party where I'm not supposed to be."

"Don't worry." Rick grinned. "I know the women working the door."

"Rick, you can't sneak in fifteen guys."

"Trust me," he said. "There won't be a head coach anywhere near the place."

And, of course, he was right. The ballroom was deserted.

One of Rick's friends at the door was a great-looking blonde named Kelly, and he introduced me, but I was so embarrassed about sneaking in that I didn't even speak to her.

At this point, Mom and Michelle had all but given up on me. Meeting a woman was still the last thing on my mind. Since I'd come to this convention to work, I made the practical decision that as soon as Rick and the rest of the guys were ready to leave for the next party, I'd ditch them and get back to my room to pack for a flight in the morning.

But somehow I was dragged along again, this time into a packed taxi and on to the Budweiser party that was being hosted in a hotel suite. This was the happening party and what would have been a huge suite was mobbed by almost a hundred people, packed up against each other like sardines.

So I'm almost six feet seven, not exactly someone who blends easily into the woodwork or who can compact myself to move well through crowds. Bottom line, this was not my scene at all. Looking for breathing room, I grabbed a beer and dodged the party room for an adjacent bedroom where all the coats were piled on the bed, and I wondered if I should bail now. True, I hadn't hung out with Rick and some of my other Princeton friends in a while. But it was getting late. Then again, now that the bedroom was filling up with people and coats falling onto the floor, I was basically trapped. The only place to sit was on a heavy nightstand.

Just then, an intern who was working the conference made his way over to me and asked, "Coach Robinson, mind if I ask you a question?"

"Sure. What's up?" I waited for what no doubt would be a question about career- or basketball-related advice.

Instead, the intern, Aaron, explained, "I'm dating this girl and . . ."

I wanted to say, "Sorry, kid, you've come to the wrong place for relationship advice."

At age twenty-one, Aaron was considering getting married and wondered what I thought.

"Are you thinking about marrying this girl because you love her or because you're getting laid on a regular basis?"

"I guess it's a little bit of both."

With that, I was off to the races, adamantly encouraging him not to be in a hurry, reminding him that he hadn't even finished college. Not holding back, I asked, "Do you know what you want to do with your life yet? Have you even dated anyone else?"

Unbeknownst to me, at that moment, leaning against the window, talking to somebody else but eavesdropping on my discussion, was Kelly, the blonde I'd met at the door at the earlier party, who was also this kid's boss.

For the next twenty minutes she listened to me explaining all the fine points of marriage and what to look for in a woman and criteria for creating a partnership in a marriage. Finally, I looked up and saw her coming over, at which point she sent Aaron to get us more beer.

As soon as he was out of earshot she said to me, "Who the hell do you think you are? What makes you such an expert on relationships? I bet you're one of those guys who's married and not wearing your wedding ring."

You could have knocked me over with a feather. Yes, even though I was at least two heads taller than this woman, she had come loaded for bear and looked to have more that she was ready to throw at me.

Fine, maybe I wasn't the most objective observer of relationships at that time. But, struggling for a snappy comeback, I had to ask, "Who the hell are you to be listening in on my discussion?"

"He's my intern," she said, "and I have to look out for him."

Once we got past that, I was able to focus more on who she was—a very self-possessed, warm, bright, strong, smart young woman—and then I noticed how much I liked her face. She was really pretty, not in a superficial way but with real intelligence going on behind her eyes. Appearing to be about ten years younger than me, she was also white. Not that such differences had to matter, but my mind didn't automatically go to the scene where we rode off into the sunset together.

Returning to her earlier remark, I asked, "What makes you think I'm married and not wearing my wedding ring?"

"Experience."

She seemed to be casting aspersions on married coaches, so I needed to clarify, "Well, as a matter of fact, I'm in the middle of getting a divorce."

"You have any kids?"

Yes, I let her know, I had two.

"You ever see them?"

Excuse me? Now I was offended. And it may have been obvious because right then, she backed off, and just in time for Aaron to return with beers—at which point she started in on him about how he shouldn't be getting married.

Next thing I knew, Kelly and I were on the same side, urging Aaron to wait to find someone who was independent and had a sense of herself. Interesting. Before long, her intern had left again and Kelly admitted that she'd been a little rough on me because she was worried about the advice I might be giving him. I admitted that some of the opinions I'd expressed might have been colored by my recent experience.

We then moved on to the next phase of the flirtation dance: jokes, laughter, a bit of small talk, and then a cab ride shared back to our hotels, which were next door to each other. Then we stood for a while in her hotel lobby, talking as if we'd known each other forever. I told her about the divorce and about juggling coaching responsibilities with single parenthood. She told me that she was at the Final Four working for the National Association of Basketball Coaches, where she used to volunteer. Her real job was as director of admissions for Monmouth University in New Jersey.

It was really late, so after a while we said good night. For whatever reason, I didn't think to ask for her phone number. We parted on a note of—"Well, if I'm ever in New Jersey, I'll look you up"—but we seemed to be two ships passing in the night.

If fate had arranged for us to meet, I sure was blowing it. Without giving me a nudge, Kelly went up to her room, and I walked over to my hotel.

A few nights later, upon my return to Chicago, Mom shared her concern with me that I was shutting out the idea of meeting another woman.

"Nah, I'm open to the idea," I told her. "In fact, I met somebody really nice just this past weekend."

"Really?" As Mom began to ask questions, I admitted that, no, I hadn't tried to call her since being back.

What I didn't admit was that I didn't even have any way of reaching her. How stupid was that? All of a sudden, I couldn't think of much else. Finally, on Thursday, I decided to Google her at Monmouth. Bingo. Kelly McCrum! Got her phone number, e-mail, and everything and just as I'm dialing her, my attention was drawn by the sound of an e-mail arriving. From? Yes, you guessed it—Kelly.

I ended my call, read her friendly note, then dialed again.

When I began my conversation by asking if she remembered me—I know, for a Princeton grad I could have been more lofty—Kelly answered, "Of course I remember you, I just sent you an e-mail. Are you calling because I sent you the e-mail?"

I said, "Not exactly. The e-mail came up while I was dialing you."

She said, "Get out of here."

And from that moment on we figured we might have something going on.

A very nice date in New York followed but we went our

separate ways after that. Our hesitation wasn't just the long-distance thing, but we were both wary of anything serious. As analytical as I was, the prospect of following my heart was uncharted territory for me, and frankly, I don't think she had ever imagined herself dating, much less marrying, an almost six-foot-seven black guy, ten years older, with two kids, no hair, and living with his mother.

But our conversations over the phone continued and I began looking forward to them as the highlight of my day. Because we couldn't date in person, we actually would go to see the same movie—me in Chicago and her in New Jersey—and then talk about it afterward. Before long, that naturally turned into live-and-in-person dates when I was on the road and closer to her, and vice versa.

During the courtship that lasted nearly five years, the big test came when I brought up her meeting the kids. In the past, women I'd dated asked about meeting my children right in the beginning. Not Kelly. I finally asked why she hadn't raised the subject.

She said, "Well, I figured when you were ready for me to meet them, you'd say so."

Having been a psychology student, Kelly had also been a child of divorce and was highly sensitive to what children go through. Her feeling was that the adults needed to determine what they felt and where they were in a relationship before bringing the kids into it.

If that wasn't an opportunity for the lightbulb to turn on that it was time to marry this wise woman, I don't know what would have been. But no rushing. And we had the family tests to pass.

Leaving Avery and Leslie for last, we made the rounds of the adults first. Kelly's mom was somewhat wary of our differences initially, but when she and a friend took us out for lunch in New York—with their own version of a "character test" like the one Michelle had asked me to give Barack—she came away pleased. Kelly's stepfather had no reservations and said so, asking, "What's everyone worked up about? Kelly's made her own decisions her entire life, and they've always worked out pretty well, so what makes anyone think this isn't a good decision?" Sounded exactly like something Fraser Robinson would have said.

The reactions of my mother and Michelle were a combination of relief and excitement—somewhere between "Phew!" and "Hallelujah." As for Barack, Kelly would be the first to tell you that he was the family member who made her feel the most at ease in the beginning. He knew what it was to become part of the loving but perhaps discerning Robinson extended family, and he knew what some of Kelly's concerns might be, coming as he did from a mixed-race background.

I wouldn't go so far as to say that Kelly's first meetings with the kids were disastrous. But I do recall seeing Leslie not budging from the spot between me and Kelly—not wanting us to be any closer. Avery, however, was kicking and screaming all the way right up to the wedding. He liked Kelly—he just wasn't ready for me to be with anyone other than his mom.

While I was upset, Kelly used basketball as an analogy and reminded me that you don't build a team overnight. Never taking any of their reactions personally, she lovingly made herself available to both of them without forcing the issue—all the while reassuring them that she wasn't there to replace their mom or to detract from their having a loving relationship with her.

After Kelly moved out to Chicago in 2003, I could see the kids starting to warm up to the idea of us as a foursome, and by early 2006, as we found our way, I began worrying a lot less. For a while there she and I were living upstairs from my mom, and Shangri-la lived again. Somehow, having people who really love each other, all huddled together in that tiny space, really was magical. With Avery almost fourteen and Leslie ten years old, Malia nearly eight and Sasha almost five, we would have all the kids for sleepovers, and listening to their laughter and young voices, it was like having my childhood all over again right in front of me.

Everything felt right in the world. I remember one night when Kelly and I promised to tell stories and the three little girls piled into one bed together, with Ave, me, and Kelly sitting on the floor. Then, while I was weaving a wondrous spell with my story, suddenly the girls interrupted to torment Avery about his girlfriend.

"My girlfriend?" Avery shook his head and started telling stories about how *somebody* he knew had a boyfriend with really big hair and big feet.

Yep, we were rocking the boat, going forward with the wedding, changing up the old status quo so that we could grow. And we were all going to be just fine.

13

A STRATEGY FOR CHANGE STARTS WITH THE BELIEF THAT YOU CAN WIN

Leadership is one of those character traits often revealed on the basketball court—as in certain other settings—and is one that Dad and I used to marvel at. It comes in many forms. Sometimes it's the quiet, unassuming fellow you never expect who loves to play on the inside and takes the ball to the basket at every opportunity. Sometimes it's that superstar who dazzles you with a certain something, beside whom all other mere mortals fade. A leader—as far as Fraser Robinson and I defined the issue between us—is someone who constantly seeks to raise their own game and who makes everyone around them a better player. They believe in themselves and their teammates and are able to infuse everyone with a sense of confidence that is required for winning at anything.

At Northwestern, I was fortunate to watch and help contribute to the task set out for head coach Bill Carmody—which was to transform a team that had stopped believing it could win. He was able to turn that around, thanks to his coaching leadership and because of his ability to cultivate leaders among his staff and among the players.

When Bill had assured me that if we did well at Northwestern there would be head coaching opportunities for me in the future, I had to believe that he was right. But then, in April 2006, while Kelly and I were in the midst of planning for our wedding on June 17, word got around that Brown University was looking for a new head coach. Not good timing. When Kelly and I talked about it, I admitted that I needed another major life change like a hole in the head. But, then again, I'd been an assistant now for five years, I wasn't getting any younger, and an opportunity like Brown didn't come along every day.

My attitude was that I might as well throw my name into the hat even for the practice of it. Actually, I might have a shot, I figured. My experience as an assistant was at a Big Ten school that, like Brown, had high academic standards. As it so happened, Brown had a basketball program that was in the basement—same as Northwestern when I arrived. On top of that, I had played in the Ivy League, knew the history and the nuances of the teams we'd be up against, and could have an edge in recruitment. Not that Brown was a plum job. This would be a turnaround assignment, taking a program from nowhere to somewhere—and without the ability to offer athletic scholarships. How many applicants would really be up to the job?

As it turned out, about seventy-five coaches applied. After the Brown hiring committee pared that list down to twenty applicants, I was still in the mix. Then they selected the top five candidates to interview and I made that cut too. My competition included an assistant currently at Brown, another assistant coach, and two lower-division head coaches. Of these, the leading contender, as I saw it, was the head coach

at Williams—with a team makeup very similar to Brown's—
and who had just taken his team to a Division III National
Championship.

But while that was the guy they might have been leaning
toward, I was out to change their mind. Unlike my tryout for
the NBA, when I played correctly but erred on the side of
unselfishness, this time I came to win and brought my full
arsenal—laying out my strategy for what a Brown turnaround
would look like, how we would take Penn and Princeton and
the rest of the Ivy League. Probably the most compelling argument I made was that, for recruiting, when you put me in
the living room of high school players and their parents, I am
Exhibit A for what Ivy League athletics are all about.

When I left the interview, as I told Kelly immediately
afterward by phone, I felt pretty darn good about it. Whatever
happened, I knew that I'd left it all on the floor and didn't
hold back. What more could I do? During the wait-and-see
period, we were kept busy with preparations for the wedding,
and my duties at Northwestern. Then, on June 12, five days
before the wedding, Brown offered me the job.

After a heart-to-heart with Avery and Leslie, who understood they would be splitting up their time between Providence, Rhode Island, and Chicago, but also understood that
this was what we'd been working toward—a head coaching
job!—I accepted the offer. That was on Monday. On Wednesday, I flew to Providence for a press conference, then flew
back for our rehearsal dinner on Thursday, and on Saturday—
stood there at the altar, early of course, watching Kelly, the
most beautiful bride in the world, walk down the aisle before
becoming my lawfully wedded wife.

The ceremony and reception were held at the Hotel Al-
legro in Chicago, an unforgettable celebration that Kelly had
planned and overseen mostly on her own—with that gift of
hers for pulling off major undertakings and making it look

effortless. My job, and it was not easy, was to contain the monumental happiness that I felt and to keep from doing victory laps around the hotel.

On the romantic relationship front, I had almost decided that the game wasn't for me; but life had given me a chance to turn that around—to start again in a new season that promised so much love and joy, it was evident to everyone who had come to share the day with us.

The bridal party included one of Kelly's dear friends as maid of honor, along with Leslie Robinson as a bridesmaid and Avery Robinson as best man. Malia Obama was a junior bridesmaid, together with Kelly's nieces, who were also junior bridesmaids. Kelly's nephew was the ring bearer and Sasha Obama was the flower girl.

Before the ceremony, Miche and Kelly carefully coached Sasha—who tends to have a mind of her own—so that she could go along with the traditional flower-girl concept.

Kelly explained, "You just drop the petals through your fingers, not too many at a time."

"I know, I know!" Sasha insisted.

Michelle demonstrated with her hands, saying, "See, just scatter them here and there."

"I know!" Sasha repeated.

When her big moment arrived in the ceremony, she stepped onto the aisle and to everyone's consternation began to drop one petal at a time, clearly with thoughtful strategy and purpose—as though she was thinking, "This flower petal should go here, and that flower petal will go there." The process seemed to take forever, with Malia trying to send her little sister signals to speed it up and everyone in attendance cracking up with rising swells of laughter. Sasha, of course, had no idea what was so funny.

We had chosen a minister we knew from Little League baseball—the sport Kelly and I were now coaching together.

Kelly had played college softball and was a natural as a coach. We were fortunate to have a minister who knew us well and knew how we felt about the importance of family and sports, and in the service emphasized the need for teamwork in our new life together—a theme that resonated with everyone. Then at the end, as a surprise right before he pronounced us man and wife, he took out a Brown University baseball cap and put it on his head.

Even Avery got a kick out of that. Going in, I had known that this wasn't going to be easy for my kids. We reassured them that whatever mixed feelings they might be having were normal. Even as they were growing closer to Kelly, they had two parents, and this celebration involved only one of them. Leslie was excited to be part of the festivities and allowed herself to be swept up in the fun the other girls were having too. But Avery not so much.

He wore a solemn expression for most of the day. Later, we would point this out to him and he would say, "Oh, no, I was happy." In looking through the wedding album, we would show him his glum expressions picture after picture, with Avery saying every now and then, "I think I was smiling hee-err." In a short time after the wedding, when he and Leslie would bond with Kelly more closely than most stepparents with their kids, we would all laugh about his solemnity when we got married. We have promised him that we will definitely smile at his wedding, a remark that always gets him to say, "Ooooh, I feel so bad."

We had decided that instead of putting pressure on Ave to give the best-man toast at the reception, those honors would go to Michelle Robinson Obama. My sister graciously agreed not only to give the traditional humorous roast of the groom but also to include a tribute to Dad—as the next day was Father's Day. This was no simple feat of oratory. She went from a very animated description of how the girls used to chase me home from school, to the Honest John ice cream story—both of which had our families and friends laughing their heads off—and segued to a more serious tone when she spoke about how happy she knew Dad would have been on this occasion.

When it came to describing Fraser Robinson to those who had never met him, Miche came prepared with notes so as not to forget anything. I knew she was holding back the tears but before long I could hear her becoming choked up, so Barack rose from his seat and went to stand next to her. Dad wasn't alive when he and Michelle were married, either, and I knew how much the loss hurt Barack too. With the residual pain of not having had his own father as a presence in his life, my brother-in-law had an immediate and special connection to Dad—short-lived though it was before my father's untimely death. Three years later he had lost his mother, Ann, to ovarian cancer.

Stoic though Barack can be, as he stood next to Michelle with her tears really starting to fall, he, too, began to wipe his eyes, and then, to give them strength, I went to stand on the other side of my sister—but I was more emotional than the two of them. And by the time Michelle was done, everybody in the place was crying like a baby.

As sad as it was that Dad couldn't be there with us, alive and in person, I felt his spirit right there with me, more strongly than ever. I could almost hear him bragging to the guests about how proud he was of his son and daughter, his grandchildren, his son-in-law and his new daughter-in-law.

To say that everything kicked into even higher overdrive from that point on would be an understatement. Who could have predicted that not many months later, in the fall of 2006, Barack and I would be sitting down to talk in their kitchen and he would ask for the kind of counsel that I had watched Fraser Robinson give to others who really needed someone whose judgment they could trust.

Of course, he didn't just come right out and say he was thinking about running for president of the United States and what did I think and could I convince my sister and mother that it was a good idea. Before we even got to that discussion, he was genuinely interested in how the head coaching job was unfolding at Brown. From the moment that I had decided to leave the business world and go into coaching, Michelle was my number-one cheerleader—with Barack a close second. As I'd come to know over the years, Barack never tired of hearing anything having to do with basketball. It wasn't just that he loved joining in on a pickup game whenever he could fit it in, given his increasingly busy schedule. He flat-out loved the game and everything about it—both as a metaphor for character, in the terms that Dad and I used to study the game, and as something that meant even more. As I understood the story, the only Christmas present his father ever gave him was a basketball—setting up a connection to the game that was, in essence, a connection to his father. So whenever he could entice me to talk about what was happening with my team, he hung on every word and I was eager to hear his strategic input—which was (and is) always brilliant.

When I arrived at Brown, it was obvious that many of my players were going though something not so different from what children of divorce sometimes experience. The previous Brown coach who had recruited them had left for Penn—a rival school—and some were feeling either confused, abandoned, or a little of both. For some it was a bruising experience of "Oh, so we didn't measure up." For others, it was a relief to have new leadership, but they were still feeling me out. Obviously, there were issues that Kelly and I were figuring out with my kids, too, as the feeling-out process continued at our new Providence home.

With the team, my focus began with fundamentals—but with new rules that required a much higher level of discipline that I tried to instill with humor, positive reinforcement, and lots of repetition. Trying to balance toughness with fairness, I sought to create an atmosphere in which everyone could thrive and shed some of the baggage of what hadn't been working before. With renewed enthusiasm and self-esteem, we could then move into the Craig Robinson–augmented version of the Princeton offense. Again, it was cultivating a mind-set in which every possession connects directly to scoring.

But as I explained to Barack that fall, right before the official start of our season, the bigger challenge had been to move out of a culture of losing. At that point a coach becomes part therapist, in helping players who have been beaten down by failure to believe in themselves again. After all, as he and I agreed, no matter what your goals, whether on the court or in a political campaign or on a personal basis, any strategy for change must start with the belief that you can win.

"What else?" Barack asked.

"Well," I said, talking about a few of the tough matchups I was anticipating in the coming season, among them some serious rivals like Providence College, "the key will be whether we can force them to play our game. With our outside shooting, they'll be forced to play zone, and we'll win. If we play their game, they're much more athletic than we are, and we'll lose."

And it was at that point, on that note, that he brought up the big subject on his mind. Besides my immediate "Wow" when I heard about the growing interest in his running, and my feeling that sometimes you have to take the shot when there is a window of opportunity, I knew his character. I believed deeply, with all my being, that he would be an inspired leader who could do great things for our country, especially at a time when it seemed we had gone so far adrift from our nation's core character.

Every time I've been interviewed about what turned out

to be a prophetic conversation in the kitchen back in the fall of 2006, the question invariably comes up about whether I knew for sure he was going to win—as if there was a specter of destiny about Barack. And the answer is no. As he and his campaign would repeatedly say—it was completely unlikely, the longest of long shots. Not only that, but as in any contest, you never know what will happen at the end until it really is the end. That said, you can always increase your chances by being the architect of a game plan for winning that can adapt easily to changing circumstances. That's one of the principles of the Princeton offense, as it so happens.

Did I have any glimmer before this conversation that Barack might go for it one day? The answer is maybe. After the attention that his speech at the 2004 Democratic Convention received and following the impact he already had been having after being in the Senate for two years, I knew the buzz had been out there. But what I didn't know was that the opportunity would come so soon.

When Barack asked if I minded talking to Michelle about how this window of opportunity might not ever be available again, I appreciated that he didn't expect me to convince her, since he himself hadn't been able to do that yet. When he added, "But let her know how you feel. She trusts you," how could I say no?

Not that I brought it up, but I sort of felt that after having put him through the test of character in a basketball pickup game years earlier, this was the least I could do. Besides, I was honored that he had come to me, just as he might have turned to Dad if he were here.

Still, for the next several days, spent traveling back to Providence and readying my team for our next game, I sweated bullets over how to approach not just Michelle but Mom— since Barack had already said he wouldn't move forward without both of them on board. If I brought it up too cavalierly, I could hear Miche saying that there was no way she was going to put the family and the girls through the ringer any more than they already had been. After setting aside a booming career in corporate law to spend more time as a mother—because that was the example set by our mom and because the window of opportunity for doing that was not always going to be open—Michelle had been devoting herself to public service and other organizations that allowed her, as a United States senator's wife, to still maintain a sense of normalcy for Malia and Sasha.

How was I ever going to convince her that the demands of a two-year campaign, not to mention what would happen if he won, could ever be anything akin to normal? Or, for that matter, how was I going to convince her that a black man with a funny name actually could win no matter how many hoops the family was put through?

The key to everything, I decided, was to appeal to the woman who had been a tireless advocate for justice and fairness throughout her life: Marian Robinson. Rather than do a song and dance, not Mom's style, I called her and let her air her concerns. They all came down to her feeling that you just couldn't do it without thinking first of the kids.

My counter was reminding Mom that I had almost stayed in a terrible marriage "thinking of the kids." My mother was the one who had wisely observed that kids thrive when their parents are happy. From there I went on to say how happy Barack was going to be if this was his dream and if he was taking his shot—and in fact the girls would grow and learn so much from watching their parents have the courage of their convictions. "Besides, Mom, you're the one who always tells us that kids are resilient. Avery and Leslie have been through a lot, but with teamwork and being relentless and a lot of love, they're going to be fine." The closer was simply, "We really can't penalize Barack for being good at what he does. What message does it send to the girls that he should limit himself? To not take it as far as he can?"

Mom was silent for a bit. Then she said, "Well, you'll never get Michelle to agree to it." Phew! In Marian Robinson terms, that counted as a victory.

My approach with Miche was to borrow from the same persuasion playbook that had worked with Mom—only better. I began by reminding her, "You were the one who persuaded me to quit investment banking." From there I recalled how she had emphasized that money isn't what was important and that what counted was to do what you're passionate about—in my case, coaching. Then I told her, "And you were right. Yes, it's harder, much harder, and it's taken me farther away from home and there are plenty of logistics to figure out, but I'm loving it, and loving life, and the kids are ultimately going to be happier for it."

Michelle sighed, letting me know—that's all well and good. The difference was, "You're not president of the United States."

"Well, maybe he won't win."

Silence. Could it be that I'd played on her competitive streak?

"Just let him take his shot," I said. "You can't deprive him of that. He wouldn't hold you back if the roles were reversed."

The real sticking point, and it was valid, was that Miche had a vision of her kids growing up like she and I grew up, ensconced in this loving and caring atmosphere, with a sense of privacy in a normal family.

I understood because it was something that Kelly and I talked about a lot. But as I said to Miche, "First of all, that's unrealistic because these are different times with different people. And second, Barack's not Fraser Robinson. Nobody's Fraser Robinson. Fraser Robinson's gone."

My sister is as tough as my mom and she, too, is a champion of justice and fairness, as well as an excellent legal mind—which means if you have a good argument, she'll give you a fair hearing. Which is what she did with me on that long but ultimately successful phone call.

And once Michelle said yes to Barack, she was his right arm, bringing a grounded, practical sensibility to the campaign and making it feel like one big extended family.

That's leadership. That's my sister.

14

PLAYING A NEW POSITION

As I like to remind my players when it comes time for on-the-court philosophy—since teaching really is the object of my game, after all—the most important races are usually marathons, not sprints. That may be confusing, because anyone who has played basketball at any level knows that it is a relentless game where speed and quickness coming down the lane can spell the difference between victory and defeat. But what I mean by marathon is in the metaphoric sense, when comparing one game to an entire season. Obviously, the more games you win, the greater the chances of ending the season with a record that gets you into the championships. So every game counts. But not all games are equal.

As I was explaining this concept one day in practice, a few weeks into our season, I noticed a blank expression on a player's face when I used the word *metaphoric*.

"Do you know that means?" I asked.

He didn't. Wow, this was the Ivy League and neither he

nor some of the other players knew what *metaphoric* meant. Suddenly, I was in the vocabulary business. And somewhere Grandpa Dandy was proud of the tradition he had created. When I told the guys, well, go look it up, I couldn't help the scowl that sprang to my face.

When Kelly found out about this, she did exactly what Mom would have done and, unbeknownst to me, conveniently left a dictionary in the locker room. In fact, back at Northwestern Bill Carmody had left both a dictionary and a thesaurus in the locker room. It caught on at Brown too. Before long, word spread that part of the Brown Bears men's basketball rebuilding magic involved improving the athletes' vocabularies.

As much as I didn't want to start celebrating until we'd finished the marathon of the season, in the early going the Brown Bears looked really good. Psychologically, that was essential because it set the tone and the tempo for everything else to come and gave us some breathing room for later on.

As I had told Barack when describing our game plan before the season started, my strategy was to maintain the discipline so that our competitors would be forced to play our game, not vice versa. The first time we proved that we could do that was indeed at Providence College—not only our crosstown rivals but a serious basketball school—and at their gym. The boost the win gave to our players' confidence was potent and it sent a message to the rest of our conference that we were not to be taken lightly. By the end of the season we would finish fifth in our league, after much lower predictions had been made. And we would sweep my alma mater, Princeton, for the season—only the second time this was ever achieved in Brown's history. It was validation that nothing I'd learned from my days under Coach Carril had been forgotten. Not an easy feat to top, we also held Dartmouth to 33 points, winning the game by 20 points. According to the history books, that was the first time in twenty-seven years that Brown had held a team to such a low score. Our overall 19-11 record for the 2006–2007 season would even earn me the honor of being named Ivy League Men's Basketball Coach of the Year.

But, of course, I was far from satisfied and knew we had a lot more work to do if we really were going to make the team the powerhouse I knew it could be. That's why, even when the season was just beginning, I became a recruiting maniac.

Meanwhile, almost two months after my conversation with the Robinson women about signing on to the idea of a presidential run, Michelle called to tell me that a conference call had been arranged between family members and some of Barack's advisors. She gave me the call-in number and said little else.

Kelly and I made the call together from home while Barack's sister Auma called from England, and his sister Maya called in from Hawaii. Miche and Barack were in Chicago with Mom, and also on the phone were campaign strategist David Axelrod and longtime friend Marty Nesbitt—both of whom were family by now.

"I wanted everyone to know it looks like this thing is going forward," Barack started in. "But before we go for sure, I feel obligated to let you guys know how considerably hard this is going to be on all of you, the people on the phone."

There was a very long pause. Conference calls are usually awkward anyway because everybody's always waiting for somebody else to say something. And in this case, everyone was genuinely struggling for something to say. How do you respond to a family member who says he's running for president?

Finally Auma broke the ice. "I think this is wonderful," she said.

As soon as she said that, everyone else chimed in with, "Yes, wonderful!" and "Congratulations!" and "Fantastic."

When Kelly and I hung up the phone, we exchanged amazed looks. As far as the family was concerned, this thing was really happening.

From the outset of the campaign, Miche and Barack knew they could count on us for everything and anything. We also knew that this was going to be a grueling marathon—and I'm not speaking in a metaphoric way either. Nonetheless, the positive energy that was generated on February 10, 2007—the kickoff day when Barack made his announcement on the steps of the state capitol in Springfield, Illinois—was electrifying. This was the same place where Abraham Lincoln had announced his candidacy. There was a feeling of history unfolding—and I wasn't even there to witness it in person!

Fortunately, Kelly and the kids flew back to Illinois to be a part of it, and to tell me all about it since the season wasn't over and I had a game to coach. The three of them came back telling me how huge and emotional the crowd had been—how diverse as well. Young and old, black and white, it was a gathering that looked like America!

As a political outsider, I didn't know what to conclude from these observations, only that it sounded great. Still, from what I was hearing, the front-runner, Hillary Clinton, was so far ahead of the pack, and already so incredibly well funded, that the groundswell of activity for Barack wasn't going to amount to much when it came time for the primaries.

But again, this was what I was seeing from a distance while catching snippets of the news between practices, games, and recruiting activities. That was until sometime in late February when I received an e-mail from a campaign staffer asking me if I could speak at an event sponsored by the Friends of Barack Obama in Providence.

When I called back, I joked that, though it was nice to be

considered influential, "no one wants to hear from a coach about politics."

"Actually," the staffer explained, "politics isn't the point. It's the human connection. You speaking from your heart about the candidate and his wife, your sister, and you talking about their character—that can be stronger than anything else anyone could say."

Thus began my new position and the new role that I would play in the campaign from then on. This, my first test as a campaigner, was at a downtown Providence loft filled with lawyers and contributors. Much to my surprise, it looked like having me on the invitations was a very good draw—partly because I was Barack's brother-in-law, and also because of my new, much-publicized role as the basketball coach at Brown, which was within walking distance of the fund-raiser.

The moment I entered the building and tried to make my way to the elevator, I was mobbed by people who wanted to talk, take pictures, and shake hands. Clearly there was a buzz growing. And though they were happy that the Bears were starting to win more than not, the excitement wasn't about me.

Within a few days, another request from the campaign came in that I do a Boston event. Again, I was happy to oblige. That was until I received a script. After taking one look at it, I called up and said, "I can't say this."

"No problem," was the official response.

So I threw away the highfalutin talking points and went with the feelings of a proud brother and brother-in-law, incorporating family stories and thoughts about character, and was an even bigger hit than before. Not only was it fun, but it was so gratifying to be able to meet people from different walks of life who were connecting to Barack and our family in a visceral way. Plus, I was inspired by the grassroots energy and the work, hours, money, and passion that people were investing into the campaign.

How could I not want to help more? The campaign kept me very busy. Wherever I went, I was introduced as someone whose authority came from being Michelle's big brother and Barack's brother-in-law. When there were questions about policy or what the Obama campaign's platform was on this issue or that, I only had to refer that person to the amazing interactive Web site that would harness energy with new technology in ways that no modern political campaign had ever mastered. But my role wasn't to sell the candidate, it was really to rally the troops to become part of the team and to work hard to be part of something that I was becoming increasingly convinced could be truly transformational.

Although I had no frame of reference for what I was seeing up close and personal—not exactly a fly on the wall, since I had something of a role to play—it became clear to me by mid-April of 2007 that the game plan developed by Barack with his closest strategists (David Axelrod and David Plouffe) hinged on changing the game of politics as usual. The Iowa caucus was eight and a half months away and they believed that if Barack could win that, it would be a game changer that could allow him to go all the way and win the nomination; conversely, if he lost, they expected he would probably have to drop out of the race. Along the lines of the Brown strategy for taking on Providence College at the beginning of the season, Barack and his strategists recognized that if he was forced to compete with six other candidates and play their game, he wouldn't have much of a chance. But if he could find the openings to play his game, and nail those outside shots, forcing the other candidates to get away from their strengths, that could give him an edge.

Easier said than done, without a doubt. Even before the first debate—scheduled for April 26, 2007, at South Carolina State University—the realities of campaigning began to set in. My sister called to check in, and from her report, it sounded like Barack's batteries were starting to run down. He missed his friends, she said, and the process was wearing him out. When I let her know my schedule was fairly flexible at that point and I'd be glad to help if possible, at her suggestion, I flew to D.C. to hang out with him. If there were concerns that this was anything more than the normal pregame anxieties making him feel weary, watching Barack during the debate prep certainly put my mind to rest. He wasn't just going through the motions or trying to master the art of the zinger. On the contrary, he was focused on his command of the issues, on grasping the complexities of a whole range of highly complicated, politically challenging problems of the day. Enthusiasm! I knew that he would be fine, and indeed, though pundits would later argue, polls conducted immediately after the first debate had him winning it over the other two frontrunners, Hillary Clinton and John Edwards.

After the debate prep, he and I and Marty Nesbitt, a Chicago-based entrepreneur, as well as the treasurer for the campaign, went out to dinner. The restaurant had blocked off the table for us where it was as private as restaurant dining can be, and the three of us had a nice meal like old times, talking about the kids, and family, and basketball. Keeping it real this way was just what the doctor ordered. Michelle knew that about her husband and was smart to keep friends and family close at every step of the game. Eventually these kinds of huddles with friends evolved into the Obama preprimary pickup basketball games that included many of the original guys who had been at the University of Chicago Lab School when I had first put Barack to the character test seventeen-some years earlier—including John Rogers and Arne Duncan. Marty Nesbitt and I were in the group as well, along with none other than Barack's nephew, Avery Robinson—who, at sixteen years old, could hold his own on the court with the best of them. And then some!

As the year unfolded and the other candidates began to ramp up their campaigns, Kelly and I were more and more drawn into what was happening and wanting to make a difference. Anything we could also do to give strength and family support in a personal way was important too. With everything starting to move at a blistering pace, it looked like we'd all catch a break in June when we went to New Hampshire to meet up with Michelle and Barack for a short RV tour in the White Mountains that would still be campaigning but in a slower, down-home friendly way.

When we first arrived and were still waiting for the rest of the entourage to fly in, Kelly and I and the kids had few options but to hang out in a small deli near the airport—and by *airport* I mean a very small private airstrip in the far northern part of the state.

The deli owner, chatting away, let us know he was a New Yorker who had moved out of the city to leave the rat race and open this small business in something he'd never tried before. By the way he was eyeing us, he appeared to be wondering who we were and what we were doing there, given the probability that there weren't too many black people up there in the White Mountains—as it were. The deli owner zeroed in on me and I could almost read his thoughts, as if he was thinking—"Looks like a basketball player, but kind of old. . . . so maybe he *was* a basketball player. . . ."

Finally, he ventured, "So, you waiting for a politician? Only politicians have been flying in here recently." The moment he asked, it clearly dawned on him that we were probably with the Obama campaign because the next thing out of his mouth was that the reason he wasn't going to vote for Barack was because he was too young. "Seems like a nice guy," he said. "I just don't think he has the necessary experience."

He had only moments earlier boasted about moving up here to the middle of nowhere to open this deli without ex-

perience. He'd never been in the restaurant or deli business
before, but he had eliminated a candidate for president because he hadn't been raised and groomed in the running-for-
president business.

So I thought that was worth pointing out. Then I went
on to talk about why character was more important than years
on the job. After all, I went on, no one really has the precise
experience required to be president unless he's already been
president—there's no other job like it. "That's why you have
to judge on the basis of ideas, values, and core character, leadership and judgment," I added. Then I wrapped it up with a
miniversion of what I'd been talking about in the campaign
events as to the amazing human beings that Barack and my
sister are.

He looked at me for a moment, and he said, "You know
what, I think you got my vote. Bring your brother-in-law by
here and I'll tell him."

A campaign staffer told me afterward, "That's what you
call retail politics."

And that's what the whole tour was like—a family affair
in the RV with all of our kids, Barack and Michelle, and stops
where we'd all pile out and meet up with staffers who tagged
along in cars. It was almost like a family vacation, only Uncle
Barack (as Avery and Leslie noted) had to step outside and give
a speech every now and then.

We all were warmly embraced everywhere—whether it
was when we stepped out to wave and shake hands with people, or enjoy ice cream cones at local creameries or hot dogs
at county fairs, or whether it was when we were leaving and
climbing back into the RV to drive to the next town. Often,
I'd joke with Kelly that it felt like we'd joined the circus. But
in fact it was a ground-level education in presidential campaigning.

Judging by the attention given to the onslaught of debates

between candidates in the Democratic Party that took place about once every three weeks, the level of scrutiny and interest in who would succeed George W. Bush was massive. But to make any kind of predictions would have been foolhardy because there were seven candidates, all energized, all qualified.

A few weeks before the Iowa caucus, I received an urgent request from one of the staffers, asking me, "Can you be in Des Moines on Friday night?" Neither Barack nor my sister could make it. Because the entire strategy hinged on an Iowa win—which was far from certain, in spite of the incredible ground operation the Obama campaign had developed early on—the folks at the Iowa campaign office felt that it would be attention-getting if I appeared at an event in Des Moines, said a few words about Barack, and then raffled off a lunch with Michelle.

We were eight games into our season—the team was then at 5-3, eventually to end up with an overall record of 19-9, ranked second in our league—so the timing was terrible. Explaining that I had a recruit coming in that day, and I had to take him out to dinner, then lead a practice on Saturday morning, I begged off.

Within the afternoon, Michelle called, asking me, "Isn't there any way you can do this? We really need you."

"Let me see what I can do."

After adding a practice early Friday morning and then shifting the Saturday practice to later that afternoon, I arranged for the recruit to have dinner with the guys and the assistant coaches and then flew to Des Moines, making it there without a lot of time to spare.

After something like forty campaign appearances by now, we had a well-established routine that included an e-mail giving me background and whatever else I needed to know—names, priorities, backstories, and subtexts. But this time, because I was trying to make this trip as fast as possible, I didn't take my computer bag. In fact, I was wearing the suit that I'd be appearing in; otherwise, all that I had with me was a pair of sweats in a duffel bag for the trip home.

A young campaign staffer met me at the airport, thanked me for coming, and began to run down the evening's itinerary and sequence of speakers. As he drove, he said, "You'll go on right after Bill Richardson and before Hillary Clinton."

I nearly fainted.

When he saw my reaction, he asked, "Oh, didn't you get the briefing?"

Of all the times not to have my laptop! This was way outside my comfort zone. Talking about two people I love dearly and telling stories about growing up in the Robinson household wasn't a problem. But speaking on equal footing with the other candidates was, as they say, above my pay grade.

However, the more I thought about it, the more I decided that if all of these Iowans could come out in the cold to support their candidate—all five thousand of them at a hall at the State Fairgrounds—I could rise to the occasion. Pumping myself up, I was all the more relieved when we arrived and Chris Dodd's wife was onstage filling in for him, talking about issues and policy positions. The waiters were serving the meal, the background noise was intense, and it seemed to me that absolutely no one was paying any attention. Phew! First of all, I wasn't the only person filling in for a candidate. And, more than that, I was in the clear, because no one would be listening to me, either, when I got up to speak.

After Mrs. Dodd, Governor Bill Richardson went to the podium to offer his remarks. Same story. The waiters were banging around and the people eating their steaks.

When Governor Richardson finished his remarks and the host introduced me, the applause was polite as I walked to the microphone. But instead of everyone returning to eat, when the clapping died down, I could hear the wind whistling through the trees outside. You could have heard a pin drop. The entire room was still, every eye glued on me.

This was when I knew something was up. Barack was the guy they wanted to know more about.

15

BE RELENTLESS: YOU HAVE TO WIN TO STAY ON THE COURT (REPRISE)

I f you were to ask five different people what is meant when a person is described as having "character," you probably would hear five very different offhand descriptions. Therefore, it would be well worth the time to do what Fraser Robinson II, aka Dandy, would have instructed us (with a scowl), and that is to go look it up.

Here is what Merriam-Webster's online dictionary says:

char·ac·ter \kár-ik-tər\ *noun*

1. one of the attributes or features that make up and distinguish the individual
2. the detectable expression of the action of a gene or group of genes
3. the complex of mental and ethical traits marking and often individualizing a person, group, or nation

Generic as that definition is, you might be curious to know the etymology of the word. It comes from the Middle English *caracter* ("a distinctive mark, imprint on the soul"), from Old French *caractère,* from Greek and Latin roots meaning "to inscribe," and from *kharax, kharak,* "pointed stick."

While I like the idea that character is a mark of who you are that is imprinted on the soul, this wouldn't be how I'd describe it in the user-friendly language that I'd want to use in discussions about basketball and life—especially when the audience is made up of college-aged athletes. Now, this is where a much-thumbed-through copy of *Roget's Thesaurus* might come in handy, where synonyms for character include words and phrases such as *nature, quality, temperament, moral fiber, personality, disposition, spirit,* and *makeup.*

Clearly, the art of defining character is not an exact science. For that reason, it would not be in my nature to try to define it for someone else. What works better for me—if I'm trying, for example, to develop team spirit or an overall temperament that would help players weather the ups and downs of any highly competitive season—is the power of demonstration. As a coach, I would want to borrow from my father's attitude of "Not too high, not too low" when reacting to wins and losses, and from my mother's version of "Let's all just take a deep breath"—i.e., when you're mad, no matter how mad you are, first count to ten.

This isn't to make a case for getting rid of passion and fire, no matter what your game. But as those of us who came up playing street pickup basketball know, you never want to let anger, ego, jealousy, or fear rule your actions in the game—because they cloud judgment. Plus, if you lose your temper and a fight ensues, playing stops and nobody wants that, and—you lose, period. So keeping your cool, in street games, is most definitely part of character.

From a coaching standpoint, though I reserved the right

to make exceptions, my players knew early on at Brown that I encouraged good judgment and even-keel temperament as traits that would come in handy in basketball, in the classroom, and in life. My feeling has long been that only a tiny fraction of my players will go on to the NBA—the reality being what it is—so the working principle is that what they learn on the court in practice and in competition should find applications in other areas.

And that effort can be truly gratifying. By the middle of Brown's 2007–2008 season, I remember watching a practice one icy Rhode Island early morning and being humbled at the trust that the players had invested in me as their coach. During the previous season, I had asked them to change—to give up the culture of losing and to start believing in themselves again. That they had done unconditionally. With a terrific work ethic, plus a willingness to play more unselfishly while pounding the fundamentals, they had come from behind to impress the naysayers.

Common sense dictated that it was all up from there. But now came a rude awakening. All of a sudden, we were on our way to being the team to beat. We had to start by keeping our cool and not getting thrown, now that we were being taken seriously. Next, we had to manage expectations—our own and everyone else's. Plus, it wasn't like we could just stick with the same game plan that had worked the year before. We had gained new players and had lost some previous players. It was a new season, a new ball game. There was no resting on laurels or coasting on momentum. If we were going to improve upon the previous season, we had to stay relentless, never forgetting that you have to win to stay on the court, and try to maintain a winning temperament.

This was obviously analogous to what was happening by the end of our season with the Democratic primaries, as the field narrowed considerably after Barack won Iowa and South

Carolina and Hillary Clinton won New Hampshire. Though the primaries would drag on and the nomination wouldn't be settled for months, by early March Barack was the electoral front-runner. As stadiums filled to unprecedented numbers in greeting him on the campaign trail, the phrase *managing expectations* took on new meanings. Just like on the court, you have to be relentless whether you are coming from behind or protecting your lead.

But the blistering pace of campaigning made doing that all the more daunting. Barack was giving three or four speeches a day, hitting three or four different states, seven days a week. Meanwhile, the decidedly negative tone in rhetoric really began to escalate once he was the front-runner. After certain media efforts to dig up dirt proved fruitless, suddenly there were out-and-out lies being reported as fact—in absurd stories about where he went to school in Indonesia, and how he was somehow both a Muslim and a devoted follower of a radical Christian preacher.

That apparently being the nature of the game, it seemed to me that if this was just the primary and it was going into double and triple overtime—with the elbows starting to fly—there came a point when you have to say, "All right . . . time to start hitting back."

With that thought, I called to talk to campaign manager David Plouffe, urging him to have Barack get mad already with something along the lines of "Listen, that's enough. No more Mr. Nice Guy."

"Calm down, Craig," David said, very calmly.

Calm down? This was my family getting trashed. They were personally going after the character of my brother-in-law and my sister. Even as a coach, I knew there were exceptions when you have to step in and say—"Fine, you want to fight? Let's go."

David Plouffe explained why that would reveal the wrong

temperament. "Craig," he said, "you just have to stay at thirty thousand feet. You can't get down into the gutter with them. Otherwise, you can get dragged into playing the other guys' game and you don't want to do that."

Oh, the irony. That was the same principle I used as a coach! David was feeding me back my own lines! Once I settled down, I could laugh at myself.

Indeed, Barack, Michelle, and all of the Obama for President staff would stay up above the fray and not get into the mud-slinging. In the general election, that quality of character—keeping your cool and having the right temperament—would help win the day. Barack's natural ability to remain calm and focused on the problem at hand—"No Drama Obama"—thus made him the leader that America needed at a time of grave uncertainties. It's one of his attributes that continues to amaze me, and I know him pretty well.

While staying above it all, however, they couldn't let up for a second and had to be careful not to get ahead of themselves, even with the momentum building for Barack to claim the nomination. If I hadn't been so invested emotionally in the outcome as a member of the family, I might have better appreciated the fascinating lessons in modern politics that played out for rest of the primary season.

And in the meantime, with Brown's season wrapped up, I, too, couldn't let up, knowing I needed to focus on recruiting and other strategies for going even farther. And that was saying a lot, after ending the year on such a high. From February 2, when Brown beat Columbia, we went on a streak of wins, taking Dartmouth, Penn, Princeton, then Columbia again, before losing to Cornell—and after that we were unstoppable, beating Princeton again, Penn again, Harvard, then Dartmouth again until the season ended on March 8. Nine out of the ten last games to end the season was exactly what I'd been talking to the guys about all year. Relentless!

On top of the world, we were invited to play in the post-season College Basketball Invitational tournament, where we faced Ohio University in the first round. After they had gotten off to a big lead, by the middle of the second half we had caught up to them and I saw a real chance for us to win the game. With the clock working in our favor, we did everything right. We made them play our game, forcing them to take bad shots and even, toward the end of the game, to run the shot clock down—resulting in their shooting an air ball, not once but twice. Our win felt so inevitable, we didn't plan for them to come back right before the last seconds were up and regain their footing and their ability to make their shots. They beat us 80–74.

The loss really choked me up. The disappointment felt was more acute than with most losses, as, for one thing, this was the end of the season, and we could have gone further in the tournament, I was sure. But as losses often are, it was also an incentive to put the pedal down on recruitment and get the Brown Bears ready to come back in top form the following year.

As I was about to learn, the team's turnaround over the past two seasons had begun to put me on the map too—with a flurry of interest in my coaching skills on the part of a couple of prominent athletic departments. According to rumors that I asked my agent, Rick Giles, to check out, one of the potential suitors was Providence College. Rick confirmed that, in fact, they were hiring a new head coach and I was on their radar. Was this flattering? Sure. Besides their strong basketball tradition, they were well-funded, and if I was going to consider it, they would have to lure me away with a higher salary. And if I was going to go anywhere, that would be the kind of move that made sense because it wouldn't involve having to pick up and go to another city and state.

Then again, I really didn't want to go anywhere. After all,

I'm the guy who doesn't like to rock the boat. And more important, I had a vision to do for Brown what Pete Carril had done at Princeton. It occurred to me, in thinking about how to respond to these potential job offers, that if money was an incentive for leaving, all I really cared about was being able to afford to send two kids to college. So, as a preemptive move, rather than have to leave or ask for a raise, I decided to see if they would work out an arrangement that if my son and daughter qualified academically for Brown, their tuition would be waived. They would obviously have to be accepted on their own merits. The answer, unfortunately, was no. The precedent, they felt, would be troublesome down the road. But the precedent for me was the priority my parents had placed on our receiving the education of our dreams.

At that point, somewhat reluctantly, trying not to let emotion cloud my judgment either way, I knew that it was time to see what the offers from others were going to entail. As Kelly reminded me, coming off two turnaround seasons at Brown was exactly when I should be testing the waters to see what was out there.

Kelly is magic—a coach in her own right but also capable of giving counsel to another coach who happens to be her husband. Kelly has an amazing level of self-confidence that she knows how to infuse in others. By the time she finished up her pep talk, I was ready to go try for the Kentucky job!

It takes a very special person with an even-keel temperament to jump into a ready-made situation like the one Kelly faced in the early going with the kids, and then be relentless enough to make it work. And this was at the point where politics was starting to make our private lives very public. Leslie and Avery were now consulting her about the routine, practical things, not me. Sometimes she would say, "Let's run this by your dad," and we would always confer, but as the trust developed, she became the one often in closest communication with them. Kelly was equally relentless in creating opportunities for the kids to see their mom and have a healthy relationship with her. She has also been very careful to describe herself as the kids' stepmother, but they started not minding it at all whenever someone said, for example, "Leslie, your mom's here."

From the start of our marriage, Kelly thought of Leslie and Avery as her children too—not biologically, of course, but in the sense that she would nurture them and be my partner in helping to raise them. Slowly but surely we had developed as a family unit even as the kids continued to have a loving relationship with their mom. Even when the final legal decision awarded me permanent custody, Avery and Leslie would be the first to say that they now have three parents who love and care for them.

Once Kelly and I had talked it out, as timing would have it, the annual coaches' meeting at the Final Four was coming up in San Antonio, so Rick Giles was able to set up meetings for me with both Providence College and representatives from Rice University in Houston, Texas, a Conference USA school that was hiring.

So with two promising meetings, I took off for the Final Four, hoping for the best. While making the rounds and keeping my ear to the ground for any other opportunities, I answered a call from Rick saying that Rice wasn't happening but he had begged the folks from Oregon State University to give me five minutes and they had agreed to thirty.

"Great," I said, flashing on the game at OSU with that sea of orange and black when I'd played there with Princeton as a senior.

Rick brought me up to date on the situation there. The men's basketball program was so bad (a record of 0 and 18 in league play for the previous year) that OSU had fired their coach midseason and had brought in an outside search firm to find the replacement. Though I was on that list, OSU blew right past me and offered it to at least four other coaches—each of whom, one after the other, turned it down. Now they were really behind the eight ball but had a new list of contenders whom they were scheduled to be meeting.

Did it bother me to be an afterthought? Absolutely not. In thirty minutes, I didn't know how I was going to dazzle them. But after all my public speaking experience, I wasn't too worried.

Sure enough, once I sat down with the athletic director and the associate athletic director, I drew from a wealth of knowledge about their program that I happened to know—and started talking about Oregon State University Men's Basketball and what a storybook history they had—and by the time we were done, two hours had gone by. Interestingly enough, it wasn't necessary to sell them on me; I was selling them on them and what this once-mighty Pac-10 conference school could be and should be.

My potential future boss, Athletic Director Bob De Carolis, said something to the effect of "Well, we know what you've done at Brown and how you played at Princeton, but the Ivy League is not an elite high-major conference."

It was reminiscent of people who said that Barack Obama might be a good senator but couldn't be president. I didn't buy it.

"Actually," I said, "I think that a coach who has come from the Ivy League will be at an advantage going to a bigger program." Then I explained that unlike the better-funded athletic departments that can give scholarships and other perks, and where coaching is less important than the star players, it's in the Ivy League where coaching really matters. You're more limited because you're recruiting without scholarships and because you have to find players who qualify academically. "Now combine those coaching skills with a program that makes recruiting more competitive. That can be a great combination."

Whether they agreed or not, I left feeling that having grown up in the Marian Robinson school of being yourself was something else to be grateful for.

Not only that, but the next day, my interview with Providence went very well and as soon as I got back to my room, the folks from OSU called to check in and get a read on how I was leaning.

"Well, I met with Providence," I said, and acknowledged that things looked promising there. Since I was supposed to hear from them later in the day, maybe with an offer, I didn't want OSU to be kept hanging but didn't want to have them lose interest if the Providence job wasn't happening. Time passed with no word, and then late in the afternoon Providence called back to say they needed another day.

Obviously, something had changed. My agent investigated and discovered what was up. Providence had suddenly developed the notion that they were going to bring back Rick Pitino, the legendary coach, now at Louisville, who had taken three different teams to the NCAA finals, including Providence College's own team years later.

The next day rolled around, and as my frustration increased, I finally told my agent, "Let's work something out with OSU."

Just like that, I signed a deal memo with them and started planning a visit to Corvallis for the next day. The university wanted to fly Kelly out to meet me for the visit as well, but she said, "I'm coming no matter what. Let's fly the kids out instead. Let's let them take a look and see if they'd like living there." Which is what we did.

At the Portland, Oregon, airport, I met Leslie and Avery, and we drove down the hour-and-a-half trip to Corvallis, past cow pastures and green fields, along a winding road off the interstate into a woodsy, small college town full of a mix of old Victorian houses and newer homes. So far so good.

The clincher was when we got to campus and arrived at Gill Coliseum, then had a tour of where my office would be. Walking through the gym, I asked the kids what they thought.

Avery said, "I love it!"

Leslie wasn't sold. She did not want to move to Corvallis. But as we talked, she admitted that it had nothing to do with Corvallis. Leslie just didn't want to move. And as we talked some more, she started warming up to the adventure of it—and decided, why not, we could give it a try.

Things were going to get really crazy, not just with moving out here but with everything we were all doing as part of the presidential campaign. But how bad could it be if we were doing it as a family?

That basically settled it. Just as I was headed toward the athletic department's main office to sit down and officially accept the offer—and then step in front of the cameras to hold a press conference—my cell phone rang. Providence wanted to offer me the job—a major program with a tradition of winning, and without the obligation of relocating yet again, clear across the country, in this semirural area we knew nothing about.

Without taking a breath, I dialed Kelly's cell, told her the latest, and asked, "What should we do?"

Kelly calmly but adamantly said, "To hell with Providence." She went on to point out that they'd known me and seen my coaching for two years and still had to hem and haw and think about their dream candidate, Pitino. OSU had just met me, talked to me long and hard, and within two hours they were ready to offer me the job. Where was I going to get more enthusiastic support?

With that, I hung up, and graciously accepted my next

post as men's basketball head coach of the Oregon State University Beavers. Everything had happened so quickly, the press conference was almost surreal.

But afterward, as I took one last look at the gym decked out in orange banners that I would be calling home soon, I started to really get excited.

Turning to Avery and Leslie, I asked them, "Did I ever tell you that orange was my favorite color, even before I went to Princeton?"

"Yes, Dad," they both said, rolling their eyes.

And before I could continue, they both jumped in together, "Because orange is a very underused color."

Relentless.

PART IV

FULL-COURT PRESS

16

WHAT WOULD FRASER ROBINSON SAY?

Over the years since my dad hasn't been with us, my role as the person whom others seek out for advice and good counsel has developed naturally. I can remember that when Grandpa Southside was alive, everyone in the community gravitated toward him for his valued input. Increasingly as he got older, it was his son-in-law, my dad, who held that role. And then, that place of honor and responsibility fell to me. Often, I wasn't sure that I deserved it, but then I'd only remind myself of the rich reservoir of conversations about basketball and character and life that Dad had left me and from which I could draw. It was as simple as asking myself, "What would Fraser Robinson say?" and I usually had an answer that was helpful for whoever was asking—including me.

This was very much the case when I arrived in Corvallis to start as head coach. Preseason nerves are commonplace for most coaches, especially in situations like the one I inherited at OSU, when I got there in the spring of 2008. After meeting with the players, both as a team and individually, it felt as if I'd stumbled into a Dickens novel—with a bunch of lost boys as my charges who had been virtually abused and abandoned. They were much better players than their dismal record indicated, but they had fallen into bad habits and were left without the discipline, structure, and support that they needed to regain self-esteem.

What I imagined Fraser Robinson would have said was that, before I could even begin working on the tough-love part, what was urgently needed was to give them a new sense of belonging to a team—a big extended family. To a certain degree, we'd had to do that at Brown. But more of my players there had come from stable "three-car-garage" homes, as Pete Carril used to say about the prep school kids. At OSU, some of my guys had never been in the kind of household like the one on Euclid Avenue where I grew up, with both a Fraser and Marian Robinson co-coaching. So, for them, this was going to be a brand-new experience.

While Bill Carmody was much more personable with players, that had never been Coach Carril's style. In fact, the whole time I was at Princeton, I saw next to nothing of his life outside of basketball. He was married with children—that much I knew. But I never met his wife, and I only met his son after I graduated.

When I got into coaching, tearing down the wall between who I was as coach and as a person became a priority. Not that the players and I were going to be on equal footing as friends. But a coach should be human. So I was all for letting my players see me not just as a basketball expert—but also as a husband, a father, and a citizen. That means that Kelly comes to my workouts, running something of a good cop to my tough cop, frequently showing up with doughnuts and other surprises for them. My kids are very much in the picture as well. The league rules limit how many times we can have the players over for dinner, but holidays and special occasions and travel to games provide opportunities for creating the one-big-happy-family atmosphere.

Call me old-fashioned, but I think the world just works better when our lives are team-, family-, and community-centered, when we feel connected to one another and when we look at problems not as "these are your issues or my issues," but as "our issues."

That, by the way, is the conclusion that I think the majority of people in America had reached in the election year 2008. During the previous eight years, amid the disastrous mess the Bush-Cheney administration had left for their successor to clean up, Americans had grown more politically divided and disconnected from one another than they had been perhaps since the Civil War.

With the yearning for connection that I saw everywhere on the campaign trail, even though obviously I couldn't be unbiased, one thing was clear—America wanted to be a family again.

This had been my observation earlier in the year when we were still in Providence and Michelle came there to speak. A staffer had called ahead of time, asking if I wouldn't mind introducing her, and of course I was happy to do it. On this occasion there was no script, no time limit, just an opportunity to talk about my sister. Not wanting to cut into too much of her time, I also wanted to give Miche the wonderful acknowledgment that she had given me with her best-man speech when Kelly and I were married.

With that planned loosely in my thoughts, I wasn't prepared for the massive, standing-room-only turnout—about the entire Democratic population of the state of Rhode Island—crammed impossibly into a community college auditorium. Hey, I figured, we could still be family and I'd make my remarks as familiar and personal as I'd intended.

No sooner had I begun to talk about our tiny apartment and what it was like growing up with Marian and Fraser as our parents—and just how proud Dad would have been of his daughter and son-in-law—than I looked out into the crowd and saw people wiping their eyes, doubtless remembering their loved ones no longer alive, connecting to our story of a working-class family's life in the Southside of Chicago. The next thing I knew, Michelle's staff were all crying, Kelly was crying, and everybody was saying how they wished they had a brother-sister relationship like ours. Miche got really choked up.

The good news was that I had anticipated how emotional she might be, so the plan was to wind up my remarks with funny stuff—the teasing, the story of her teaching me to dance, all that. The bad news is that the best my funny stuff earned was some polite chuckles.

Yikes. When Michelle came up to the stage to speak, she embraced me with a warm hug—mainly a don't-leave-yet, let-me-get-myself-together hug. And the crowd was going crazy.

After she did get herself to speak, talking completely from her heart, the crowd went even crazier.

In the hand-shaking and picture-taking that followed, I was overwhelmed by the number of people who thanked me for reminding them of funny and touching things that had happened in their homes when they were growing up. And as I looked around and saw people connecting to one another, it really did feel like what it was becoming—a movement.

When Kelly and I went to say good-bye to Michelle, pushing through the crowds, she again thanked me profusely for giving her the intro.

"Anytime." I grinned.

Well, apparently, she took me at my word. Months after I'd made that comment, a request was issued from the planning committee for the Democratic National Convention that they wanted me to introduce her.

At first, I thought they meant that I'd introduce her to the delegates before the cameras turned on, something informal. No. Michelle was going to headline the opening night of the convention during primetime and they wanted me to come on first to introduce her.

"Wait." I laughed, certain that this was either a joke or a colossal mistake that would blow the election. "I'm a basketball coach."

Yes, the reply came back, that's what made me just right for the job.

"I'm honored, but you should get someone like Oprah."

There was nothing I could say to convince anyone that there was someone better than me for the job. They wanted a tighter version of the introduction I'd given in Providence. If I could give them notes, they'd sketch it out and put it on the teleprompter and it would be a piece of cake.

Cut to: Monday, August 25, 2008. Denver, Colorado. And there I am, onstage in the darkness at the Pepsi Center where the Democratic Convention is being held, right before the lights come up for my speech.

Earlier in the afternoon, when I was in one of the hotel suites practicing, Michelle had entered and interrupted, saying, "I have to come in here and listen to you practice so that I'll have heard it a million times when you go on and it won't make me cry."

I thought about that onstage in the darkness, hoping that her strategy worked. The main thing that we had to remember was that after this bruising, grueling, and protracted primary, the party was reuniting as a family—even with the reluctance of some fervent Clinton delegates, as well as delegates still loyal to other candidates.

Everything that Michelle said and did from the moment of her entrance would set the tone for the party unity that had to be on display during the rest of the week and that was needed to effect the transition to the general election. All of a sudden, after standing in awe of her all this time, the worrier and protective big brother in me decided that this wasn't fair and it was too much to ask of anyone.

But then I thought of Mom and could just hear her say, "Stop worrying!" And I thought of Dad, wondering what Fraser Robinson would have said if he had lived to see this day. The thought made me smile, just imagining how he would have been so out of his mind with the thrill and pride of seeing his daughter and son-in-law arrive at this place, at this time in history, that the excitement would have probably killed him!

With that, the lights came up and it was like being in a much bigger living room, but right at home. Directly in my sightlines was the Oregon delegation, which began to chant my name, "Robinson! Robinson!" Delegates were calling out, "That's our coach! That's Michelle's brother!"

It didn't go ignored that I had worn the black suit with the orange tie that Kelly and the kids had picked out.

"Good evening," I began, "I'm Craig Robinson and Michelle Obama is my little sister." The delegates roared. I could have just said that I was Superman and they wouldn't have applauded so much.

Wow. Then I proceeded to explain that I wasn't just going to introduce my sister, rather, "I want to introduce *you* to my sister—the girl I grew up with, the poised young woman I saw her grow into, the compassionate mother, aunt, and sister-in-law she is, the passionate voice for women and children she has become, *and* the type of First Lady she will be."

I wove in a few stories about growing up in our home, about Christmas mornings when Miche had to wake me up so that we could open our presents together, and how she played the piano to calm my nerves before basketball games. Right at that point, a cheer went up from the Oregon delegation and I couldn't help interjecting an ad-libbed "Go Beavers!" The audience loved the spontaneity and applauded wildly.

And then the speech turned to character and family, as I continued, "When I really think back, I can also see how the person she is today was formed in the experiences we shared growing up: working hard, studying hard, having parents who wanted more for us than what they had. And always being reminded that in this country, of all countries, those things were possible."

What came next was a quiet that washed over the audience when I talked about how neither of our parents had gone to college and about the sacrifices they made for us:

... We lost my father in 1991. And I know he's looking down on us tonight, so proud of his daughter, not because of who she married, though he was a big fan of Barack—but because of the hardworking, brilliant woman she is, what she's accomplished in her own right, the mother she's become, and the values she's instilled in her daughters.

My mother, Marian, is here tonight. She remains our family's anchor, and the sole reason Michelle was willing to campaign at all was because she knows that Mom is there to help take care of the girls.

When we were young kids, our parents divided the bedroom we shared so we could each have our own room. Many nights we would talk when we were supposed to be sleeping. My sister always talked about who was getting picked on at school, or who was having a tough time at home. I didn't realize it then—but I realize it now—those were the people she was going to dedicate her life to: the people who were struggling with life's challenges. . . .

After then detailing some of Miche's public service record and how she and Barack met, as well as the story of the basketball test of character, I reached the conclusion by describing, from my heart, how Barack and Michelle had strengthened each other and created a home together, filled with love and grounded in faith.

And only at the end, right before I brought my sister on, who was so extraordinary that she was the proverbial game-changer, did I start to get choked up. As I said the last words, I knew that Dad would have allowed himself to be emotional, too, simply because they were and are so true:

During challenging times I've watched Michelle and Barack stand by each other. And I know, they'll stand by you—the American people—now and in the future.

17

HARNESSING ENERGY, SEIZING MOMENTUM

Even though Mom never professed to be an expert in matters related to sports, it is to her credit that I have come to appreciate what may be one of the most important, yet much overlooked, aspects of character needed for winning on the basketball court and in every other arena.

Wonder what that might be? If so, you already have it! It's called "curiosity." Marian Robinson not only valued it in a way that motivated us to want to learn but managed to design her own homemade curriculum for cultivating this golden commodity. She did it partly, of course, with the energy of relentless parenting; she was always there to listen to us and pay attention to our questions, subtly encouraging them and feeding us enough tasty morsels of knowledge to create a hunger for more. It was no easy job to cultivate inquisitiveness and a desire to investigate or explore new ideas and subjects of interest to others, to egg us on in our search beyond the boundaries of what we had already learned. What made Mom such a wiz at it was that she was and is a genuinely curious person who was always challenging herself to grow and learn, constantly investigating ways to be a more effective mother, grandmother, teacher, and human being. Indeed, no matter at what stage of her life, she has never stopped looking for ways to expand her own horizons, to help her family, and to continue to whet our curiosity in the process.

Now, there may have been a time when Mom had some ideas of retiring into a quiet life of catching up on a lot of reading, but that didn't last long.

In fact, when we were first getting settled in our home in Providence and Mom started to say how much trouble it was to fly, Avery took the initiative to call Grandma and ask when she was coming to visit. Next thing we knew, she had booked a flight. Then, of course, there was this thing called a presidential campaign, and just a few other things that followed to keep her even busier.

As for spotting the attribute of curiosity in a basketball player, it so happens to be one of the hallmarks of unselfishness on the court. On the flip side, Dad and I used to observe how lack of curiosity as to what others are doing on the court usually goes hand-in-hand with the selfish player who hogs the ball, argues with calls, or is too busy showboating to care to see that his teammate is open.

Interestingly enough, for those who are curious, if you look at the etymology of the word *curiosity* its Middle English root also means "*to care.*" The two really do go hand-in-hand, or so I believed in developing my strategy for how to begin the turnaround at OSU.

The operating principle was that if I demonstrated curiosity in my players, in how they were doing in their studies and in other aspects of their lives, the caring would be evident. Then I could implement a level of discipline that had been missing and we could start shedding some of the bad

habits. The challenge was not to do it in a punishing or boring way but within an innovative, even fun, structure that
managed to feed curiosity, engage their learning curve, and
motivate them to want to build the better habits. Fortunately,
the Fraser and Marian Robinson playbook was at the ready.

"Five thirty . . . ?" Lathen Wallace, the very talented, fearless but—at the time—sort of surly six-three guard asked incredulously when I announced to the team when practice
time was going to begin from then on. Lathen asked, "You
mean, five thirty P.M., right?"

From the Netherlands, Roeland Schaftenaar, our six-foot-
eleven center/forward, speaking in proper but accented English, corrected Lathen, saying, "Coach Robinson does mean
five thirty A.M."

"That's right, guys," I echoed. "See you in the morning." To
reboot their attitudes, I had to go for a little shock and awe.

Bewildered, the rest of the team exchanged is-he-kidding?
expressions, but as a sign of respect, everyone nodded in understanding. A few of them may have even been curious as
to how a major new regimen was going to dig us out of the
5-23 overall loser's pit of the season that had just finished up,
with zero wins and eighteen losses in the Pac-10 conference
games.

To combat the psychological hopelessness of how tough
it is to rebuild from there, you have to take drastic measures.
And they probably were desperate enough to accept that they
needed an overhaul approach.

Early practices—like the schedule I instituted upon my
arrival that spring at OSU and continued, with full-court-press
training, when school began in late summer—were what the
doctor ordered. Partly because these sessions exist in their own
time-and-space continuum, when the concerns of the day and
coursework and body fatigue haven't set in, once the guys got
used to the regimen, they seemed to develop by leaps and

bounds, both with fundamentals and also in starting to learn the principles of unselfish basketball, with the augmented version of the Princeton offense.

That next morning, I came up with a schedule for myself that I continue to maintain: a four fifteen A.M. alarm, followed by breakfast alone, before slipping out of the house while my wife and kids are still in bed.

For that first week or so, most of the players dragged in half-asleep at five twenty-five, so to give them a jolt, we launched right into running drills. Pretty soon, thanks to their curiosity as to what was going to advance them in the cause of improvement that they cared about, everyone got the message that five-thirty practice meant being on the court at least by five-ten for warming up, stretching, and shooting around. The deeper message was that as players, they were taking responsibility for their own preparation in order to be accountable, not just to their coach, me, but to the rest of the team.

These are some of the basics of unselfish basketball that are mental, not physical, when you begin to ask yourself, "How can I contribute, how can I assist, how can I learn?"

And, yes, from a discipline standpoint, I created tough guidelines. Everyone quickly understood the rules—that if anyone was late, or if there were reports that someone had skipped a class or otherwise screwed up, everybody faced the consequences. All of that has continued, because it was effective. If one player arrives late or is skipping class, practice is moved to five o'clock. If there's no turnaround in behavior and performance, practice moves to four thirty. Do I love having to arrive ahead of the players, opening up the gym and turning on the lights? Hardly. However—and this goes back to Johnnie Gage in my days traveling to play on the Westside at the Boys Club—when a coach shows up for the team, they show up for themselves on the court.

When I came home from practice one day not long before our preseason games got rolling in the fall of '08, I told Kelly, "They're getting it, I think. But sometimes, they look at me when I say something, and I'm not sure they know what I'm saying."

Just as at Brown, Kelly tried the old dictionary-and-thesaurus trick, nonchalantly leaving them in the locker room without saying anything. Before long, curiosity did its wonders and the guys were coming back to me with words they were discovering on their own.

Another strategy that proved useful was based on something that Kelly had developed when Avery and Leslie were younger and going through the toughest part of dealing with the aftermath of divorce. In that period they were taking their frustration out on one another and were sometimes hitting each other, so Kelly started fining them whenever she caught the instigator in the act. Then she gave them journals and created an incentive for them to do some writing. Kelly didn't ask that they let her read what they'd written. All they had to do was show her that a page had been filled, and she would refund the money that they'd been fined. From what I recall, Avery was so motivated, he wrote almost an entire book's worth.

Out of my own curiosity, I wondered how something along those lines might benefit the Oregon State Men's Basketball Beavers. When I announced to the players, "I want you guys to keep a journal," the range of expressions on their faces was pretty hilarious. Everything from *Say what?* to *What the . . . ?* to *Why not?*

Fortunately, having a business and sales background, I was able to sell the idea as a way to chronicle the incredible turnaround adventure we were embarking upon. It was all I could do to keep from using the phrase *Yes We Can,* but I knew that if the players kept a journal of their progress, and developed an awareness of the accomplishments and achievements they were making as a team, they would begin to believe in their ability to win. And that was everything. If we believed that we could make history and rise from the ashes as a team, confident that we would have a story to tell, what was wrong with that?

While this was great for boosting team spirit, we soon saw that being overly lofty or ambitious could be self-defeating if we didn't have more realistic goals and benchmarks. Based on some of the more ambitious goals the players were writing down, one of my assistants, Doug Stewart, suggested we come up with a business-modeled strategic plan. With coaching staff employing more curiosity, we did just that—after research and analysis of our upcoming schedule, the competition we'd be facing, and where we had opportunities and challenges. Instead of creating a goal to become national champions, which wasn't realistic, our objective for the 2008–2009 season was simply that we finish NOT in the bottom of the Pac-10.

So, how did we ultimately achieve a .500 record and, indeed, go on to make history, in what was to be declared one of the nation's best single-season turnarounds, with eighteen wins—marking the first time in eleven years that OSU had won that many games in a season? We did it with all hands on deck, with some audacity, yes, and with incredible character, caring, and commitment on the part of the players.

From start to finish, I had no way of knowing if we were doing what we all needed to do in order to harness the energy and seize the momentum of a very unique season. But in order to keep a careful gauge on what was working and what wasn't—and to keep everything out in the open, Honest John style—I instituted a weekly open evaluation with the players. Not everyone loved it, but it kept us all on the same page and removed the guesswork. Everybody knew now why Coach was making changes as to who was starting and who wasn't, The lines of communication were open.

At Princeton, Pete Carril had used a similar method of evaluating each player in front of the whole team, so everybody knew where we stood. Coach Carril did this on a daily basis but I've adapted the approach by keeping it to once or twice a week. That's enough. Yes, it's important to know the reason why you're getting squeezed to the bottom of the team, but on a daily basis you don't have time to improve. Over the period of a week, in open evaluation you can assess whether you're doing the right things to reverse the slide.

Just as it was with Coach Carril, Player 15 hears what I've got to say to Player 1, and vice versa. Sometimes it's fanning a few flames of competition, too, when, for example, you tell the Tarver brothers you want more hustle by saying, "Josh, you're not showing it to me. And, Seth, you are. So tonight, Seth, you're going to start."

And this kind of change should come as no surprise, because, with the ongoing evaluations, it's clear who's coming on strong and who's slipping, who's getting the praise, and who's getting the "You have to show me more."

Honest evaluation includes giving people not just what to work on, but also some specific instruction on how to gain the improvement they need. If they have their grades and academic assignments in order, and they want you to work with them up to the limit that the NCAA regulations will permit, then you gladly give them that time. You have to be like Marian Robinson, continually engaged and exploring different avenues for developing and helping. You have to be like Fraser Robinson, coming home from working a double shift and still going outside and playing with the kids. You have to care because it's what you do—what you're there for.

When did I know we were going to have the turnaround

that we had only dreamed might be possible? Not until the very end of the last postseason game, at the very end of the game. But I will say that at about the ninth game, when we went on a four-game winning streak, I saw a different kind of confidence in the OSU Beavers.

The question now arises, naturally, as to when I knew that my brother-in-law, Barack Obama, was going to win the election and become president of the United States. Here, too, it's important to say that there was no way I was going to predict what would happen on Election Day until the shot clock ran out and he or the other guy was declared the winner. However, by October 7, when the second debate between him and Senator John McCain took place at Belmont University in Nashville, Tennessee, I was starting to think along the lines of—*Wow, Barack could well win this.*

Four days earlier, when the vice-presidential debates between Joe Biden and Sarah Palin were broadcast, it seemed to me—among other reactions—that it showed a stark contrast between the kinds of judgment employed by the two heads of the ticket in their selection process for who they wanted as a running mate. And that comparison favored the Obama-Biden ticket considerably.

But then a week earlier, the real glaring comparison had come in the midst of the Wall Street collapse and the economic crisis that had Senator McCain first saying that the fundamentals of our economy were sound and then suddenly suspending his campaign because of the crisis. To me, that was the moment when the nation saw Barack tested at the highest level even before the election—and because of his composure and leadership, and his command of highly complicated concerns that needed thoughtful deliberation and probing investigation, he was no longer the young guy without experience but a candidate qualified to handle the highest office in the land.

Then, during the second debate, in the town hall setting, it seemed to me that the contrast was just as stark between one candidate who wasn't engaged and Barack, who showed great curiosity and caring in the way that he engaged with the audience members, listening intently to their questions, remembering names and details, connecting to their experiences. Knowing him as I do, I thought that night, especially, of his mother and grandparents, who had lovingly cultivated those capacities in him.

In the following weeks, as the clock ticked down to Election Day, with OSU's preseason games beginning, I kept a few balls in the air and managed to also crisscross the country, making recruiting stops wherever the campaign trail took me. Every now and then, I'd get a chance to jump into a pickup game with Barack and staffers, when we happened to be in the same state. But mostly I was interacting with state and local volunteers when I came in for events and was astonished at the sheer numbers of people who were pitching in, walking neighborhoods, making phone calls, throwing fund-raisers— with young kids showing up at phone banking centers, singles and families, young and old, well-to-do and struggling, every ethnicity and background, all hands on deck.

When I looked at the volunteer schedules and saw that people were planning to work up to the last minute on Election Day—calling voters and making sure they had gone to the polls—and that they weren't going to stop until they knew who had won, I was almost brought to tears. This was energy that had been harnessed and the momentum seized that could not just win elections but could move mountains, change the world, do anything we put our minds toward— just by asking how.

When, out of curiosity, I asked folks what had brought them to volunteer, I heard a few different answers. Some said that they had never worked on a campaign before and just wanted to get involved. Others said that they couldn't sit at home and NOT get involved because this was the most important election of their lives.

Without reservation or qualification, I felt the same way.

18

THE CHARACTER OF
A NATION

As much as I have scoured the various dictionaries and thesauruses that have been left for my own and others' perusal in various settings, I have not yet come across the exact word that sums up the essence of character—which I understand to be that quality of a player who squeezes every last drop of energy and ability out of himself or herself, then goes back and finds an extra reserve tank and gets some more, and leaves it all out on the court, never holding back, never having to regret that they didn't give their all when the game was on.

What is that word?

It is akin to *relentless,* but is something more—a word to describe the act of showing up and playing a game of full-court press not just in one particular area but with everything. The word should also encompass courage, purpose, and vision, qualities that lend themselves to a life attitude equivalent to what in basketball we call "court-sense," or the uncommon ability to see the whole game and all the moving parts at once.

Dad lived his life that way, day in and day out. Perhaps that was why, when he left us too young, the loss was not as painful as it might have been, because we knew that he'd lived his life so magnificently and completely, and touched everyone who came within his sphere while he was at it.

When the sun rose on November 4, 2008, it was time to conclude the full-court press played by the leaders on the Obama team, back and front office, including Barack and Michelle, Joe and Jill Biden, along with everyone in the inner circle who had been there from the start and those who had come on board later, everyone who had poured his or her heart and soul into the effort. They all had to know that the marathon had been run, the work for the election was done, and it was now time to leave the decision in the hands of the voters.

As I was thinking about the past two years that had transpired—everything that had happened from the time that Barack had first raised the possibility of his running for president, when he talked about the window of opportunity—what stood out for me were the admirable traits of all the candidates who had been his opponents, from Hillary Clinton to John McCain, and the others who had also left their all on the playing field in this contest. These were all individuals of character, so many of whom dedicate their lives to public service, which is what the quest for political office is or should be about.

What I also thought about was the character of a nation, the United States of America, and the strength and resiliency of our democracy that gives us the opportunity and the responsibility to participate in the electoral process—to choose our own leaders. Regardless of political differences, in my comings and goings over the course of this time, the chance to tag along with the campaign and travel the country let me be reminded of the basic goodness, courage, hopefulness, and decency of the American people.

These thoughts were percolating inside of me, in fact, on Monday, November 3, when Kelly, Avery, Leslie, and I flew out to Chicago from Oregon. Since I'd given the team Election Day off, we had moved practice to Sunday. Our season was beginning this same week and I had to trust that we were prepared.

Kelly and I had voted by mail, so we didn't have the experience of going to the polls, but we had the vicarious pleasure of being there when Michelle and Barack went out early to vote. Upon their return, the smiles on their faces were all we needed to know that the reception at their polling place had been incredibly gratifying. Then Michelle, keeping a light schedule, went to get her hair done and took Malia and Sasha with her.

The morning provided an opportunity for Avery and Leslie to go visit with their mom. After they returned, Ave and I headed off to a pickup game called for one P.M. How long ago had it been since Michelle had asked me to set up the first game to check out what kind of a guy Barack Obama was? A few lifetimes ago. Over the past year, it had become an Obama campaign tradition to play basketball whenever there was a primary or caucus, wherever Barack was that day. Instead of the usual ten to fifteen guys, however, on November 4, 2008, the BIG day, there were forty of us invited. Accordingly, instead of playing at the East Bank Club—where we regularly played—we gathered at a huge facility in Chicago that had a handful of NBA regulation courts.

It was surreal enough to be playing pickup basketball tournament-style with multiple games going on. Then add to that the really crazy part that no one addressed outright—the fact that we were playing hoops with the man who might be the next president of the United States! Nobody said as much, but I'm sure we were all trying to ascribe some significance to whose team was winning, who was making their shots, and who wasn't.

Actually, there were some moments when Avery noticed that I wasn't playing with all of my usual full-court-press intensity, almost cautiously.

Well, heck, what kind of brother-in-law would I be if Barack turned an ankle, pulled a muscle, or did anything to bang himself up in a way that might jeopardize this big day and the evening to follow? Barack, in contrast, played as hard as ever. You would have thought that this was hard-core street basketball and he had to win to stay on the court and keep on playing. No Drama Obama, he played as he always did, with calm, focus, curiosity, and—even though it was half-court— with a full-court press that was reminiscent of the nonstop, full-out effort of his campaign ever since he'd become a viable candidate.

Winning on the court that day was not my goal at all. I just wanted to experience the moment, to share it with my son, and imagine that this was a game that would be talked about for years, in barbershops, and in bars and gyms all over the country. No one would remember who played or what the score was, who hit what shots and who didn't. All that would be remembered was that on the day history was made, and the first black president of the United States was elected, before the outcome, he had played all-out in a game of pickup basketball with forty of his closest friends.

After heading back to Michelle and Barack's house, I found Leslie and her cousins playing some kind of board or card game, and Avery soon joined in. The plan was that we would have dinner and watch the results together, but once I had showered, I couldn't wait and turned on the television to try to get a sense of what was going on. Kelly came in to give me a bit of a nervous hug, asking, "Well?"

"No news," I said, feeling almost shaky with anticipation. There had been reports of polling places where people waited to vote for hours, lines that stretched around city blocks, ballots running out, even some machines breaking down. Given the scarred memory, for many, of the 2000 election, with its hanging chads and the horrible, divisive battle to determine who had won the presidency—the Supreme Court giving it to Bush over Gore, who had overwhelmingly won the popular vote—it was hard not to worry about all kinds of things going wrong. But the media reported no real cause for concern.

"Are you okay?" Kelly asked, feeling my forehead to see if it was warm.

It occurred to me then that I was having total election anxiety. My stomach was churning, like being on a speedboat in choppy waters. We turned off the TV and she left me on the sofa to chill out for a while. Thinking that it would be good to try to doze off, even though that was going to be hard, I closed my eyes. What do you know? Turned out to be easier than expected as I drifted off. A twenty-minute catnap felt like a two-hour snooze.

When I woke up, the house was bustling with dinner preparations.

"Uncle Craig," Sasha called, "Grandma said to tell you it's time to eat!"

And so there we were—Mom, Michelle, Barack, Kelly, me, and the kids—all sitting around the table as if we were in my mom's kitchen at home on Euclid Avenue, way back when. Mom asked the kids all the usual, curious questions—how was school, what were the teachers like, what were everyone's favorite subjects? And then the girls were teasing Avery about how many girlfriends he had and you would have never known that there was a national election happening and the members of the next First Family might well be dining with us.

One of my explanations for the calm that enveloped us is that for anyone on the verge of winning or losing an election of this magnitude or even less, there is no playbook, no set of guidelines for how to gauge feelings or what exactly to do. Barack had won most of the races he had run, but not all. So perhaps this was a defense mechanism for both him and Michelle. Then again, when primary votes had come in, I seemed to recall them staying very much on top of the data. But perhaps the real reason for the quiet dinner, and the conscious decision not to talk about how the returns were going, was the loss the day before of Barack's grandmother, Madlyn Dunham—Toot, as he affectionately called her, short for Tutu, the Hawaiian word for "grandma."

From everything that I had heard, Toot had that quality of character hard to describe in one word, someone who left her indelible mark on everyone who met her and someone whom Barack called his most important influence. With condolences pouring in from around the world, and, memorably, a most gracious note from Senator and Mrs. McCain, I knew that the emotions had to be raw for him, even on what soon might turn into one of the most euphoric occasions of his life. With Barack's "court-sense," he had known Toot's death was coming and ten days earlier had left the campaign trail to go see her. That said, I think we were all hoping that she would live to see her grandson, into whom she had poured her all, come into his own and make history.

Later, Barack and his sister Maya would describe in writing how their Tutu would have wanted to be remembered, and this said a lot about the atmosphere at our dinner table that night: *"When Tutu found out that she had little time remaining, she insisted that we dispense with excessive solemnity or sorrow. She was not afraid of any storm and withstood many in her eighty-six years. We feel fortunate to have had so much time with our Tutu."*

While we ate dinner, though the TV wasn't on, both Michelle and Barack had their BlackBerrys sitting on the table. Every now and then, we'd hear a buzz, and Barack, calmly, would pick his up and check out the message. Then another buzz followed, and my sister would look at hers, with similar calm, and then put it down.

As the pace of the buzzing picked up on Barack's Black-Berry, he finally stood up and went to turn on the tiny little television set in the kitchen. At that moment, I heard the sound of helicopters overhead, circling over the house.

From where I was sitting, it was hard to hear or see what was being reported, but Barack let us know what was happening. "Well," he said, his gaze fixed on the TV screen, "looks like we're going to win this thing."

Michelle's cell phone rang and she picked up, smiled, turned from the phone to Barack and said, "Congratulations, Mr. President."

In spite of the extraordinary normalcy of this dinner and the unbelievable calm we had witnessed in Barack and Michelle, we momentarily allowed a wave of full-court emotion as we all hugged and let forth a round of "Congratulations!" and "Way to go, Barack!" and "Oh my God!" It was definitely a mix of rejoicing and relief still colored by disbelief. The reality was going to take some time to set in.

Without further fanfare, we finished eating, and then Michelle smiled, took a deep breath, and said, "Time to go get ready."

Unbeknownst to us, a crowd that would later swell to more than a hundred thousand was gathering for a rally at Grant Park that was intended, unless there was some sudden reversal, to be a victory celebration. Even more unbeknownst to us, spontaneous and planned rallies, parties, and dancing in the streets would be erupting in major cities and small towns across America and around the world.

In the days to come, I would hear the accounts of how the vote had come in, how the networks reported the results for states where polls had closed, and the euphoria that exploded once Ohio went for Barack. These stories about "where I was when history was made" almost made me envious! We were definitely inside the bubble, just all getting dressed and heading down the stairs and out into the brisk Chicago night air—where it finally began to sink in for me that this was not an everyday motorcade waiting for us but *the presidential* motorcade.

As the limousine pulled out of the driveway and we started off along Lake Shore Drive, we were struck silent by the sight of hundreds of Chicagoans out lining the streets, cheering and waving. Kelly and I grabbed hands, laced our fingers together, but said nothing. The silence in the car was almost funny. Words had truly failed us.

After a while, as we sailed forth at a smooth and steady pace, finally Malia broke the silence. "Hey," she said, peering out the window, "how come there are no other cars?"

All at once, the answer registered. Traffic along both sides of Lake Shore Drive had been cut off for the motorcade. It was real. Barack had just been elected president of the United States!

While that marked the moment when it dawned on me that the words written two hundred and thirty–something years earlier by Thomas Jefferson in the preamble to the Declaration of Independence—"We hold these truths to be self-evident, that all men are created equal"—had been borne out with the election, it wasn't until the Inauguration two and a half months later that I could sit and reflect about what it all meant. And it wouldn't be until then that I would finally be able to celebrate; not so much that this was happening to my sister and her husband and kids, and our family, but celebrate as a citizen of the United States of America.

During the interim, it was time to get back to the real world and go to work. Though we didn't win any of the first slate of games, there were some encouraging signs that the lights had turned on upstairs for the players and they were starting to know what they were doing. In our game with Nevada, for instance, we played very good basketball for thirty-seven minutes. Against an excellent team like them, the take-home message was that if we could do for forty minutes what we had done in thirty-seven, we could win. Full court, all out. The next two games we lost but each time it was by only one point, and in overtime.

Finally, in our fifth game of the season, on the road against Fresno State, we won, and it was medicinal and visceral. Our guys played well, and perhaps just as important, they *knew* that they played well. They had begun to believe that they could win and were starting to see the big picture, how all the parts fit together, how to master execution and maintain the winning mind-set.

After that, we won six of our next eight games, including an overtime win against USC on our home court. This was Oregon State's first conference win in more than two years, and everybody in Corvallis went wild. It was huge! Still, we had a long season ahead.

With momentum working for us, I actually was torn about leaving for the Inauguration. But after juggling practices and scheduling, I wouldn't have missed for the world the opportunity for me, Kelly, and the kids to join with two million Americans to celebrate history and what we as a nation had accomplished and were preparing to do together in the coming term. It was awe-inspiring, humbling, unforgettable, and oddly restful. Seeing my sister step into her role as First Lady so effortlessly was no surprise. Nothing had changed about her in who she was and what she stood for. True, the White House was not the upstairs tiny apartment where we grew up, and Pennsylvania Avenue in the District of Columbia was a far cry from Euclid Avenue on the Southside of Chicago. But one thing clearly had remained the same in the two settings and that was the importance of family. Our country needed children in the White House, a reminder of why we strive and need to strive for the next generation coming up behind us.

With the fuel-injected inspiration of Tuesday's Inaugural events, I kissed my wife and kids good-bye on Wednesday before flying from D.C. to Oakland, where I met the team at the airport. On Thursday night we would be playing against none other than the University of California, Berkeley—the team that then held first place in the league—and on their home court.

There were plenty of reasons for me to worry, starting with the mini media circus that had begun to follow me. If that wasn't enough of a distraction for the team, I had to hold my tongue when I found out that the only gym available for us to have a special practice in was at an Oakland-area high school—where a game was scheduled. That meant we were bumped over to using an auxiliary cage that would have been more suited for middle school kids.

But what really could throw my guys, I worried, was the fact that the former OSU head coach who had been fired the previous season was now at Cal as an assistant coach.

Watching my players in practice, I liked what they were showing me. But even as I gave them a "That's what I'm talking about!" here and a "Now, that's thinking of the other guy!" there, I was cringing inside at what a grudge match they were heading into, with their former coach and all. There was nothing to do, other than to remind them to play our game, and for me to start mentally writing my mea culpas to the sportswriters, taking full responsibility for setting us up for a poor showing. There was simply no way the OSU Beavers could do their best in these conditions.

When we arrived at the Cal gym and the team hit the floor for their shoot-around, I snuck a peek and saw that the stands were packed, heard the band jamming, and sensed that everybody seemed juiced. Oh . . . (insert expletive)! All I could do was exude calm and confidence and hope that when we limped out of here we wouldn't be permanently damaged. With my pregame ritual of letting the team get ready in their locker room without me hovering around them, I stayed in my locker area alone. The plan, as usual, was I would wait until just a couple of minutes before it was time to head out to take my seat and then call everybody over for a quick huddle.

Consumed with guilt that we had to go through this ordeal, my mind-set unable to shake off a sense of doom, I left the locker room and headed into the arena when, to my speechless amazement, the minute I stepped out onto the floor I heard a ferocious roar come from the crowd.

Oh, right, it had to be for the entrance of the Cal team. But when I glanced behind me, there was nobody there. Blinking into the lights, I looked back up into the stands and beheld a sight that I'd never forget: Every single person in the entire arena from the University of California, Berkeley, had taken to their feet and they were giving me a standing ovation. It wasn't really for me, of course—it was for Barack and Michelle, and, more than that, for our country.

Nothing had prepared me for this reception and I was so

proud and choked up that I had to really work to hold it together. After all, it was game time.

Nearing the end of the first half we were down by eleven.
Things did not look too good, clearly. But then something
happened. Some extra something clicked and OSU suddenly
looked like they were champions on the floor, playing unselfishly and also making those choices that weren't correct but
were right—finding those open outside shots and making
them! There in front of my eyes, I saw the Beavers start turning it around. After the half they blew through Cal's lead with
a 16–4 run, and they played their hearts out, leaving it all on
the floor. Maybe some of this was to show their former coach
what they could do. Maybe not. But whatever it was, I saw
them play with a mix of pride and defiance that lifted them
to a new level. We won, 69–65.

Everyone contributed. As I told the press that night, "I've
got a locker room of guys who think they're going to be
in every game." And it was that attitude—along with great
execution—that made all the difference.

What I loved most, though, was how they handled themselves in victory. I expected to see them dancing around like
they'd just won the NCAA tournament. Instead, they were dig-
nified and poised, as if they had become who they were meant
to be all along—winners in the game of character. There were
high-fives, then they all lined up to shake hands with their opponents, cool and collected. Once in the locker room, well,
then we all went nuts with jubilation. OSU hadn't won at Cal
in more than ten years!

How much better could this season—in all aspects—
become for my players and my family and my country? It was
in the midst of our locker room celebration that the true test
of character became clear to me, just as greater tests were up
ahead for the president and First Lady, and for the rest of the
nation. We had come a long way over the span of an election

to create change, and now there was a lot of work to do that would require all hands on deck.

After the celebration subsided, that was the gist of what I saw scrawled on the chalkboard as I left the locker room to go talk to the media: "*It's not enough. We have another game Saturday night.*"

POSTGAME:
WE ALL HAVE A
WINDOW OF
OPPORTUNITY

C hange isn't easy.

Understanding that, accepting it, yet still striving to change for the better is one last aspect of character that I'd like to offer here at the end.

And it's not an overnight process either. I give enormous credit to my players at OSU for what they achieved in a turnaround in our first season together. Two days after our momentous win against Cal in January, we went on to win against Stanford. Later in the season, we beat both Cal and Stanford at home. The season was so phenomenal that we landed an invitation to the CBI, the same invitational tournament that I'd attended the year before with the Brown Bears but in which we didn't make it out of the first round.

At first, I considered the fact that the incredible turnaround the Beavers had achieved in one season might have worn them out. But when I asked my players if they were up for the tournament, they were unanimous in wanting to go.

The guys definitely showed up with something to prove, winning the first game against Houston and then beating Vermont in overtime. Not to be stopped there, we took on Stanford next, beating them for the third time that season. With that, we made it into the championship, a best-two-of-three play-off against the University of Texas at El Paso. For game one, we beat UTEP on our home court. Then we went to their place and they beat us. Now it was all down to the wire. The final game was at their gym, in front of twelve thousand highly partisan fans, and we won, the first postseason championship victory for OSU, ever.

Our Cinderella story, for that season, had come to an end. But the next season was going to be a whole new set of challenges and opportunities, a new cast of characters. And we had to know that going in, to manage expectations from others and ourselves. It was going to be harder than the year before, much harder.

At Thanksgiving time, early in the '09–'10 season, the team and I, along with my family, had the honor and pleasure of visiting the White House. Barack, Michelle, Mom, Malia, and Sasha then surprised us by showing up at our game in D.C. against George Washington University. It was a once–in–a-lifetime experience for my players. For me, it was pretty funny to hear my sister telling me, after all these years, that I was much too tough on the guys! Mom only smiled, suggesting that I must be doing something right—since we won the game!

The funny thing about having an "in" at the White House is that it has nothing to do with politics, only with family. Often it's the elephant in the living room during conversations. After all, as I told the staffers during the campaign, "I'm just a basketball coach." At the same time, I am amazed and incredibly proud of what my brother-in-law and his allies from both sides of the aisle have accomplished in a very short period during a time of both needed change and ever-growing global challenges. It may appear that the typical gridlock and partisan infighting has slowed down progress in efforts toward the big change that many desire. But in addition to bringing us through a disastrous economic crisis, righting our ship of state and guiding it into calmer waters, the leadership Barack has shown in moving forward the agenda he ran on has been remarkable. What the media doesn't report is the work ethic that is now back in fashion. Behind the scenes, an array of individuals of high character have come together and decided that it's time to roll up their sleeves and do the people's business.

To those who want to complain and criticize, fine, have at it; freedom of speech is a protected right. But what bothers me are those who go beyond criticizing policy and launch personal attacks, who spread lies and make money stirring up hatred and violence, and who are happy to see change fail—even if it hurts the country. Wouldn't it be better to use that energy toward doing some good?

For all of us who embrace change and accept that it's not easy, I think the character test to note is that we can't just assume that creating the change we want is only the job of elected officials. Not only do we miss out in shaping the kind of change we want if we don't play a part, but it makes us weaker to just sit around and expect others to make it happen. That was the point of all the chores we had to do when we were growing up. And I know that our family wasn't alone in that respect.

Creating change also doesn't require an Ivy League degree or a background in government. And if you're wondering what you can do to pitch in, you don't have to go very far.

For example: How about volunteering in the classroom? Or what about signing up to coach a Little League team? Don't know anything about sports? Not a problem, you can learn! There are food drives that can use you. There are groups gathering items needed for our soldiers and their families. There are organizations working to raise awareness about climate change that need you. There are charities raising funds to cure diseases that you can also help. Surprisingly, what may feel like duty might actually be fun. You might be excited by the team effort out there that could put you to work. And if you are already a teacher or a parent or a coach or a community organizer or working with the elderly or doing something that impacts others, you can feel free to twist some arms and bring more on board.

Change takes everyone making a contribution, all hands on deck. These aren't like other times when the status quo is acceptable. Much as we may not like the idea, we have to rock the boat if we want to confront big challenges to make the world safe and stable for our children. The good news is that we all have a window of opportunity. You don't have to be a basketball player to look for your open shot and take it.

That's the secret of the game of character. Anyone can play.

ACKNOWLEDGMENTS

In the past, whenever I heard authors compare their literary undertakings to the act of giving birth, I frankly thought they were protesting too much. But that all changed after experiencing the mental labor required to bring this book to life, during a time period in which my wife, Kelly, was pregnant with our son Austin—who was born just as *A Game of Character* was readying to go to press. And, yes, it turns out that writing a book really is a lot like giving birth!

This is all by way of saying that the first person I must acknowledge herein is Kelly—who was reading the final copyedited version in between contractions! Thank you, thank you, thank you, Kelly, for your constant encouragement, insights, and belief in this endeavor from start to finish. Loving thanks extend to Avery and Leslie, for being troopers and coming along for the ride—no matter what.

Profound gratitude goes to Gotham Books publisher, Bill Shinker, for your vision, and to our indomitable editor, Lauren Marino, for your passion in seeing to it that we lived up to that vision. To everyone at Gotham who really went beyond the call of duty on this book, I salute you for your character and your commitment. Thank you.

It is no exaggeration to say that without a handful of individuals, *A Game of Character* wouldn't have made it to the shelves. At the top of that list is my literary agent, Scott Waxman, who had the audacity persuade me to write it in the first place. Also key in the process early on were Andy Katz of ESPN and writer William Patrick, each of whom helped stir up the memories that I'd forgotten and made for great company in the process. Thank you to Mim Eichler Rivas, the point guard on this project. Without your diligence, speed, and velvet touch, *A Game of Character* would not exist. My voice has never been so clear. My sincerest gratitude.

A big shout-out must go to my lifelong friend and sports agent, Rick Giles, for being a "coach's coach" and continually reminding me to push my game. And to all my buddies, particularly everyone in the ongoing pickup games that helped make history these past couple of years, thank you. We're overdue for a game!

There really aren't enough words of thanks to express my appreciation to everyone at OSU, especially Dr. Ed Ray and Bob De Carolis, for giving me a wonderful opportunity. To my assistant coaches, Doug Stewart, Nate Pomeday, and David Grace, for all of your loyal support. It is my good fortune to know you have my back in every way on a daily basis. Also, to my right hand, Jaimee Colbert, who takes care of everything—and I mean everything—thank you.

Finally, I want to acknowledge all the basketball players of every team that I've coached. Your character and your effort shine through in my memories and make me prouder than you know. Keep playing!